WITHOUT FEAR

Hockey's 50 Greatest Goaltenders

Kevin Allen and Bob Duff

with Special Commentary by
Johnny Bower

TRIUMPH
BOOKS
CHICAGO

Library of Congress Cataloging-in-Publication Data

Allen, Kevin, 1956–
    Without fear : hockey's 50 greatest goaltenders / Kevin Allen and Bob Duff,
with special commentary by Johnny Bower.
        p. cm.
    ISBN 1-57243-484-8 (hard)
    1. Hockey goalkeepers—Biography. 2. Hockey goalkeepers—Rating of.
I. Duff, Bob. II. Bower, Johnny, 1924– III. Title.

GV848.5.A1 A44 2002
796.962′092′2—dc21
[B]

                                                                    2002074310

CONTENTS

INTRODUCTION

All goaltenders are going to heaven. Hall of Famer Glenn Hall used to preach that gospel during practices when pucks were whizzing past his nose.

"I'm the only one here going to heaven and you shooters are all going to hell," Hall would bellow when slap shots would rise too high for his liking.

Former NHL netminder John Davidson, now a respected television analyst, has insisted that goaltenders have two missions each day they strap on pads: "To stop the puck, and to not be killed stopping the puck."

Truly the real miracle on ice is that no National Hockey League goaltender has ever been killed in the performance of his duties. Bobby Hull told us he was frankly stunned that he hadn't killed one. Remember that, in the days before accurate radar guns, Hull's slap shot was listed at 118.3 mph in the *Guinness Book of Records*. The chatter in the sixties was that his shot was 35 mph faster than the average player's. We couldn't determine whether that assessment of Hull's shot was accurate or even how that conclusion was reached, but goalies didn't need an understanding of physics to appreciate that Hull's wicked riser could test Hall's theory. Hull won't deny that he liked to spray a few high shots at the net just to give goalies something to think about.

Says Hull, "Looking back at the equipment in those days, it was crap. It was unbelievable what they wore. The equipment was held together by dust. Kids' equipment today is better than what they were wearing."

It was clear that to play goal in the NHL required a man to be without fear. That was particularly true in years gone by when a goalie's armor had all of the protective qualities of a bundle of rags.

Trying to explain why a man would play goal in the NHL is like trying to explain why a police officer would aspire to join the bomb squad. Maybe they crave danger. Maybe they just want to be in the center of the action. Maybe they never entertain the notion that they could be seriously injured. Whatever the reason, goaltenders clearly have always led the league in bravado. Clint Benedict wore a mask briefly after an injury, but it wasn't until Jacques Plante donned a primitive mask in 1959 that goalies began to think it was a reasonable idea to cover their faces. And it wasn't until 18 years later, when Andy Brown retired from the World Hockey Association, that the last maskless wonder was gone.

These were indeed men without fear.

The price players have paid to be NHL goaltenders for the past nine decades has been ghastly. In 1989 Buffalo Sabres goalie Clint Malarchuk almost bled to death when a skate cut his throat. When Frank Brimsek was playing minor league hockey in Pittsburgh, he once played with an eyelid so badly cut that he could see with his eye closed.

Goalies essentially did whatever it took to stay in the lineup. When former NHL goaltender Eddie Johnston played for the Boston Bruins, he had leeches applied to his swollen face to suck enough blood to allow him to see. He also broke his nose in two different places in the same week and didn't miss a minute of action.

In the midst of his record 502 consecutive-games-played streak, Glenn Hall had his mouth ripped open from a blast by Jim Pappin. About 40 stitches were required to close the wound. But he played on. Goalie Bruce Gamble suffered a heart attack while playing for the Philadelphia Flyers in a February 9, 1972, game. That ended his career, even though he finished the game.

Goaltender is a unique position in sports. A coach can spend hours fine-tuning a defensive strategy, but if his goalie surrenders a couple of soft goals, the coach's labor is rendered useless. Likewise, a coach can spend days ratcheting up his power-play efficiency, but if the rival goaltender is at the top of his game, that labor is also wasted energy.

"Goaltending is the one factor a coach has no control over," says former NHL coach Al Arbour, who earned four Stanley Cup championship rings with the New York Islanders. "You can't control how well your goalie plays, and you can't control how well their guy does, either."

If there is but one trait that unifies all goaltenders, it is an indomitable competitive spirit. No one illustrates that more than Johnny Bower, who agreed to provide technical analysis of the goaltenders in this book. Bower was 45 when he wore the pads for the final time in an NHL game in the 1969–70 season. Leafs coach/general manager Punch Imlach called him the "world's greatest athlete," and Bower was indeed a rare physical specimen. His combination of agelessness and impenetrability earned him the nickname the "China Wall."

Greatness in goal can be defined by myriad factors, not the least of which is performing well at the most opportune time. We believe that that by itself is a talent. All goaltenders give up bundles of goals. But what separates the very good goalkeepers from the exceptional goalies and the exceptional goalies from the legendary goalies is the ability to bar the door at precisely the right time.

In ranking the top 50 goaltenders of all time, we interviewed scores of folks and looked at a mountain of statistics. We weighted several key factors, including, but not restricted to, Stanley Cup championships, Vezina Trophies, All-Star selections, goals-against averages, save percentages (when available), and, to a lesser extent, longevity. We also considered reputation, stature, and aura. But in the end, the selection process came down to just one simple question: if you were in Game 7 of the final, who would you want between the pipes?

Given the history of each of the men on our list, it became easier than we had suspected to fold each man into a ranking.

Clearly, many will disagree with us. Who do you like as the greatest impact player in baseball? Babe Ruth? Mickey Mantle? Ted Williams? How about the number one quarterback of all time? Joe Montana? Or, are you partial to John Elway? That's the same struggle that we face in determining a ranking for men who played in different eras, under different rules, and with different equipment. Today's goalies have personal coaches and consult sports psychologists, while goaltenders of past eras were primarily self-taught.

"Gump Worsley told me that he never had any coaching at all," says former Montreal broadcaster Dick Irvin Jr., son of the late NHL coach Dick Irvin. "Neither did Glenn Hall or Terry Sawchuk, or any of the guys from that era. Gump told me that when he came to Montreal, he was thinking, 'Now I will be able to talk goaltending because I have Toe Blake and this guy is a genius.' The first time that something went wrong he went to Toe and asked him, and Toe said, 'Don't ask me. I don't know anything about goaltending,' and walked away."

That wasn't uncommon. "When I was growing up, I remember thinking my father knew everything about hockey," Irvin says. "When he told me he knew absolutely nothing about goaltending, I was shattered."

Modern goaltenders will seek advice on every aspect of the game, from how they hold their stick to precisely where to drop the puck behind the net for a defenseman. "The position of goaltender today is very mechanical, very methodical," says Philadelphia coach Ken Hitchcock. "Goaltenders play percentages now. The technical aspect of goaltending is now just so elevated from where it was before. It's not the same as it was when it was very athletic, like in the days of Glenn Hall, Roger Crozier, and others."

We tried to judge the men, not the equipment or the era. And rather than looking at the hardships each man endured, we preferred to judge these athletes on their ability to handle hardship, regardless of what form it came in.

Choosing the best goaltender of all time is like trying to choose the most lethal poison of the 20th century. The world's 50 deadliest poisons all have different styles and methods of burying you, but each is amazingly proficient at doing you in. That is also true of these 50 goaltenders. On a day-to-day basis, each of these goaltenders inflicted agony and torture on his opponents in a variety of styles and forms. But regardless of which method was employed, each of them was amazingly proficient at doing you in.

THE
RANKINGS

1 PATRICK ROY

With his incredible focus and devotion to technique, Roy is the yardstick by which all other goaltenders are to be judged. His greatest single talent is his ability to win at all times, regardless of circumstances or challenges. He won in Montreal. He won in Colorado. He has no peers in his number of victories—regular-season or playoff.

2 TERRY SAWCHUK

The NHL's all-time leader in games played and shutouts put up astonishing numbers during his first five full NHL campaigns—56 shutouts, 195 wins, and a 1.93 goals-against average.

3 GLENN HALL

Probably the most indestructible goalkeeper in NHL history, Hall blended durability, moxie, and an unorthodox style to earn the apt nickname of "Mr. Goalie."

4 JACQUES PLANTE

In the early years goaltending attracted thrill seekers. Plante viewed goal-tending as a craft. He studied it and worked to improve the position, including using a mask and playing the puck outside his goal crease.

5 DOMINIK HASEK

The "Dominator" (1996–97 and 1997–98) and Jacques Plante (1961–62) are the only goalies in NHL history to win the Hart and Vezina Trophies in the same season.

6 BILL DURNAN

Durnan won the Vezina and was a first All-Star choice in each of his first four NHL campaigns. He helped the Montreal Canadiens win their first Stanley Cup in 13 years as a rookie in 1943–44.

7 KEN DRYDEN

While it would be impossible to prove that Dryden was the most intelligent man ever to play between the pipes, he clearly was the first to intellectualize the position. He is capable of writing a doctoral thesis on goaltending, and essentially did in a book entitled *The Game*.

8 GEORGE HAINSWORTH

Hainsworth retired as the NHL shutout leader in 1936–37 with 94 and held the honor until Terry Sawchuk shattered it in 1964.

9 GEORGES VEZINA

Vezina took the Canadiens to consecutive Stanley Cup finals in 1923–24 and 1924–25. When illness ended his career the following season, Montreal missed the playoffs.

10 BERNIE PARENT

The only NHL goaltender to be Stanley Cup MVP in consecutive seasons, Parent grew up idolizing Jacques Plante and shared goaltending duties with him in Toronto.

11 TURK BRODA

Toronto's fabulous fat man was the first goalie in NHL history to backstop his team to three successive Stanley Cups.

12 GRANT FUHR

While facing the Edmonton Oilers' ferocious offense in the eighties, opponents never lost sight of the fact that Grant Fuhr was the best goal-keeper in the world during that period. He could dive across the net like lightning rippling across the horizon.

13 FRANK BRIMSEK

With his shy, unassuming nature and handsome face, Brimsek looked more like a Fuller Brush man than an NHL goaltender. But six shutouts in his first eight starts with the Boston Bruins in 1938–39 proved how competitive he was.

14 BILLY SMITH

"Battling Billy" could beat opponents both literally and figuratively. A feisty, highly combative athlete, he was just as likely to use his goal stick like a hatchet to cut down forwards as he was to make saves with it.

15 TONY ESPOSITO

Espo's 15 shutouts in 1969–70 remain a mark for rookie goalies and are tied for the second-highest total by a goalie in a single NHL season.

16 CLINT BENEDICT

Benedict left the NHL in 1930 as the all-time leader with 15 Stanley Cup shutouts. He led the NHL in shutouts in each of the league's first seven seasons.

17 CHARLIE GARDINER

Gardiner's peers selected him as the starting goalie in the 1934 Ace Bailey Benefit Game in Toronto, the first NHL All-Star Game.

18 JOHNNY BOWER

Bower turned pro during the Truman administration and was still stopping pucks at the NHL level in the midst of Richard Nixon's presidency.

19 GUMP WORSLEY

The "Gumper" came out of retirement three times and played in five Stanley Cup finals, even though he didn't win a playoff series until he was 36.

20 CECIL "TINY" THOMPSON

The Boston Bruins finished in first place in six of the ten seasons that Thompson manned their goal. He was a winner in his first five Stanley Cup games.

21 MARTIN BRODEUR

Posting 200 regular-season wins before his 27th birthday, Brodeur established his potential to chase Patrick Roy for the league's all-time victory record. He might handle the puck better than any goalie in league history.

22 GERRY CHEEVERS

Perhaps the world's worst practice goalie, Cheevers was at his best when it mattered most, winning titles in junior hockey, the minors, and the NHL.

23 ALEX CONNELL

Recognized by the familiar black cap that always adorned his head, Connell posted 50 shutouts during his first four NHL seasons.

24 VLADISLAV TRETIAK

An intimidating force in international hockey, Tretiak forced the National Hockey League to recognize that Europe also boasted high-caliber goaltenders. He is undeniably the most dominant figure in international hockey history.

25 TOM BARRASSO

Barrasso's ability to jump directly from high school to the Buffalo Sabres and win the Rookie of the Year award in 1983–84 helped change the way NHL scouts viewed the draft. Although Barrasso started his career as a high-profile player, his contributions to Pittsburgh's back-to-back Stanley Cup championships in 1990–91 and 1991–92 sometimes get lost in the glare of the Penguins' offensive brilliance.

26 HARRY LUMLEY

Lumley made the NHL at 17 and helped the Detroit Red Wings win a Stanley Cup in 1949–50 at age 23. Although his accomplishment might not be on par with Tiger Al Kaline winning a batting title at age 19, it is certainly one of the significant stories in Detroit sports lore.

27 ED BELFOUR

Once he harnessed his nuclear intensity, Belfour earned a reputation as one of the league's best big-game goalies. This introvert never endeared himself to the media, and has probably never received all the accolades he deserves.

28 HARRY "HAP" HOLMES

Holmes came up big at the most important time of the year. He posted a playoff goals-against average below 2.00 in six of his ten pro seasons.

29 ROY WORTERS

Worters won every trophy a goalkeeper could win in his era except the Stanley Cup. Off the ice, he was a tireless worker for charitable causes.

30 AL ROLLINS

Rollins might have accomplished even more had he not played for the dismal Chicago Black Hawks in the early fifties. Some might argue that his ability to lead the Hawks to the playoffs in 1952–53 was a greater achievement than his helping the Toronto Maple Leafs win a Stanley Cup in 1950–51.

31 MIKE VERNON

The list of storied Calgary Flames players starts with the diminutive and well-spoken Vernon. He is the Flames' all-time wins leader and was in net for the franchise's only Stanley Cup championship in 1988–89. He entertained fans with his stingy netminding and wit.

32 RILEY HERN

The father of professional goaltending, by some accounts, Hern knew how to take care of business on and off the ice. He was the first to translate sports fame into profitability.

33 ROGIE VACHON

While most of the hockey world was sleeping, Vachon produced some of the NHL's most spectacular goaltending in the seventies with the Los Angeles Kings. He is underrated, primarily because Ken Dryden erased memories of Vachon's Stanley Cup championships in Montreal, and the results of Kings games rarely were carried in East Coast papers.

34 LORNE CHABOT

Referred to frequently during his era as having "mournful eyes," Chabot probably had as much misfortune as any goalkeeper who has ever donned the pads. But he had enough accomplishments in the thirties to be considered one of the greats of the game.

35 DAVEY KERR

Rebelling because of his belief that the New York Rangers management was treating him like an indentured servant, Kerr retired early—otherwise his statistics would be more eye-catching. His pride might have cost him a place in the Hall of Fame.

36 ROGER CROZIER

Defying conventional wisdom that goalies should set up for shots as if they were standing at attention, Crozier left crowds gasping with his acrobatics around the goal crease. He was like an Olympic gymnast between the pipes.

37 MIKE RICHTER

If a coach had a century of professional goalkeepers to choose from, Richter might be the one they'd use to face anyone on a breakaway. Throughout his career with the New York Rangers, he has used his elasticity and quickness to frustrate many breakaway artists.

38 CHUCK RAYNER

NHL fans and players from the forties have fond memories of seeing Rayner bolt from his New York net to chase down the puck. He didn't just trigger offensive rushes with his puckhandling; occasionally, he would lead the rush. He was one of the most respected goaltenders of that era.

39 EDDIE GIACOMIN

Another goalie who didn't feel he needed to be tethered to his net, Giacomin could both excite and petrify fans when he skated after the puck. He clearly was one of the most popular players in New York Rangers history.

40 HUGH LEHMAN

Lehman jumped to the Pacific Coast Hockey Association when it was organized in 1911 and played every season until the Western league folded in 1926.

41 PERCY LESUEUR

LeSueur was a thinking man's custodian, a goalkeeper in the era when rules prohibited netminders from lying down, sitting, or kneeling to stop the puck.

42 MIKE KARAKAS

By signing with the Chicago Black Hawks in 1935, this Eveleth, Minnesota, native earned his place in hockey history by becoming the first American to become a number one goaltender in the "Original Six" era.

43 RON HEXTALL

When Hextall arrived with the Philadelphia Flyers in 1986, he was viewed as the prototype for the 21st-century supergoalie. He was tall and powerful, and he skated like a defenseman. He also handled the puck more smoothly than many defenders.

44 NORMIE SMITH

With a 9–2 career playoff record, Smith proved that a small man could have a huge impact for an NHL club. He guided the Detroit Red Wings to back-to-back Stanley Cup titles in 1936 and 1937.

45 CURTIS JOSEPH

Breaking into the NHL with the St. Louis Blues, Joseph recorded 100 wins in his first 209 games with the Blues, a club record for the fastest to 100 wins.

46 JOHN BOWER "BOWSE" HUTTON

Hockey's first John Bower to guard the nets, Hutton played his entire career in Ottawa and never recorded a losing season.

47 PADDY MORAN

Moran led the National Hockey Association in losses with Quebec in 1910–11, then took that club to a pair of Stanley Cup championships over the next two seasons.

48 CHRIS OSGOOD

Osgood ranks second on the Detroit Red Wings' all-time wins and shutouts lists and shares the New York Islanders' single-season win mark (32) with Billy Smith.

49 BILL RANFORD

For a brief spell in the early nineties, Ranford was considered the game's best netminder. He jumped right from the junior ranks to the NHL.

50 JOHN VANBIESBROUCK

Vanbiesbrouck played the position with the bravado of a Wild West gunslinger. He was poised and polished, and confidence oozed from every gland, particularly when he played for the New York Rangers and the Florida Panthers. Go ahead. Shoot on him. Make his day.

PATRICK ROY

GLENN HALL

JACQUES PLANTE

TONY ESPOSITO

INNOVATORS

CLINT BENEDICT

CECIL "TINY" THOMPSON

VLADISLAV TRETIAK

HUGH LEHMAN

PERCY LESUEUR

RON HEXTALL

1 | PATRICK ROY

BORN: Quebec City, Quebec, October 5, 1965		
SHOT: Left	**HEIGHT:** 6′	**WEIGHT:** 192 lbs.
Stanley Cups: 4		Vezina Trophies: 3
Conn Smythe Trophies: 3		Jennings Trophies: 5
NHL First All-Star Team: 4		NHL Second All-Star Team: 2
NHL All-Star Games: 9		

NOTABLE ACHIEVEMENTS: Only NHL player to win three Conn Smythe Trophies; NHL leader in career wins; only player to win Stanley Cup and Conn Smythe Trophies as a rookie; one of only three NHL goalies to play 900 games (with Terry Sawchuk and Glenn Hall); holds the NHL record for most 30-win seasons (12); one of three goalies with seven consecutive 30-win seasons (with Tony Esposito and Martin Brodeur); NHL All-Rookie Team selection, 1985–86; leader in Stanley Cup playoff wins (148), shutouts (22), and minutes (14,786); tied for most consecutive playoff wins (11, with Ed Belfour and Tom Barrasso); third-youngest goalie to win 300 NHL games (the two younger being Brodeur and Sawchuk); holds a 2.30 playoff goals-against average.

Johnny Bower's Commentary on Roy

"Patrick Roy is one of the greatest competitors of all time. He hates losing, and sometimes people misunderstand that intensity and consider him temperamental. But I believe that he has the right attitude to win. He pushes himself to be the best and it shows because he seems to be getting better with age. That's why he has been the backbone of both of his NHL teams. Roy is a butterfly goaltender who has some of the quickest feet in the game. He's a solid skater who is able to go post to post in an instant and make key saves. He can be beaten top shelf, but it's a lot easier to say than do, especially with the speed of his glove hand."

Second Opinion: Former Montreal Coach Jacques Demers on Roy

"Patrick is just a winner. He wasn't perfect. I knew if he made a mistake, he would work that much harder to make up for it. You are never going to get Patrick to lose his concentration—even if he makes a bad play. That's what happened in the [2001] Stanley Cup final [against New Jersey]. He made a bad puckhandling play, but that just made him stronger. In 1993, when we won the Stanley Cup, we were down 2–0 against Quebec and [Quebec goaltender coach] Daniel Bouchard said, 'We found a weakness in Patrick Roy.' Boy, did that get him going. He wanted to prove Daniel wrong. One thing you don't ever want to do if you are Patrick's opponent is to challenge him. He always wants to prove you wrong. And he will."

As much as everyone in the hockey world understands that Patrick Roy is not omniscient, there is a sense that he knows all and sees all in this sport.

He has long been able to predict the movements of forwards before they actually occur. He is blessed with a sixth sense for locating the puck in traffic when others can't seem to find it. His focus is panoramic. While some goalkeepers struggle to maintain their concentration on the play, Roy seems to be able to take in every event in the building. His observation skills rival those of a New York City beat cop. Nothing escapes Roy's notice.

"The popcorn guy could drop a bag in the second period and Patrick will have seen it," says former NHL player Peter McNab, now the Colorado Avalanche's broadcast analyst.

No disrespect is intended toward Roy's athleticism or his mastering of the "butterfly" style that has been copied by hundreds, perhaps thousands, of young goaltenders. But a case can be made that Roy's mental game, more than his physical tools, have put him in position to have 600 wins before he retires. This is why he is viewed as hockey's all-time greatest netminder.

Patrick Roy won his first Stanley Cup as a rookie with the Montreal Canadiens.

It has become almost a game to those around Roy to test the outside limits of his awareness. His mind is almost like a video camera, able to record every moment of every game in every season.

"I try to pick up the most obscure thing that happened," says McNab, "[and] I will say to him, 'Did you notice that a player dropped his stick for just a second in the game?' And he will say, 'Oh, yeah, it led to two scoring chances. Dominik Hasek made a great save on one, and we almost scored on the second one. But then they came down, and we made a defensive mistake.'"

This is a man who devours statistics as if they are Holy Scripture. He worships the game's traditions and pageantry. He adores the game's psychology and lives to play the game within the game. All the trappings that often seem to distract others only seem to heighten Roy's awareness. The more immersed he can get into hockey's culture, the better he seems to perform.

"He's one of those guys who when he's not playing is in here reading *The Hockey News*, or looking at stats, or watching how other players are playing," says former Colorado teammate Aaron Miller. "He knows what happened before just as much as what is going on around him now. A lot of what he does [on the ice], he does with his mind."

When a biography on Terry Sawchuk hit the bookstores, Roy was there because he wanted some insight on the man he's always compared with.

There's definitely an aura about Roy that everyone has felt since he won the Stanley Cup as a rookie with the Montreal Canadiens in 1985–86. What he says and how he acts define him as much as how he performs on the ice. It seems to fuel how he performs. Telling Jeremy Roenick he couldn't hear his razzing because he had two Stanley Cup rings in his ears explains Roy's success as much as the fact that when he is kneeling in his butterfly position, the bottom portion of the net seems to have been boarded up and nailed shut.

"I knew Patrick was a fearless competitor," former teammate Ray Bourque says. "But [after I got to Colorado], I saw what a competitor he really is. He's just a winner and doesn't accept anything else."

Roy was the one who called Bourque and told him he wouldn't be sorry if he agreed to play for the Avalanche after 21 seasons in Boston. "If Patrick Roy was a forward or a defenseman, he would be a great captain," coach Bob Hartley says.

NHL rules prevent goaltenders from being commissioned as official captains, but Roy always has held the unofficial rank. In the midst of the battle, he seizes command and finds a way to rally the troops. "He knows when it's time to shake things up," Bourque says. "I'm impressed at how well he picks his spots."

St. Patrick, as he has been called, can drive the snakes out of the dressing room as efficiently as the original St. Patrick herded them out of Ireland.

"Especially in the playoffs, he changes his character," Miller says, smiling at the memory. "I remember a couple of years ago, we were playing Detroit in the playoffs. We were up 5–1 going into the third period and we ended up winning 5–2. We had a bad third period, and he just snapped. You could just see how upset he was at how we played in that third period. That's how competitive he is."

Roy's cockiness is a weapon every bit as dangerous as Barry Bonds' swing or Michael Jordan's jam. Roy doesn't believe in pilot error. As long as he is at the controls, he believes nothing will go wrong.

"First and foremost, when you look at Patrick, you see a very confident person," says former Avalanche teammate Warren Rychel. "You see a winner."

Roy beats teams with bravado. He has the words "Be a warrior" inscribed on the underside of his blocker pad. He has an inner confidence second to none in the NHL, and maybe all of professional sports. He's driven by the need to succeed.

"There is no greater feeling than holding the Stanley Cup and knowing you have earned the right to hold it," Roy says. "You do that once, and you want to do it again and again."

On the ice, Roy's biggest change through the years is how he handles the puck. He likes to move out of his net and play the puck like a defenseman, a style that fits well with his desire to be as involved as possible.

"In Montreal, they didn't like me handling the puck very much," Roy says, smiling. "Here they accept my mistakes more. I might make six or seven mistakes a year, and I try to cut down on them. But I know that I also might save a couple of injuries a year because the defenseman doesn't have to get hit playing the puck. And I might save a few goals a year by coming out to play."

That's how Roy approaches the game. Details are as important to him as the brand of pads and stick he uses.

"It's not an understatement to say that Patrick is still a student of the game," Hartley says. "He is always looking for little details to get his game better, to get his technique better, to get his equipment [better]. That's what makes Patrick Roy special. He wants to do more than just stop pucks. He strives to be the best.

"Four Stanley Cups, three Conn Smythes, how many All-Star Games? Most wins in NHL history. And he's a guy who, after a game, will be in the video room to see how he made a save or how a guy scored on him."

Roy is always looking for an edge. At age 36, he embraced a diet and changed his training regimen from running and riding the stationary bike to weightlifting. Clearly, Roy's motive in tweaking his training strategy was his desire to play longer than might once have been thought possible. Now that Sawchuk's wins mark is behind him, he's embracing the goal of playing 1,000 games. He should get there during the 2002–03 season.

"I'm a person who always looks ahead, never behind," Roy says. "It's important that I keep my game at the highest level. Guys like Hasek and others have raised the goaltender bar. That's a challenge for me."

Through the years, Roy has been successful by working his way into the minds of his opponents. Call it the Roy Mystique.

He is generally more proficient when he is challenged or when his team isn't favored. "Patrick may be the best pressure goaltender in the history of the league," McNab says.

In 1986 the Canadiens had the NHL's seventh-best regular-season record and Roy, then 20, posted a 1.92 goals-against average to help them win the Cup. In 1993 Montreal had the sixth-best record, and Roy had a 2.13 goals-against average to help the team win. In 2001 a horrid puckhandling mistake, which led to a New Jersey goal, seemed like it would cost Colorado the series. But he kept his composure. That's the secret of his success: confidence in the face of chaos.

But Roy is anything but a robot. For all of the composure he displays on the ice, he's a caldron of emotions away from it. As much as he loves playing in Colorado, there is still some Canadiens blood in him, according to his agent, Bob Sauve. Roy has long regretted the circumstances of his departure from Montreal.

"As a French Canadian, you can't play for the Montreal Canadiens and have the success Patrick Roy did and just say, 'I'm walking away, that's it,'" Sauve says. "Most of him is with the Avalanche; there is a part still in Montreal."

Roy had a public meltdown on December 2, 1995, when he was left in for nine goals of an 11–1 blowout by the Detroit Red Wings. He brushed past coach Mario Tremblay and told team president Ronald Corey that he had just played his last game with the Canadiens. Roy was traded on December 6 to Colorado, along with Mike Keane, for Jocelyn Thibault, Andrei Kovalenko, and Martin Rucinsky. The Montreal newspapers covered those events as if they were the start of World War III.

The transition from Montreal to Denver wasn't easy for Roy, who appeared to thrive in the media frenzy of Montreal. He seems to love the roller coaster, not the merry-go-round. When he first came to Denver, he could walk down the streets without being recognized, and he didn't like it.

"What you also have to remember," says Sauve, "is that the reason that some players are good is because they love that attention. Superstars thrive on that stuff. That's why I was glad he ended up with a contender."

Although Roy's outburst triggered the trade, he believes his departure was inevitable. "I think it was their plan to trade me," he says, "and they used that as an excuse to do it."

Does Roy have regrets? "The only one I have is the way it ended in Montreal. I deserved a better end in Montreal," he says.

The remaining challenge for Roy is winning a fifth Cup—one more than won by Sawchuk. During the 2001–02 season, Roy shocked the hockey world by telling Team Canada executive director Wayne Gretzky that he wouldn't play in the 2002 Olympics. Columnists suggested he was miffed that Gretzky refused to designate him as the number one goaltender. But those who know him best say his quest for back-to-back Stanley Cups played the biggest role in his decision. Having played in Nagano in 1998, Roy knew that trying to win the Olympic gold medal was mentally draining. He recalled that the Avalanche had been knocked out in the opening round of the 1998 playoffs. He believed that most of the premium players in the NHL would be weary in April. He also realized that by taking time off, he could see his son, Jonathan, play in the Quebec Peewee tournament.

"He is the perfect example of total loyalty," Avalanche general manager Pierre Lacroix says. "He's loyal to his team, loyal to his teammates, loyal to his friends and family. This is the guy you have no worries about loyalty."

Perhaps the reason why Roy loves hockey's ambience is that he carries the same passion for playing he had as a Peewee. He might understand the business side of the game as well as anyone, but he hasn't forgotten that the best aspect about hockey is feeling the ice beneath your feet. The impish, youthful side of Roy hasn't been lost through almost two decades in the NHL.

To offer insight into Roy's demeanor, Lacroix, who was the goalie's agent years ago, tells the story of Roy taking apart the Stanley Cup after the Canadiens won in 1993. Seeing the Cup's keeper distracted by his wife and a few friends, Roy looked at Lacroix and said, "Let's get a special look."

He grabbed the Cup and whisked it off to his garage.

"He took a screwdriver and unscrewed the bottom," Lacroix says. "He just wanted to see what was inside. To him, that was a very big deal. He was like a kid in a candy store." Roy has to know everything about the game—even what's scrawled in the Stanley Cup's underbelly.

3 | GLENN HALL

BORN: Humboldt, Saskatchewan, October 3, 1931

SHOT: Left	HEIGHT: 5'11"	WEIGHT: 180 lbs.
Stanley Cups: 2		Vezina Trophies: 3
Conn Smythe Trophies: 1		Calder Trophies: 1
NHL First All-Star Team: 7		NHL Second All-Star Team: 4
NHL All-Star Games: 13		

NOTABLE ACHIEVEMENTS: Hall of Famer; played an NHL-record 502 consecutive games; the only goalie to be a first All-Star selection with three teams (Detroit, Chicago, and St. Louis); most first (7) and overall (11) All-Star selections of any NHL goalie; one of only three NHL goalies to play 900 games (with Terry Sawchuk and Patrick Roy); third on the all-time shutout list (84); fifth in all-time wins (403); played in five Stanley Cup finals; his No. 1 sweater was retired by the Black Hawks.

Johnny Bower's Commentary on Hall

"Glenn Hall was the first goaltender that I saw play what I call the spread eagle, or the butterfly. But that's not to say he was a flopper, because Glenn would only go down when he had to. He was a tremendous competitor who played the game to stop every puck that he faced, no matter the score. He had two of the quickest hands I've ever seen in the game. Couple that with his ability to go down and cover the bottom of the net in the butterfly and it's no wonder that the Chicago Black Hawks were so good when he was in goal."

Second Opinion: Former Teammate Stan Mikita on Hall

"Glenn used shorter pads than everyone else. When he went down in the butterfly, it would expose the top of his knee and leg. In one game someone tried to jump over him and sliced him open with a skate. I don't know how deep the cut was, but you could have put your finger in it. But he kept playing. It was one of the most outrageous acts of—you think I'm going to say courage—but I'm going to say one of the most outrageous acts of stupidity I've ever seen."

Glenn Hall played without a mask for 15 of his 18 National Hockey League seasons, and yet he insists that all goaltenders in that era—himself included—were mindful of self-preservation.

"Your first priority was staying alive," he says, "and your second priority was stopping the puck."

But what Hall says and what he actually did on the ice don't match up. Hall seemed to have his own priorities backward; most of his peers say he was one of the most fearless goaltenders ever to play the game. He vomited before every game and would routinely refer to hockey games as "60 minutes of pure hell." Yet this was an athlete who seemed to put winning ahead of safety.

"He was the first to really challenge the compromise of safety versus effectiveness," says Hall of Fame goaltender Ken Dryden. "The way it was defined in hockey, as a goalie you played a stand-up style. It seemed like it was for effectiveness. Unspoken was that it was a safety compromise. It was a way of putting your head as far away from the puck as you could. You put it above the bar. Glenn Hall decided he would put his head below the bar sometimes."

His NHL record of 502 consecutive regular-season games played in goal from 1955–56 to 1962–63 might be the safest record in professional sports. When his playoff starts are included, the total is actually 551 complete games. That's more than 33,135 minutes of continuous play.

Cal Ripken's baseball record of 2,632 consecutive games is quite impressive, but Hall's mark might be more impressive when you factor in a goaltender's potential for injury during the "Original Six" era. Remember, Hall was competing when Bobby Hull and Gordie Howe were both shooting the puck at more than 100 mph. Hall was Hull's teammate during the majority of this streak and Hull was known for firing for effect, even in practice. He wasn't shy about getting a puck up around a goalkeeper's ears. Hull used a curved stick and the puck would rocket off it like a supersonic knuckleball. The puck would dance, dip, and twist several times before it reached Hall.

"There are always lots of very good goalies and a few great goalies," says Dryden, now president of the Toronto Maple Leafs. "But there are very few important goalies. Glenn Hall is not only a great goaltender. He's an important one. He changed how goaltending is played. With the exception of Jacques Plante, I don't know if there is another important goalie in that way."

Hall Was an Innovator Because . . .

He was a pioneer in the butterfly style of goaltending.

Plante changed the sport of hockey by making it acceptable for goaltenders to wear a mask. Hall's contribution to goaltending came through defying the conventional wisdom of the time by embracing a courageous playing style that put him in harm's way more frequently. While most goalies today swear by the butterfly style, it's important to remember that Hall was considered both unique and foolish for playing a butterfly style in the fifties and sixties. Many of his contemporaries believe he was begging for a serious injury by playing low in the crease.

In the butterfly position, goaltenders play on their knees and then kick their legs parallel to the goal line to cover the lower regions of the net. "If the shot came in and it was low on the ice, I didn't feel strong enough to stop it," Hall explains. "If it hit the stick, it would still go in. With the knees behind the stick, it didn't go in."

Most goaltenders played a stand-up style in that era and then would occasionally go low to block shots during goalmouth scrambles. Although Hall is lauded for the courage he showed by putting his face lower at all times, he contends that he embraced the butterfly style to keep his face farther away from the ice. In the butterfly, he didn't have to dive after pucks the way some goaltenders did. He wasn't always in the butterfly like modern goaltenders. He was known as being an athletic goaltender who could make acrobatic saves.

"Hall played the way Dominik Hasek plays," says former NHL player Bill Gadsby. "Roger Crozier was like that, too. They were flippy, floppy guys. They would have one arm and one leg up and they looked like they were being stretched out. Their arms, legs, and body were always going in different directions."

What makes Hall's streak more impressive is that he maintained his level of excellence throughout the run; he was a member of the NHL's ruling class during that period. He won a Calder Trophy (rookie of the year) and a Vezina Trophy (top goaltender) and led the NHL in shutouts five times during the streak. During seven seasons of playing every minute of every game, Hall had 45 shutouts. He never had a goals-against average over 2.97, and he made the first or second All-Star team six times. To appreciate the respect that Hall commanded, remember that the Red Wings traded Sawchuk in 1955 to make room for Hall.

The Red Wings traded Hall in 1957, primarily to punish him because he didn't get along with the tyrannical Red Wings boss, Jack Adams. The trade was meant to be an insult because Hall was going from one of the league's best teams to a team that always seemed to be struggling.

"I didn't like Jack Adams any more than he liked me, so it was nice to get away from that situation," Hall says. "I always said my loyalty was to whoever signed my paycheck."

Revenge was achieved in 1961 when the Hall-led Black Hawks defeated the Red Wings for the Stanley Cup championship. "I always said it didn't matter who we beat," Hall says. "But I suppose it's satisfying to beat the team that didn't want you."

Hall says it was exhilaration—not terror—that prompted his bouts with vomiting. He would throw up before every game, and sometimes between periods. He sometimes sipped tea between periods in an effort to control it. "[The vomiting] got worse later in my career," Hall says. "I found that I played better in those conditions. I didn't try to control or stop it. I encouraged it because I felt I was ready to play then."

Hall doesn't recall—or chooses not to—too many narrow escapes during the streak, although he does remember a Jim Pappin drive that caught him in the mouth and ripped open both lips. About 35 to 40 stitches were needed to close the wound, and Hall spit out a tooth, the only one he lost during his career. He recalls that the attending dentist told him that given the severity of the wound, he was fortunate that more teeth weren't knocked loose or out. With his face ballooned to twice its normal size, he says it was difficult to feel "lucky."

Hall's most gruesome injury happened in junior hockey, long before he got to the NHL. During a goalmouth frenzy, his right cheek was sliced open by a skate. The hole was wide enough that he could poke his tongue through the wound.

Hall is humble about his reputation for being fearless. "You could tough it out and play around injuries easier back then than you can today," he says. "We got shots from all over back then, but the velocity wasn't on them the way it is today. You could concentrate on the good players."

Hall recalls that goaltenders in that era feared eye injuries because they could potentially end a career. But they didn't fear facial injuries as much as they did knee injuries or broken bones. "Facial injuries just involved pain," Hall says. "It was just stitches. They didn't restrict your movements. You can forget about pain."

One irony of Hall's streak is that it ended with an off-ice injury. He spent seven years in the combat zone, sometimes using his face to stop shots. In the

Hall was the first goalie to drop his head below the crossbar while making saves.

end, an act as innocent as tying a shoe took him out of the lineup. He merely bent over to lace up a toe strap when he felt a debilitating pain in his back.

"You always felt you could play around it," Hall says. "When the adrenaline is flowing, you don't feel anything. I felt like, 'Hell, when you get into the game, you won't notice.' But that wasn't true. I couldn't move."

Wanting to play immediately, Hall sought a medical solution. He remembers a doctor "requesting an inch and a half needle and grinding it in my back."

Hall tried to play the 552nd consecutive game, actually starting against the Boston Bruins. But in the first period, Murray Oliver scored on him between his legs, and Hall was convinced that he had given up the goal only because he couldn't bend down. He wouldn't keep playing if he wasn't effective. The streak ended.

Hall played for five more seasons with the Black Hawks after the streak ended, but his reward at the end was to be left exposed in the 1967 expansion draft. He was making $35,000 at the time, and the Hawks were looking to go in another direction. He was going to retire, but the St. Louis Blues made him reconsider with a salary offer of $47,500. Hall helped the Blues reach the Stanley Cup final in their first year, and he won the Conn Smythe Trophy, even though the Canadiens swept them. The Canadiens outshot St. Louis 151–91.

4 | JACQUES PLANTE

BORN: Shawinigan Falls, Quebec, January 17, 1929

DIED: February 27, 1986

SHOT: Left	HEIGHT: 6′	WEIGHT: 175 lbs.
Stanley Cups: 6		Vezina Trophies: 7
Hart Trophies: 1		NHL First All-Star Team: 3
NHL Second All-Star Team: 4		NHL All-Star Games: 8

NOTABLE ACHIEVEMENTS: Hall of Famer; first netminder to don a face mask on a regular basis; only goalie to win five straight Stanley Cups; played in eight straight finals; holds the mark for most Vezina Trophies won; third in all-time wins (434); had seven 30-win seasons, including six in a row; shares the NHL record for most 40-win seasons (three, with Martin Brodeur and Terry Sawchuk); fourth in all-time shutouts (82); led NHL in goals against nine times, including a 1.88 GAA with Toronto in 1970–71 at age 42; fourth in Stanley Cup shutouts (14); his No.1 sweater was retired by the Canadiens.

Johnny Bower's Commentary on Plante

"We all know that Plante was the first goaltender to wear the goalie mask on a regular basis, but what is often forgotten is that he was one of the first wandering goalkeepers to play in the National Hockey League. Jacques would come out and stop the puck behind his net and leave it there for a defenseman. He was a tremendous angle goaltender. He could match an attacking forward move for move. He was a strong skater who would come out and challenge a shooter and force him to make the first move. He was great on the ice, but off the ice, Jacques was one of the most superstitious people I'd ever met. When he came to Toronto in the early seventies, you'd walk into the dressing room to find his equipment laid out on the floor in the order that he would put it on. If anyone accidentally touched or moved the equipment, you might as well have left him on the bench for the rest of the night because his focus would have been disrupted."

Second Opinion: Hall of Fame Defenseman Bill Gadsby on Plante

"You never really talked about where to shoot on goaltenders in my era, but we did talk about Jacques Plante. It was said that he didn't like the high shots. I remember Andy Bathgate a few times would fire a puck right at his head. He would then come in the next two or three times and put it along the ice. I think he got some goals against Plante that way. . . . But I say he was one of the top three goaltenders I ever played against. I thought it was Terry Sawchuk, Glenn Hall, and then Jacques Plante. Plante was a great goaltender."

As much courage as it took for goaltenders to play in the National Hockey League without a mask, it probably required more for Jacques Plante to be the first to wear one regularly in 1959.

Covering his face in an era when nonconformity was considered a sign of weakness required a player who had the fortitude to challenge authority. It required a man who wasn't afraid to lose his job and marched to his own cadence. It required an eccentric.

Plante was such a man.

"He did it his own way, and he was so damn good, he could do it his way," says Hall of Fame sportswriter Red Fisher. "As much as [coach] Toe Blake hated the guy, Blake still said that Jacques Plante was the best goaltender he saw in the five years they won the Cup. For Toe to say that was quite an admission."

Plante donned the mask after Andy Bathgate hit him in the nose with a shot on November 1, 1959, when the Montreal Canadiens were visiting the New York Rangers. Plante had been wearing a mask in practice, but Blake had forbid him to wear it in a game. Officially, he thought Plante wouldn't be able to see low shots that hugged the ice. But Blake and Plante never really got along, and this was just the latest source of friction.

"Bob Turner [a friend on those Canadiens teams] . . . told me that Plante was the happiest guy in the rink that he got cut," says longtime Canadiens broadcaster Dick Irvin Jr. "He said, 'Don't ever feel sorry for him because he was looking for the opportunity [to put on the mask].'"

Plante Was an Innovator Because . . .

He was the first goaltender to regularly wear a mask.

After receiving his stitches, Plante told Blake that he couldn't go back in unless he could wear a mask. With no other option available, the coach gave his blessing and Plante officially became the first goaltender to wear a mask since Clint Benedict used a leather one to protect a broken nose in 1930.

He won that game 3–1, but Blake still didn't want him to wear the mask. Eventually, the coach relented when Plante said that the Canadiens would get him with a mask or not at all.

Maybe Blake and Plante were destined to be at odds. Blake was an old school athlete, a man's man, set in his ways. Plante was an eclectic citizen of the world. He knitted for a while, and then started painting. He liked to lie down for a couple of hours before every game and listen to records. When he showed up in the National Hockey League in November 1952, he insisted on wearing a wool stocking cap on his head. The *touque*, as it is called in Canada, was a source of a controversy before the mask ever was.

"My father [Canadiens coach Dick Irvin] told him he couldn't wear his *touque*," Irvin Jr. says. "He just thought it was bush league, not an NHL thing to do. He probably did Plante a favor by getting rid of it right away."

Although the Blake/Plante scrap over the mask would generate attention, the coach's chief complaint was that he never knew when the goalie was going to play, according to Fisher. Debates continue even today about the severity of Plante's asthma, but the condition gave him license to keep Blake guessing about his availability.

"He would come to the rink and say he didn't feel so good," Fisher recalls. "He would say he would go on the warm-up and if I can't play, you will have to use someone else. Of course 99 percent of the time he would play, and he would play brilliantly. But it was something that really bugged Toe."

The sourness of the Plante/Blake relationship was always evident, but Plante's brilliance kept him in Montreal until he was traded to the Rangers on

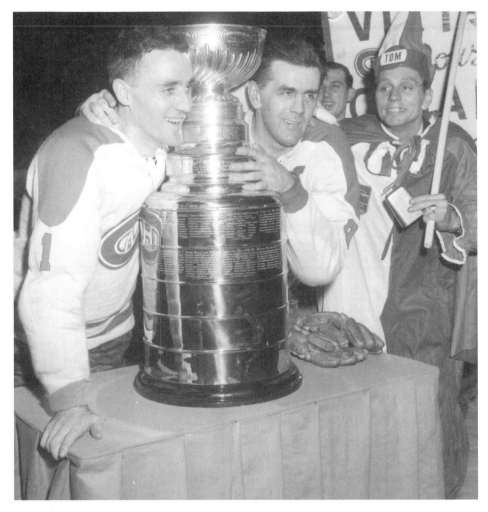

Plante (left) and Maurice "Rocket" Richard embrace the Stanley Cup.

June 4, 1963. That was just one year after Plante had won both the Vezina and Hart Trophies as the top goaltender and the league MVP.

Per his style, Plante didn't go gently into the night. He told New York journalists: "I'm glad I left the Canadiens. The Canadiens don't have a team anymore. They've gone down, and the Rangers are coming up."

Plante was never short on boldness in his words or actions. "He had more confidence in his ability as a goaltender than any goaltender I ever met," Fisher says.

When Doug Harvey was dealt to the Rangers in 1961, Fisher recalls asking Plante how the loss of one of the all-time greatest defensemen was going to affect his performance.

"Remember this guy had won the Norris Trophy every year," Fisher says. "Jacques said, 'We all know what a great defenseman Harvey is, but I tell you what: I'm going to win the Vezina Trophy without Doug Harvey."

Plante went 42–14–4 and won both the Hart and the Vezina.

"Maybe he wasn't a great team player, but players tolerated him because he put money in their pocket," says Ron Caron, a former Montreal scout and St. Louis general manager. "The Canadiens made their money on bonuses for Stanley Cup championships. They respected that about him."

Plante, who unofficially became a pro at 15 when he persuaded his coach to pay him 50 cents a game, was also noted for leaving his crease to play the puck.

Irvin Jr. recalls that when he watched Plante playing for the Montreal Royals, he was flabbergasted by the goalie's habit of directing traffic like a street cop and wandering well out of his net. "I thought he was a bit of a nut case," he jokes.

In an interview published in *Hockey Night in Toronto* magazine, Bathgate recalled what an advantage the Canadiens had because Plante could stop the puck behind the net or play it quickly to defensemen. He seldom made a puck-handling blunder.

"The puck moved automatically out of their zone," Bathgate said. "It was very difficult to play against that, especially with the caliber of team Montreal had. [We] were very hesitant to shoot the puck in because he handled it so well."

For all of Plante's boasting, he truthfully didn't enjoy the same success in New York as he had in Montreal. The Rangers eventually demoted him to Baltimore in the American Hockey League with the hope that he could restore his game. He played 17 games in Baltimore in 1964–65.

"He really didn't produce in New York," says Rangers defenseman Harry Howell. "Gumper had far better success in Montreal than Plante did in New York. He was injured quite a bit and missed a lot of games. I think he missed Montreal, too. He really wasn't the goaltender he had been in Montreal. When he moved to St. Louis, he went back to his old ways."

Before being sent to the minors, Plante had endured more bouts with asthma. In 1963–64, he had to leave the team to be treated in Montreal. "If I get another asthma attack, I may quit," he told the Associated Press. "I don't want to die in the net."

He retired in the summer of 1965, although he did come out of retirement briefly in 1966 to produce one of his greatest performances. With only four days of practice and playing with a patchwork junior lineup, he beat a Soviet national squad 2–1 at the Montreal Forum.

"When he came out after the game, it was like the pope blessing the crowd in Rome on Sunday morning," Caron says. "He was on his knees giving the benediction. It was great drama."

Although Plante's decision to wear a mask is said to have revolutionized the game, it was truly a trudging movement toward change. Andy Brown was the NHL's last maskless goaltender, and he was still in the league in 1973–74.

"The first time [my team] played against Plante and he was wearing that mask, I thought to myself, that guy has no balls, but he has brains," jokes Emile Francis, a former NHL goaltender, coach, and general manager.

Caron says Plante was probably the only goaltender who could have won that battle to keep his mask. "It was taboo," Caron says. "But Plante said, 'I'm strong enough, and good enough, they will have to live with that.'"

Clearly, Plante didn't think much of the notion that playing goal without a mask was a symbol of bravery. He would often say, "If I jump out of a plane without a parachute, does that make me brave?"

Plante had a sharp intellect. "My father thought Plante had as good a grasp on hockey as any young player he had ever met," Irvin Jr. says. "He thought he would make a good coach. He was wrong about that. But Plante was a good teacher."

Irvin recalls doing a television report on the art of goaltending and Plante was simply spellbinding when talking about his profession. "He had made a study of his craft," Irvin said. "I wonder if there was a goaltender before him who did that to the degree he did."

Most people remember Plante's quirkiness, particularly his reputation for cheapness. Caron says it is true that Plante would take the free tickets he received from the Canadiens and sell them for above face value.

Money was what brought him out of retirement when the league expanded from six teams to twelve in 1967. The St. Louis Blues persuaded him to play again. Some say he was paid $35,000. Others say he received even more.

Plante, then 39, played exceptionally well for the Blues, leading the league with a 1.96 goals-against average. The Blues also had Glenn Hall, and in 1970–71, they traded Plante to Toronto, where he posted a 1.88 GAA to lead the NHL. The Boston Bruins gave up a first-round draft pick to land the 44-year-old Plante in 1972–73. He went 7–1 for them for the remainder of the season. That's why they were furious when Plante retired to become general manager of the World Hockey Association's Quebec Nordiques. The lure of a $150,000 contract put him back in uniform for the WHA's Edmonton Oilers in 1974–75. He retired before the following season.

It certainly didn't seem to be out of character when cosmopolitan Plante moved to Switzerland after his final retirement. The hockey world was stunned when he died of stomach cancer in 1986 at the age of 57.

"He almost died in my arms six weeks before," Caron says. Plante had become ill while visiting Caron in St. Louis to tutor Blues goaltenders. The Blues' team physician had treated Plante, and Caron knew he was seriously ill because he looked emaciated.

Plante was among the first goalies to venture from his net to play the puck.

Nothing illustrated how obtusely Plante viewed the hockey world better than one of his last conversations with Caron. He had won six Stanley Cup championships with the Canadiens, but when he and Caron reminisced, the focus was on Plante's one game against the Soviets.

"He was sensational in the game, and Jacques remembered each detail very well," Caron says. "He thought maybe it was his greatest achievement."

15 | TONY ESPOSITO

BORN: Sault Ste. Marie, Ontario, April 23, 1943

SHOT: Right	HEIGHT: 5'11"	WEIGHT: 185 lbs.

Stanley Cups: 1	Vezina Trophies: 3
Calder Trophies: 1	NHL First All-Star Team: 3
NHL Second All-Star Team: 2	NHL All-Star Games: 6

NOTABLE ACHIEVEMENTS: Hall of Famer; played for Canada in 1972 Summit Series and 1977 World Championship; played for USA in 1981 Canada Cup; his 15 shutouts in 1969–70 are the most by an NHL goalie in the past 73 seasons; shares the NHL record with seven consecutive 30-win seasons (with Martin Brodeur and Patrick Roy); fourth on NHL's all-time wins and games-played list; seventh on all-time shutout list; led the NHL in goals-against average once and in shutouts three times; three-time All-American at Michigan Tech; won the NCAA title in 1965; fourth goalie to win both the Calder and Vezina trophies as a rookie (with Frank Brimsek, Tom Barrasso, and Ed Belfour); his No. 35 sweater was retired by the Black Hawks.

Johnny Bower's Commentary on Esposito

"Tony Esposito was much quieter than his brother, Phil, but you can't mistake that for lack of intensity. He hated losing, which I guess must have come from playing all of that hockey against his brother on the outdoor rinks in the Soo. Tony meshed the traditional stand-up style with that of the modern butterfly. He was incredibly tough to beat when forwards were in tight on him because of his quickness. He could drop down into the splits and then be back up in the crouch before a second shot could be fired upstairs."

Second Opinion: ABC Analyst John Davidson on Esposito

"When Tony played, he would smell like old horse liniment because he would get the rubdown all over his arms and legs from the training staff. At a time when goaltending wasn't a great deal of fun because shots were getting harder and higher and the equipment wasn't better, Tony was always messing around with equipment. He had stuff to cover the toe caps of his skates. He had little bars to cover his eyes on the outside of his fiberglass mask. He always had little additions to his equipment. When you watched him play, he looked like a big guy in the net, spread out with big pads and arms. But when you met him, he really wasn't a big guy."

Tony and Phil Esposito's epic NHL battles had roots in the basement of their Sault Ste. Marie, Ontario, home. Tony, falling victim to little brother's syndrome, would find himself guarding the nets, doing his best to prevent Phil from having any reason to gloat.

"He was younger," Phil explains, "so he had to play goal. Somebody had to stop pucks for me."

Years later they would take their one-on-one duels to hockey's biggest stage, while in cellars across North America, brothers would emulate Phil and Tony's act, pretending they were the Espositos. There had been other NHL brother combinations to feature a goalie and a shooter (Paul and Tiny Thompson in the twenties and thirties and Brian and Gary Smith in the sixties). But none attained the heights that the Espositos combined to scale—an unprecedented relationship in professional sports history.

The NHL's most prolific shooter and its preeminent stopper, both from the same home, sharing the same parentage. Imagine Dick Butkus and Bart Starr as gridiron brothers, or Bob Gibson and Willie Mays as baseball siblings.

By the time Tony made the NHL grade for good, Phil was already established as the game's number one sniper. He won the Art Ross Trophy as league scoring champ in 1968–69 while registering 126 points, becoming the first NHL player to hit triple figures in a single season. Two of those points came at the expense of his little brother.

When the Montreal Canadiens lost Gump Worsley and Rogatien Vachon to injury that season, they summoned Tony from their Houston farm club in the Central League. Tony debuted in a mop-up role against the Oakland Seals and was handed the starting assignment on December 5, 1968, against the Bruins at Boston Garden. He shut out every Bruin that day except one. "Phil got both their goals," Tony recalls of that 2–2 tie. "His little brother, making his first NHL start, and he shows me no pity."

Brotherly love does have its limits, Phil suggests. "When it came to goalies, I wouldn't even give my brother a break," he says.

Not that Tony needed any. The following spring he moved to Chicago in the NHL intraleague draft. Word was that Montreal general manager Sam Pollock owed Tommy Ivan (his Chicago counterpart) a favor. The Black Hawks were a last-place team in 1968–69 and in desperate need of a goaltender. Tony more than filled that bill. By the end of the 1969–70 season, the Black Hawks were in first place and Tony was the most talked-about rookie goalie since Frank Brimsek unseated Thompson as Boston's netminder in 1938. They also attached Brimsek's nickname—"Mr. Zero"—to this new phenom, with good reason. Tony posted 15 shutouts. In NHL history, only George Hainsworth, with 22 in 1928–29, ever hung up more zeros in a single season.

As Brimsek had done 31 seasons earlier, Tony won the Vezina Trophy as the league's top goalie and the Calder Trophy as its outstanding rookie. A graduate of Michigan Tech, he emerged as the first NHL netminding star who played U.S. college hockey.

From 1968 to 1974 Tony captured three Vezina Trophies, and Phil won five Art Ross Trophies.

Esposito spreads out to make a glove save.

On game day, Esposito's focus was all-emcompassing.

Between them the brothers appeared in six Stanley Cup finals. They also fought several sensational head-to-head bouts. Boston swept Chicago in the 1970 Stanley Cup semifinals. Phil fired a hat trick past Tony in Game 1, then spent the night at Tony's place, worried about his brother's condition after a Ken Hodge slap shot blackened both of Tony's eyes. "It's tough to have a lot of success when your brother's such a big scorer," Tony says of Phil.

The 1968 night that Phil drilled a pair past Tony was their first experience as opponents, other than those cellar-dwelling sets. "He played junior and I played college," Tony said. "Before that, we were always on the same team."

While leaving Chicago was the best thing that ever happened to Phil—his record-setting scoring ability emerged after a 1967 trade to Boston—getting to the Windy City was Tony's break. He tended to Chicago's goal for 15 seasons, taking the Black Hawks to a pair of Stanley Cup finals. But their performance in Chicago wasn't the only difference between the pair. Phil was easygoing, the life of the party. On game day, Tony went into complete external shutdown mode. He talked to no one, not even his wife and children. "I was all business," he explains. "I needed that time to myself."

Tony's unique style of goaltending—the butterfly, in which he formed an inverted V with his pads—evolved from watching Glenn Hall play goal for Chicago when Phil was with the Black Hawks. Tony modified Hall's version of the butterfly more dramatically, crouching low and flopping to make almost every save. "Aggressive goaltending," Tony calls it. "Attacking the puck."

In the days before goaltending equipment was inflated to epic proportions, Esposito developed gimmicks to heighten his advantage over the shooters. "He had a plastic pad he'd wear on his arm at the end of his blocker, which he used as a ramp to send pucks flying out of play," Hall of Fame NHL linesman Matt Pavelich says. "He used to sew fishnet between his legs and under his arms.

"We checked his pads all the time, because we were sure he was using illegal pads, but they always measured out to be correct. . . . We couldn't figure it out; then one day, we discovered his secret. He had zippers in the side of his pads and he'd just fill them with stuffing after we measured them."

His methods and his style were certainly unconventional, but it would be sheer madness to suggest that Esposito doesn't deserve recognition as one of hockey's greatest goalies.

"I respect him so much because he came up in an era when the hockey mind-set jumped to the conclusion that you couldn't play if you were on your knees," ESPN analyst and former NHL forward Bill Clement says. "Tony went against the grain. He swam upstream like a salmon, but fortunately for him, he didn't die when he got to the top. He beat all the odds to be successful."

16 | CLINT BENEDICT

BORN: Ottawa, Ontario, September 25, 1894

DIED: November 12, 1976

SHOT: Left	HEIGHT: 5'11"	WEIGHT: 185 lbs.
Stanley Cups: 4		

NOTABLE ACHIEVEMENTS: Hall of Famer; first NHL goalie to post back-to-back shutouts; first to post three straight Stanley Cup shutouts and four in one playoff year, both still records; only goalie to post four shutouts in a playoff season on two occasions; first NHL goalie to wear a mask; second on all-time list with 15 career Stanley Cup shutouts; runner-up for the 1926–27 Vezina Trophy; one of only eight NHL goalies to post three shutouts in one Stanley Cup series (with Davey Kerr, Martin Brodeur, Turk Broda, Frank McCool, Felix Potvin, Brent Johnson, and Patrick Lalime); one of only five goalies to post three consecutive shutouts in Stanley Cup play (with John Ross Roach, McCool, Johnson, and Lalime).

Johnny Bower's Commentary on Benedict

"A strapping six-footer, Benedict was one of the game's first big goalies, during an era when the short kid or the fat kid was usually shunted into the nets. His flopping style was in sharp contrast to the stand-up style performed by his peers, but Benedict's size enabled him to adopt this more radical approach to puck-stopping. He also stayed with the thin, cricket-style pads throughout his career, even after larger leather leg protectors came into vogue, feeling the lightweight pads allowed for quicker movement. Benedict was a scrapper who'd tangle with anyone who came too close to his net. He was also a superstitious sort and throughout his career hung a horseshoe in the webbing of his net during games."

Second Opinion: The Windsor Star's *Jimmy Thompson* on Benedict

"Clint Benedict is a man whom shrewd critics have called hockey's greatest goaler. Benedict and the late Georges Vezina were acknowledged kings of the net. . . . Benedict possesses an eagle eye and the quickness of a cat. Benny's famous splits in front of the net still give the fans a big thrill."

Clint Benedict was acknowledged as hockey's first inventive goaltender—both in how he changed the game and in how he went about changing it. Fear never prevented him from trying something new or forcing others to see things his way, even if it meant bending the laws of the game to open their eyes.

This pioneering puckstopper entered the big-league ranks with the National Hockey Association's Ottawa Senators in 1912 at a time when netminders would receive a minor penalty if they sprawled on the ice to make a save. Viewing this prohibition as outlandish, Benedict was determined to get it overturned. He developed a knack for taking a fall and making the spill appear to be accidental.

"What you had to be is sneaky," Benedict said in a 1976 interview with *Hockey Digest*. "You'd make a move, fake losing your balance or footing, and put the officials on the spot—did I fall down, or did I intentionally go down?"

Critics chastised Benedict's rule violations and gave him nicknames such as "Praying Benny" and "Tumbling Clint" because he spent so much time on his knees. But his efforts were gaining a foothold with frustrated referees, who took their complaints to National Hockey League president Frank Calder during the 1917–18 season. Calder, equally dismayed by his officials' inability to accurately determine Benedict's intent, took the rule off the books on January 9, 1918. "In the future, they can fall on their knees, or stand on their heads, if they think they can stop the puck better in that way than by standing on their feet," Calder told the *Montreal Star*.

In 1930 Benedict briefly employed this crude leather mask.

Benedict's success at changing the rule drew mocking comments. A day before Ottawa's January 12, 1918, game in Montreal, the *Star* quipped, "Many people will go to tomorrow's match no doubt with no other purpose than to see how often Benedict . . . will fall in the nets, now that president Calder's new rule permits him to do so."

Benedict wasn't the only Senator to go down that night. They were routed 9–4 by the Canadiens, but Ottawa was about to rise to the top of the NHL behind the stopping abilities of their sprawling sensation. Benedict served notice that Ottawa was the team to beat during the 1919–20 season, opening with a 2–0 win over the Toronto St. Patricks, followed by a 3–0 whitewash of the Canadiens, the first back-to-back shutouts in NHL history. Ottawa just kept rolling, capturing both halves of the NHL's split schedule, then dropping the Pacific Coast Association's Seattle Metropolitans in the Stanley Cup final.

Another Cup win followed the next season, this time over Vancouver. In these interleague series, alternating games were played by each league's rule-book. Always seeking an edge, Benedict the improviser quickly took advantage of the more offensively advanced western regulations, which permitted forward passing in all zones. "The Ottawa goalie made good use of the forward pass allowed by the coast rules," the *Winnipeg Free Press* noted during the 1921 Cup final. "Benedict used it at first experimentally, but finding it useful, made it a very effective part of his game." As was Benedict's nature, he also sought to discover exactly how far he could push the envelope. "[Benedict] even took to throwing the rubber by hand, until stopped by the referee."

Rising to become the NHL's first dynasty, the Senators won the Cup again in 1922–23, defeating the Edmonton Eskimos in the final. During this series, another side of Benedict's edginess came into evidence—his dogged determination to protect the front of his net. "Benedict, you wouldn't fool around with him, because he'd cut you in half," Hall of Fame Ottawa defenseman King Clancy told Karl-Eric Reif and Jeff Z. Klein during a 1986 interview.

Benedict Was an Innovator Because . . .

His flopping caused the NHL to change its rules in 1917–18 to allow goalies to leave their feet to make a save.

In the second period, Benedict clobbered an Edmonton player with his stick and was assessed a two-minute penalty by referee Mickey Ion. "He chopped some guy down and I was the closest one to him," Clancy said. In those days, netminders sat out their infractions. "He handed me the stick and says, 'Take care of this place until I get back,'" added Clancy, who held the fort and shared a 1–0 shutout with Benedict, as Ottawa won its third Cup in four seasons.

Between the 1918–19 and 1923–24 seasons, Benedict led the NHL in wins and shutouts every season and in goals-against average five times. "I think that he was on about a par with [Georges] Vezina," was Clancy's estimation of Benedict's ability. But Ottawa had discovered a new hot-shot amateur goalie named Alex Connell, and just as Benedict had pushed peerless Percy LeSueur out of a job 12 years earlier, he was about to give way to Connell. His contract was purchased by the expansion Montreal Maroons, and it proved to be one of hockey's wisest investments.

The Maroons won the Stanley Cup in 1925–26, in their second season of existence, thanks to the almost impenetrable wall Benedict threw up in front of their net. He established two playoff records that have never been bettered, posting four shutouts, including three in a row. His goals-against average for the Cup final series against the Victoria Cougars was a piddling 0.75. "His saves were spectacular and to the Victorias, heart-breaking," wrote the Toronto *Globe*.

That would be the last time Benedict would lift Lord Stanley's mug, but he still had one more history-changing moment to add to his repertoire. Battling Boston midway through the 1929–30 season, Benedict dove to save a point-blank shot from the Bruins' Dit Clapper and was struck square on the head. He finished the game and two nights later, still woozy and probably suffering from the effects of what is now known as post-concussion syndrome, he assumed his position in front of the goal to face the Canadiens. Ten minutes into the contest, Benedict took a Howie Morenz howitzer flush in the face, shattering his nose and cheekbones. He didn't play again until a 3–3 tie February 20 at Madison Square Garden against the New York Americans, making 30 saves and hockey history.

"Benedict, the Maroons goalie, played his first game since his injuries over a month ago, wearing a huge mask to protect his injured nose," noted *The New York Times*.

The first NHL goalie to don facial protection, Benedict wore a leather contraption that looked hauntingly similar to Hannibal Lecter's muzzle in *Silence of the Lambs*. "It was leather and wire with a big nosepiece," Benedict recalled of the mask, constructed by a Boston firm, but soon discarded by him. "The nosepiece proved the problem, because it obscured my vision."

Years later, when Jacques Plante received credit for making the mask a standard piece of goalie equipment, hockey's original masked man nodded in admiration. "If he has perfected it, if he's making money on it and protecting goalers, good luck to him," Benedict said.

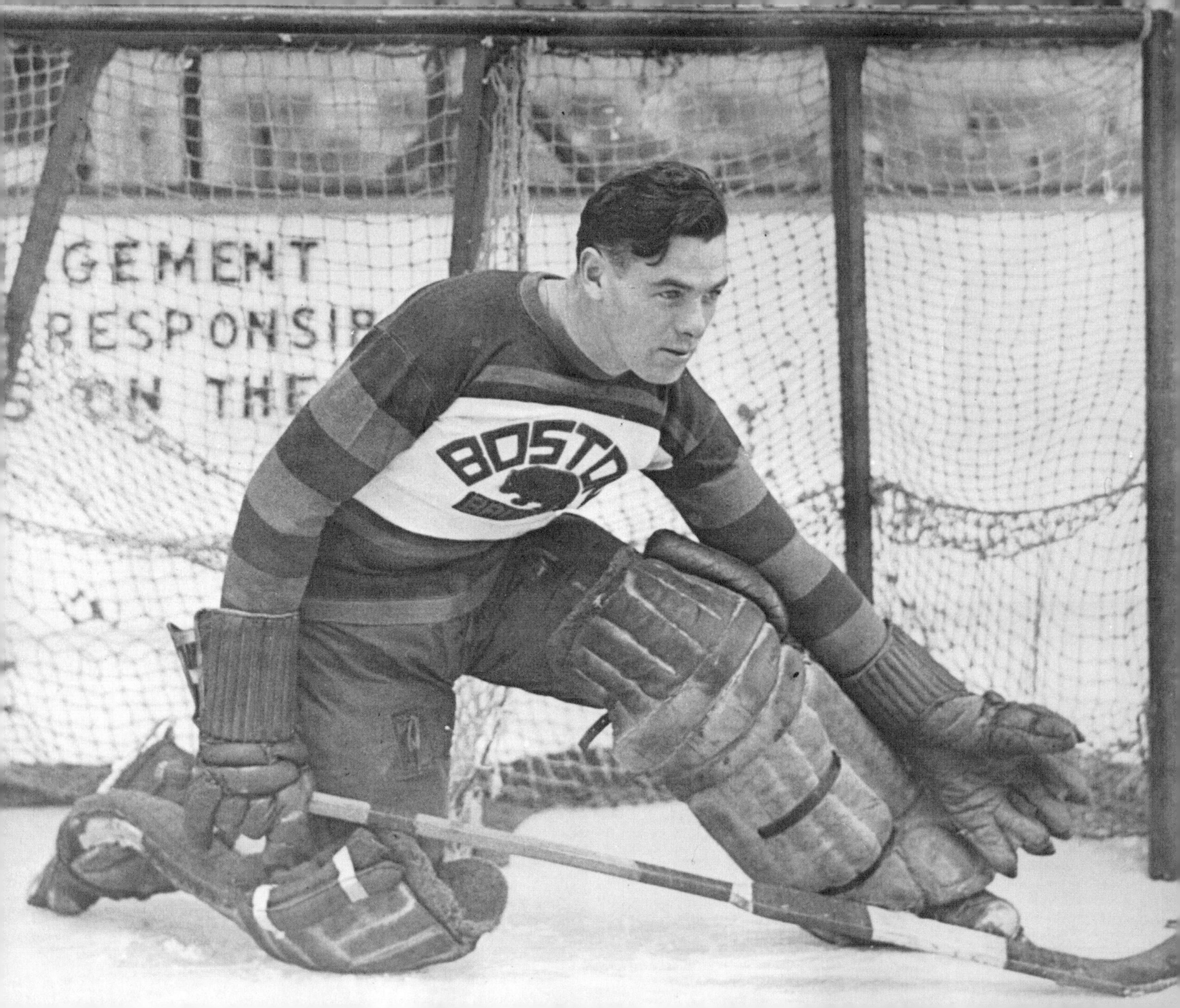
GEMENT
RESPONSI
ON THE
BOSTO

20 | CECIL "TINY" THOMPSON

BORN: Sandon, British Columbia, May 31, 1905

DIED: February 9, 1981

SHOT: Left	HEIGHT: 5′10″	WEIGHT: 160 lbs.
Stanley Cups: 1		Vezina Trophies: 4
NHL First All-Star Team: 2		NHL Second All-Star Team: 2
NHL All-Star Games: 1		

NOTABLE ACHIEVEMENTS: Hall of Famer; only Hall of Fame goalie to post a shutout in his NHL debut; led NHL in wins five times, including each of his first three seasons; part of the first NHL brother combination in which one was a goalie—his younger brother, Paul, was a left wing with the New York Rangers and Chicago; led the NHL in shutouts four times and in goals-against average four times; 5–0–0 with three shutouts and 0.60 GAA in 1928–29 playoffs as a rookie; posted a career 1.88 GAA in Stanley Cup play; missed just one game in his first 10 NHL seasons; his 14-game unbeaten streak in 1929–30 was an NHL record at the time, and his .875 winning percentage from that season is an NHL single-season record; fifth on all-time shutout list.

Johnny Bower's Commentary on Thompson

"In reading some of the work of writer Vern DeGeer of *The Windsor Star*, I got the impression that Thompson was ahead of his time as a puckhandler. DeGeer said Thompson was the best at his time at forward passing. Thanks to DeGeer we also know that Thompson used ordinary gloves, even smaller than those used by forwards. What was handed down about Thompson was that he had one of the quickest glove hands in that era, honed by years of playing baseball."

Second Opinion: Former Detroit Teammate Carl Liscombe on Thompson

"He was strong and he could really handle the puck. Tiny was a big, stand-up goalie. He was tall and he'd catch everything. He almost never, ever went down to his knees to make a save. He loved to play the game, he loved to be on the ice, and he was always willing to help you to get better. I could always score goals, but Tiny was the one who taught me how to be a top goal scorer, how to beat the best goalies. Every day after practice he'd take me out on the ice for about an hour, line up some pucks, and have me just come in on him. He showed me the weak spots to go for against certain goalies. By the time we were done, I knew what every goalie in the league was going to do."

Cecil "Tiny" Thompson's work with the Boston Bruins turned him into a larger-than-life hero to thousands of wide-eyed youngsters. But when Tiny was tiny, it was his work behind the Calgary Tigers net that gave birth to his immense talent. From the time he was big enough to see over the boards, Tiny idolized Charlie Reid, the goaltender for the Western Canada Hockey League's Tigers, the 1923–24 Stanley Cup finalists in Thompson's adopted hometown of Calgary. At every Tigers home game, Thompson could be found in the front row, directly behind Reid's cage, seeking to learn the nuances of the position. Reid took a liking to the ambitious boy. They grew close and the two would talk goaltending before, during, and after every game.

Thompson proved a good listener. When he donned the pads he quickly advanced through the amateur ranks. With the roles now reversed, Reid situated himself behind Thompson's goal. Cecil earned a spot with the junior club in Canmore, Alberta, but when Reid ventured there to watch his protégé in action, he was shocked to discover Thompson skating on the forward line.

"You'll just be an ordinary hockey player as a forward," Reid said, lecturing his pupil after the game. "You should be a great goaltender. Now you go in there and tell the manager that he has to put you in goal. And if he won't do it, then quit the team."

Thompson issued his ultimatum to the Canmore coach and from that day on he was a goaltender. A great goaltender, as Reid predicted. With the Bruins Thompson led the NHL in wins in each of his first three seasons. Debuting in 1928–29, Thompson posted a 1.15 goals-against average and 12 shutouts in 44 games. He went 5–0 in the playoffs and his minuscule 0.60 goals-against average backstopped the Bruins to their first Stanley Cup. "When your team finishes first and goes on to win the Stanley Cup in your rookie season, that's quite a thrill," Thompson said in a 1976 interview with *Hockey Digest*.

His .875 winning percentage in 1929–30 remains a league record. His experience on the forward line gave Thompson the ability to play the puck—he was credited with an assist in a January 14, 1936, game against the Toronto Maple Leafs—and few netminders of his era could boast that they devoted more time to refining their craft. "He works in practice just as he works in a game," Boston teammate Jim "Peg" O'Neil told *The Windsor Star* in a 1936 interview. "We'll go for long stretches without scoring on him while drilling. He loves to engage in battles of wits with his teammates. He lays wagers that no one can score on him within stipulated times. Every player on the club will take his turn rushing, but the result is usually the same—no goal. He's poison at close quarters."

The exception was when Boston winger Woody Dumart was winding up. "The pads he was wearing were nothing like the pads they are wearing today," recalls Boston teammate Milt Schmidt. "Tiny used to step out of the net all the time when Woody Dumart would shoot. Woody had a very heavy shot. When it would hit Tiny's pads, it would go right through the pads and he would say, 'To hell with that, I'm not staying in there for that.'"

Thompson won the Vezina Trophy four times and was a four-time league All-Star. "Thompson was good at everything," NHL opponent Clint Smith says. "He was a great angle player, had a great pair of hands, and was exceptionally good on his feet."

Thompson picked up his famous nickname in midget hockey. His teammates jokingly labeled him Tiny because at 5′10″, he was the tallest player on the team. But as Thompson advanced to the pro game, his nickname came to represent the odds of enemy scorers getting the puck past him.

"I bought Thompson sight unseen from Minneapolis and never regretted it," Boston manager Art Ross told the Associated Press, insisting Thompson was the greatest NHL netminder since Georges Vezina.

Thompson spent 11 seasons with the Bruins, leading the NHL in wins five times and in shutouts on four occasions, before moving to Detroit in 1938. "This is the greatest goalie in the world," Detroit coach Jack Adams exclaimed, finding few willing to engage him in debate.

Thompson Was an Innovator Because . . .

As an astute baseball player who played semipro ball on the sandlots of Calgary, he was the first to use catching the puck with the glove hand as a defense mechanism.

24 | VLADISLAV TRETIAK

BORN: Dmitrov, Soviet Union, April 25, 1952

SHOT: Left	**HEIGHT:** 6'1"	**WEIGHT:** 202 lbs.
Olympic Gold Medals: 3	Olympic Silver Medals: 1	
World Championships: 10		

NOTABLE ACHIEVEMENTS: Hall of Famer; first European player elected; four times named the best goalie at the World Championships; MVP of the 1981 Canada Cup; drafted by Montreal Canadiens, but never played in the NHL; debuted in Soviet Elite League at 17 and won 13 titles with Central Red Army.

Johnny Bower's Commentary on Tretiak

"I saw him play in 1972 live when the Soviets played at the [Maple Leaf] Gardens. He was the star of the series until Paul Henderson scored the winning goal. He wasn't really an angle goaltender at the time; he'd stay in his crease and rely on his quick reflexes. He had big quick hands and would make the big saves when he had to. I had a chance to meet a lot of the players in 1972 at the

Gardens, and he's a nice fellow to talk to and is willing to share his knowledge of the position with almost anyone. That's why he's helped develop goaltenders like [Dominik] Hasek and [Ed] Belfour into top-notch NHLers."

Second Opinion: 1980 U.S. Olympic Coach Herb Brooks on Tretiak

"I know Tretiak was an incredibly patient goaltender, and that's something that is very important. We talk about patience all the time for shooters, but it's just as important for goaltenders. He always let the play come to him. He didn't jump or guess. Too many athletic goaltenders start guessing too soon. They become acrobats before the fact. Tretiak used his athletic ability in the right sequence. He only reacted to rebounds or shots off passes. You never caught him guessing. And, of course, the psychology is part of the equation. He had that mystique. The intimidation factor he had on the other team was significant. But would it have mattered if [Viktor Tikhonov] had kept Tretiak in the game? We will never know, but the odds say we could have had some trouble."

In a world where athletes are playing again three weeks after knee surgery, Vladislav Tretiak still nurses a festering wound from a game 22 years ago.

Tretiak is the only non-NHL Russian elite player to be named to the Hockey Hall of Fame, and he was voted as the best Russian athlete of the 20th century. He owns three Olympic gold medals and one silver. His life is wrapped in glory, but he is still angered that Soviet coach Viktor Tikhonov yanked him after two periods against the Americans at the 1980 Olympics in Lake Placid, New York.

"I would have four gold medals if not for Tikhonov's bad judgment," Tretiak says.

Tretiak's pride was severely sprained when Tikhonov opted to switch to Vladimir Myshkin after Mark Johnson scored late in the second period to tie the game 2–2. "I'm never going to forget that," he says. "Me coming out? That had never happened before."

The Americans ended up scoring two goals and beat the Soviet Union 4–3 in the greatest upset in international hockey history.

The rawness of Tretiak's two-decade-old anger speaks to how driven he was to be the best at his craft, and why he deserves a place among this collection of NHL standouts because he was the first European to earn NHL respect.

He is undeniably deserving of respect, even though the North American hockey community didn't want to give him any heading into the 1972 Summit Series.

In a Canadian Press story published before Team Canada faced the Soviets in this historic series, Toronto Maple Leafs coach John McLellan and scout Bob Davidson, who had gone to the Soviet Union to evaluate the Russian players, said they weren't impressed with Tretiak.

"We saw Tretiak, and he didn't look particularly good," Davidson was quoted as saying. "He let in eight goals, some high over his shoulders and a couple between his legs."

As it turned out, the scouts had witnessed Tretiak when he was in the midst of angst over his pending nuptials.

In the first game of that series, the Soviets defeated Canada 7–3. Tretiak has called that game "my best ever."

Tretiak Was an Innovator Because . . .

He was the first European goaltender

to gain the respect of NHL players.

The Canadians had underestimated Tretiak, who performed well enough that the Canadians needed a dramatic goal by Paul Henderson to win the eight-game series 4–3–1.

Tretiak played on 10 Soviet World Championship teams, but one of his most memorable international performances came when he played for Red Army against the Montreal Canadiens in a 3–3 tie that probably was one of the most exciting hockey games ever played. Tretiak made 35 saves.

As familiar as Montreal fans were with Tretiak's mystique, it seemed appropriate that the Canadiens drafted him in 1983.

After the Soviets won the 1984 Olympic gold medal, even Tretiak was convinced they would allow him to play in the NHL. Their refusal produced another level of bitterness that still exists today.

He responded to the Soviet rejection by retiring at the height of his career at age 32.

"I had at least five or seven good years left in me," Tretiak said. "I was still very fit and in excellent shape. Montreal's general manager, Serge Savard, was in Moscow to negotiate my release, but it was useless. They wouldn't let me go."

The presumption is that Tretiak would have been a standout NHL goaltender, perhaps in the mold of a Ken Dryden. We will never know for sure, just like we will never know if Tretiak would have made a difference had he played the third period in 1980.

USA 1980 captain Mike Eruzione likes to remind folks that Myshkin was considered the Soviets' best goaltender, which means theoretically it would be like an NHL team pulling Patrick Roy in favor of Martin Brodeur. Says Eruzione: "Who knows, we might have gotten six against Tretiak."

TRETIA

40 | HUGH LEHMAN

BORN: Pembroke, Ontario, October 27, 1885

DIED: April 8, 1961

SHOT: Left	HEIGHT: 5'8"	WEIGHT: 168 lbs.
Stanley Cups: 1	All-Star Selections: 11	

NOTABLE ACHIEVEMENTS: Hall of Famer; selected to Pacific Coast Hockey Association All-Star team 11 times; led PCHA in wins six times and in shutouts five times; played in eight Stanley Cup finals; one of only two goalies (with Percy LeSueur) to challenge for the Cup with two teams in the same season (1910, with Berlin and Galt); first former NHL goalie to coach an NHL team (Chicago, 1927–28); led the NHL in games played and minutes, 1926–27; played in major league ranks until age 42, performing in 22 pro seasons.

Johnny Bower's Commentary on Lehman

"Hockey was a seven-player game when Hugh Lehman took up the sport, and the roles of each skater were clearly defined. The goaltender protected the net and the defensemen protected the goal area, seldom venturing into the attacking zone. Wingers moved up and down the ice along the boards, while the center took care of the middle ice. The rover, a position later eliminated, was the only one with the freedom to move around the rink. At least that was the way it was drawn up on the chalkboard, but Lehman was a fellow who blurred those lines. A strong skater and skilled puckhandler, Lehman used his abilities to chase down loose pucks, to chip them away from enemy attackers with his stick, and to quickly headman them to his own attackers, catching defenders flat-footed. The Ron Hextall of his day, he scored a goal as an amateur. Lehman could also stop the puck with the best of them."

Second Opinion: *The* Winnipeg Free Press *on Lehman*

"Lehman's work in goal bordered on the marvelous. While he is older than most men who participate in active sports, he is justified to the title 'Eagle Eye' bestowed on him by coast league fans. He stopped shots from all angles, all distances, and even came out of his goal to clear shots that had dribbled through the outer defense line. He was as valuable to his team as almost any two of his teammates. The long forward passing of the goalkeeper was a feature. Not content with turning aside numerous shots that rained in on him, he frequently left his net and carried the loose puck and passed it out to his forwards. This was a risky performance, but he got away with it every time."

Lehman Was an Innovator Because . . .

He was the first goalie to roam from his net and play the puck up to his forwards.

His nose a disheveled mess after it was broken in a collision with teammate Art Duncan during Game 1 of the 1924 Stanley Cup semifinal, Vancouver goalie Hugh Lehman laughed heartily when a *Winnipeg Free Press* reporter asked if he'd be able to play in Game 2. "Sure, I am going to play," Lehman cackled. "What's the use of living if you don't take a chance?"

Lehman's theory on life also applied to his philosophy for puckstopping. He believed in risk management. Why wait for them to bring the puck to you, he reasoned, when you can go get it yourself?

"Old Eagle Eyes," as they called him, was free to fly. He would roam from his net to corral loose pucks, dart out to check it away from onrushing forwards, and race into the corners of the rink to battle startled opponents for possession of the puck. Then he would confidently send his team out on scoring forays through his hard, accurate forward-passing skills.

"Lehman was leaving the goal continuously, checking Ottawa men who broke through," the *Winnipeg Free Press* noted in its coverage of the 1921 Stanley Cup final, though not everyone found his wandering ways so entertaining. "Lehman was just as effective as ever," the Vancouver *Province* wrote in its report on Game 4 of the series, "but the fans would be more pleased if he stuck a little closer to his goal job. It was the greatest piece of good fortune that Ottawa did not score when Lehman was 20 feet to one side in the middle period."

Lehman's teams participated in Stanley Cup competition eight times during his 21-season pro career. In the span of two months in 1910, Lehman backstopped separate Stanley Cup challenges. He came up short in both bids—with Galt against Ottawa and for Berlin versus the Montreal Wanderers—but his performance raised eyebrows. "His work has all been of the gilt-edged variety, his stopping being generally recorded as phenomenal," the *Montreal Star* noted after Lehman's efforts on behalf of Berlin.

His pioneering, frontier spirit carried Lehman to the West Coast in 1911 when the new Pacific Coast Hockey Association was formed, and in 1914–15 he guarded the twine for the Vancouver Millionaires, the first PCHA club to capture the Stanley Cup. Every regular from that team—Lehman, Frank Nighbor, Fred "Cyclone" Taylor, Si Griffis, Barney Stanley, Frank Patrick, and Mickey MacKay—earned Hall of Fame recognition. "We were beaten by the best team we ever played," Ottawa coach Alf Smith confessed.

Vancouver was invited to play an exhibition series in New York against the Montreal Wanderers. Lehman, who maintained money in his wallet about as long as he kept his feet planted in front of his net, took his wife on a Manhattan shopping spree, buying her the pick of designer outfits. Taylor, a Canadian immigration officer, advised his netminder that he'd never get his booty across the border without paying duty. So Lehman farmed out the dresses among his teammates—most of whom were single—leaving puzzled Canada customs officers to wonder whether Canada's best hockey team was made up of the nation's most famous drag queens.

When the western league folded in 1926 Lehman joined the Chicago Black Hawks, leading the NHL in games (44) and minutes played (2,797) in 1926–27. When the 1927–28 season commenced, Lehman, 42, was handed the task of schooling newcomer Chuck Gardiner. One afternoon he happened upon Black Hawks owner Major Frederic McLaughlin, who was sketching out plays. "What do you think?" McLaughlin asked. "That's the craziest bunch of junk I've ever seen," Lehman responded.

Realizing he'd just suggested the man who signed his paychecks was nuts, Lehman began packing his gear, when he got the expected call to come to McLaughlin's office. Anticipating a pink slip, Lehman instead received an offer. "Hughie," McLaughlin bellowed, "you are the new coach of the Black Hawks."

Another chance well taken in the life of "Old Eagle Eyes."

Lehman backstopped Vancouver to the 1915 Stanley Cup.

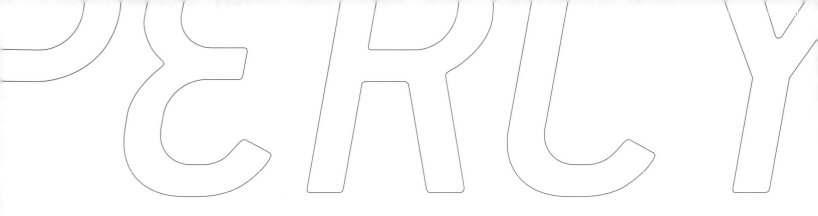

41 | PERCY LESUEUR

BORN: Quebec City, Quebec, November 18, 1881

DIED: January 27, 1962

SHOT: Left	HEIGHT: 5'7"	WEIGHT: 150 lbs.
Stanley Cups: 3		All-Star Selections: 1

NOTABLE ACHIEVEMENTS: Hall of Famer; led Eastern Canada Hockey Association and National Hockey Association in wins once each; played four times for the Stanley Cup; posted a 7–2 record in Stanley Cup play; captained Ottawa Senators for three seasons, also serving as player/coach in 1913–14; selected to play goal in 1908 Hod Stuart Memorial All-Star Game, hockey's first All-Star Game; penned a hockey handbook during his playing days that was a popular read for youngsters; designed goal nets used in NHA and NHL from 1912 to 1925 and gauntlet-style goal gloves used by netminders during his era; served as referee and coach in NHL; managed Windsor Arena, Peace Bridge Arena, Syracuse Arena, and Detroit Olympia; helped assemble an ownership group that acquired Detroit Cougars in 1926–27; also worked as a newspaper columnist and broadcaster (an original member of *Hockey Night in Canada*'s Hot Stove League).

Johnny Bower's Commentary on LeSueur

"The gifts Percy LeSueur provided hockey extended far beyond his peerless ability to stop the puck. LeSueur was athletic enough to parry two and three shots in succession, even from close range, and was an able puckhandler, capable of clearing the biscuit to safety. LeSueur served as an NHL referee, coached the Hamilton Tigers, penned columns for *The Hamilton Spectator*, and was the first reporter to tabulate shots on goal as part of his game summaries. He managed arenas in Windsor, Ontario; Detroit; Fort Erie, Ontario; and Syracuse, New York. As a minor league coach in Buffalo and Syracuse, LeSueur employed spare players on the ice during intermissions to explain the nuances of hockey to newcomers and utilized afternoon games and radio broadcasts to help sell hockey in nonhockey environments."

Second Opinion: Hockey Historian Bill Fitsell on LeSueur

"LeSueur was a pioneer and an innovator, par excellence. He was a stand-up goalkeeper in the era when the rules prohibited netminders from lying, sitting, or kneeling in stopping the puck. He had an intense, roving style later attributed to Jacques Plante. 'He played with the alacrity of a tiger,' reported the *Ottawa Free Press* in 1907. 'He played with his hands, head, and feet. He never throws the puck away and in the tightest corners carries [it] to the back of his net and gives it to one of his forwards.' Facing a breakaway against Quebec, he ran out on the points of his skates and floored the attacker before he could shoot. As a player he developed a pad for the goaltender's gauntlet and in 1911 designed and patented the LeSueur net, with a 17-inch-deep top and a 22-inch-deep bottom. He was a keen observer of the game and in 1909 wrote and published a 48-page booklet called *How to Play Hockey*."

In the early days of Stanley Cup competition, any team could issue a formal challenge. If the trustees of the trophy found the squad to be worthy, they would order the Cup holders to arrange dates for the competition.

Such was the case in March 1906, when the tiny central Ontario town of Smiths Falls bid to do battle with the mighty Ottawa Silver Seven. Holders of the Stanley Cup for the previous four years, Ottawa had successfully defended its title seven times during that span, but the boys from Smiths Falls figured they had a secret weapon that would give them a fighting chance against hockey's first great dynasty—goaltender Percy LeSueur.

Despite being decidedly outplayed in the opener of the two-game, total-goals series, Smiths Falls came away 6–5 losers, thanks to the work of LeSueur.

"The most spectacular saves of the match were made by LeSueur," noted the *Montreal Star*'s account of the game. "Three of Ottawa's forwards got right down on him when there was no defenseman near enough to help him. First [Frank] McGee, then [Rat] Westwick, then [Harry] Smith shot, but on each occasion, though they were only a yard or two away, he managed to stop the puck and get it to safety. The way he stopped the most dangerous shots was a sight rarely seen."

Although Ottawa overpowered Smiths Falls 8–2 in Game 2, the credentials of the man who would become known as "Peerless Percy" were established. The Silver Seven were so impressed that they decided it might be best for all concerned if LeSueur joined them. Less than a week after their successful defense against Smiths Falls, the Silver Seven absorbed a 9–1 drubbing at the hands of the Montreal Wanderers in their next Cup challenge. Determining that goalie Billy Hague wasn't up to snuff, a call went out to the sensational saver from Smiths Falls.

Ottawa claimed that LeSueur's arrival in town was a coincidence. He'd moved to Ottawa anyway, so the Silver Seven figured they might as well sign him up. Owning an eight-goal lead in the two-game set, the Wanderers didn't protest his eligibility too vehemently. Montreal's Moose Johnson tallied an early goal, then LeSueur erected a barricade in front of his cage, as Ottawa poured in nine successive tallies to tie the count. Only a pair of late goals by Lester Patrick prevented the Wanderers from blowing the biggest scoreboard advantage in Stanley Cup history.

Amazingly, LeSueur came to Smiths Falls to play right wing and was converted to goal at the age of 21, when the regular netminder fell ill. He brought along his goal stick from Smiths Falls to Ottawa and was still using the same stick when he retired in 1916, keeping it for years as a souvenir. "The club bears slight resemblance to the present-day cudgel wielded by professional netminders," Vern DeGeer of *The Windsor Star* noted when LeSueur showed him the ancient piece of lumber in 1931. "It reminds one of the handle of an umbrella."

LeSueur performed in Ottawa's goal for eight seasons, leading the team to a pair of Stanley Cup titles, working as Ottawa's captain, coach, and manager during his tenure. "He is as sharp as a needle and recovers quickly," commented the *Montreal Star*. "He is a goaltender of high class."

LeSueur left pro hockey in 1916 for combat duty with Canada's 48th Highlanders during World War I, returning to serve the game as a referee, coach, arena operator, and journalist for nearly 50 years.

LeSueur Was an Innovator Because . . .
He changed the way the position was played by designing the first goalie gloves. A thinking man's goalie, he continued to come up with alterations that improved the game during and after his playing days.

43 | RON HEXTALL

BORN: Brandon, Manitoba, May 3, 1964

SHOT: Left	HEIGHT: 6'3"	WEIGHT: 192 lbs.
Vezina Trophies: 1		Conn Smythe Trophies: 1
NHL First All-Star Team: 1		NHL All-Star Games: 1

NOTABLE ACHIEVEMENTS: Scored two goals in NHL competition—once in the regular season, once in the playoffs; appeared in two Stanley Cup finals; led the NHL in wins, 1986–87; led the NHL in goals-against average, 1995–96; named American Hockey League top rookie and All-Star goalie, 1984–85; a third-generation NHLer, his grandfather, Bryan Hextall Sr., played with the New York Rangers and his father, Bryan Hextall Jr., played 11 NHL seasons, but neither were netminders.

Johnny Bower's Commentary on Hextall

"When I was scouting for Toronto, they'd send me to Brandon [Manitoba] to go watch Ron Hextall. The Wheat Kings were a lousy team at the time, and it seemed that every time I saw him, he'd give up five or six goals. It seemed that no matter what he did, the puck would somehow take a funny bounce and end up in the cage. I thought that he had potential, but he'd have a tough time making the NHL. Shows you how much I know about goaltending. The kid goes on and wins the Conn Smythe Trophy in 1987. What allowed Hextall to become one of the best goaltenders of his era was his desire to improve himself."

Second Opinion: Former NHL Player Peter McNab on Hextall

"Ron Hextall was the original outlet pass goalie. I remember Brad McCrimmon telling me they would peel off to the boards and Hextall would just hit them. They would hit the guy cutting through the middle and off they would go. Hextall took the concept of a goalie playing the puck and took it to the next level. They weren't just those push passes. He would drop his hands into a shooter's position and bang. If he had to throw an aerial, he did. If he had to bounce off the glass, he did. It was stuff we hadn't seen before from a goalie. We would see a goaltender go to a backhand and kind of clumsily lift it out of the zone. Now here's this guy who is snapping passes to defensemen."

Hextall Was an Innovator Because . . .

He handled the puck better than any goaltender who had come before him.

Ron Hextall will be recalled as one of the most memorable villains in goal-tending history.

"Ronny Hextall was a great character," says former NHL goalie John Davidson. "When he came to town, fans would want to race to the arena to boo him. He was the guy wearing the black hat. Hextall thrived on that."

Hextall was a tall, strapping athlete who punished opponents in many different ways. Nobody had ever seen anyone use his goalie stick in the manner that Hextall did. In addition to using it in the traditional manner to make saves, Hextall brandished it as a weapon. He was ruthless in cleaning goal scorers out of his workspace. Most important, he used his stick the way forwards and defensemen used theirs: to move the puck, to pass the puck, and even to score. Hextall's puckhandling was revolutionary for a goalie.

The first time former NHL goaltender Darren Pang witnessed Hextall wrist a puck up ice during a minor league hockey game, he felt as if he had just witnessed Superman flying out of a phone booth. "My jaw dropped," Pang says. "I'm thinking, 'You got to be kidding me.' I was considered a good puckhandling goaltender and I was a peewee compared to him."

Never short on confidence, Hextall would boldly handle the puck in many situations where other goalies wouldn't consider it. On December 8, 1987, late in the third period after Boston had pulled Rejean Lemelin for a sixth attacker, Hextall fired the puck the length of the ice for a goal. Billy Smith had once been credited with a goal because he was the last to touch a puck before a Colorado Rockies defenseman put it in his own net. Hextall was the first to actually steam a shot down the ice for a goal.

"I don't mean to sound cocky," Hextall told the media that night. "But I knew it was just a matter of time before I flipped one in."

As well as Hextall's stick served him, it also got him into trouble. He will be remembered for his slash against Edmonton's Kent Nilsson in the 1987 Stanley Cup final that earned him an eight-game suspension the following season. Especially in his early days, his temper could explode like Mount St. Helens. Other incidents included attacking Chris Chelios during a playoff game in retaliation for what the Montreal defenseman had done to a teammate and making a berserk dash after Pittsburgh forward Rob Brown during a playoff game.

Hextall had always been like that. He would tell the story about how classmates razzed him when his father, Bryan, played on a bad Pittsburgh Penguins team in the seventies. Hextall's brother would just agree to avoid a confrontation, but Hextall always wanted to argue the point.

One debate about Hextall is whether his emotions hurt him as much as they helped him. "Ron Hextall was a tremendous competitor," says former NHL coach Jacques Demers. "But the reason why he didn't reach the level of a Grant Fuhr or a Martin Brodeur was that he lost his cool if you got in his face. And it's funny because off the ice, he is a great guy."

Demers recalls that the Canadiens rallied against the Quebec Nordiques in a 1993 playoff series with a game plan of riling up Hextall. "If you just disturb him, bump him, you could get to him," Demers says.

TURK BRODA

GRANT FUHR

BILLY SMITH

MARTIN BRODEUR

WINNERS

GERRY CHEEVERS

HARRY "HAP" HOLMES

MIKE VERNON

RILEY HERN

JOHN BOWER "BOWSE" HUTTON

PADDY MORAN

11 | TURK BRODA

BORN: Brandon, Manitoba, May 15, 1914

DIED: October 17, 1972

SHOT: Left	HEIGHT: 5'9"	WEIGHT: 180 lbs.
Stanley Cups: 5	Vezina Trophies: 2	
NHL First All-Star Team: 2	NHL Second All-Star Team: 1	
NHL All-Star Games: 4		

NOTABLE ACHIEVEMENTS: Hall of Famer; led the NHL in shutouts twice and in goals-against average twice; ranks 11th on the NHL's all-time shutout list; tied a Stanley Cup record with three shutouts in 1950 semifinals against the Detroit Red Wings, but the Toronto Maple Leafs lost the series, including a 1–0 overtime decision in Game 7; one of only eight NHL goalies to post three shutouts in one Stanley Cup series (with Davey Kerr, Martin Brodeur, Frank McCool, Clint Benedict, Felix Potvin, Brent Johnson, and Patrick Lalime); won consecutive Memorial Cups (1955, 1956) as coach of the Toronto Marlboros; his No. 1 sweater was honored by the Maple Leafs.

Johnny Bower's Commentary on Broda

"I met Turk my first day at Maple Leaf Gardens. I had arrived early for a practice and I was sitting on the bench watching the Toronto Marlies' junior practice. Turk skated over to the bench and introduced himself to me. I'll never forget the two pieces of advice he gave me that day. He said, 'Johnny, Toronto is the greatest place in the world to play. They know this game and love this team. If you work hard and play hard, this city will give you all of the credit you deserve.' He then told me that he wanted me to wear the No. 1. He said, 'You're going to wear that No. 1 sweater and don't you ever, ever let anyone take that from you. . . . Don't you ever give up that sweater.' While I was with Toronto, I never gave up that sweater and that's why it was the greatest thrill of my life to have my No. 1 raised to the rafters at Maple Leaf Gardens the same night as Turk's No. 1. I only wish he could have been there that night with me."

Second Opinion: Former Teammate Harry Watson on Broda

"Turk was the best goalie in the playoffs of all time. Playing with him back there, you knew they weren't going to be able to get any by him. The thing I liked about him most was that he never blamed the forwards or defensemen when he gave up a goal. It was always his fault. One time in Detroit, I went to clear the puck and accidentally drove it past him, just inside the post. I felt terrible, but as we were going to the dressing room, Turk said, 'Don't worry about it, Harry. I should have stopped that shot.' Before every game and after every period, he'd sneak into one of the washroom stalls and light up a cigarette. Hap Day, our coach, he wasn't a smoker and didn't want anybody smoking, but he wasn't going to say anything, because of what Turk did for us on the ice."

Providing aid to the Red Cross and its war effort, the Montreal Canadiens and a group of NHL All-Stars staged an exhibition series in Hollywood shortly after the 1942–43 season. Toronto Maple Leafs netminder Turk Broda, never one to turn down an invitation, accepted the nod as the All-Star goalie.

Always the life of the party, Broda happened upon an American GI, and the two embarked on a tour of duty through Hollywood's most famous nightspots. In the wee hours, as dawn was about to break, an MP searching for missing soldiers found Broda's buddy passed out in the orchestra pit at one popular nightspot. Broda, meanwhile, was seated at the piano, tickling the ivories in a duet with that night's headliner, legendary jazz pianist Hoagy Carmichael.

Later that day, in typical Broda fashion, he blanked the Canadiens 1–0 in the deciding game of the series. Turk never missed the opportunity to lift a mug, whether he was on or off the ice. "He sure liked his beer," says Carl Liscombe, Broda's minor league teammate in Detroit and his NHL opponent for seven seasons.

Broda won five Stanley Cups with Toronto.

And he sure liked to win.

Detroit was called the city of champions during the 1935–36 sporting season—for good reason. The title roll started in the fall, when the Detroit Tigers upended the Chicago Cubs to win the World Series. A couple of months later, the Detroit Lions reigned supreme over the NFL, downing the New York Giants 26–7 in the championship game. On the ice the Detroit Red Wings captured their first Stanley Cup, and on the same weekend, the Detroit Olympics, the Red Wings' farm club, were crowned International Hockey League champions, spawning Broda's title-winning legend.

Broda's Olympian effort in goal against the Windsor Bulldogs brought the Olympics that championship, earning him a promotion to the NHL, albeit completely by coincidence.

Toronto Maple Leafs manager Conn Smythe, whose club was waging a futile battle with the Red Wings for the Stanley Cup, knew his goaltender, George Hainsworth, was nearing his 41st birthday and that his days as a premier puckstopper were dwindling. Smythe received promising reports about Bulldogs goalie Earl Robertson and decided to go to the IHL finals to take a look for himself.

Unfortunately for Robertson, he chose that night to cluck like a turkey, while Turk stood on his head in an 8–1 victory. "When Smythe came to that game, he'd never even heard of Turk Broda," recalls Liscombe. "He was there to see Robertson, who was the more seasoned goalie, but Turk, he was hotter than a pistol that night. We knew after the game that he'd be gone."

The Leafs paid Detroit $8,000 that spring to acquire Broda's rights in one of the most lopsided deals in NHL history. The move would come back to bite Red Wings boss Jack Adams where it hurt the most—in the Stanley Cup finals, where Broda backstopped Toronto to three titles at Detroit's expense.

Yet in Toronto, where Broda gained his fame, they frequently meddled with his winning ways. His excitable manner between the posts was the antithesis of his predecessor—the stoic, relaxed Hainsworth—and made Toronto's hockey minds cringe with disdain.

"When he first started out, they'd always be after him to try to do something different," recalls Lorne Carr, a right wing with the Leafs in Broda's early years. "He would do it and then they'd score on him and he'd be pretty mad after that. Finally they learned to leave him alone and that was a good idea, because to tell you the truth, we didn't care what he did in there, as long as he stopped the damn thing. And he sure did that."

Just as he had come to Toronto's attention by accident, Broda's introduction to goaltending was also happenstance. A pudgy boy who carried a spare tire around his midsection throughout his adult life, he was cut when he tried out

for defense with his school team in Brandon, Manitoba. Offered the goalie position, the youngster seized the opportunity.

Broda's extra girth remained a sore spot with critics when he was a pro. Smythe benched his goalie early in the 1949–50 season until he dropped his weight from 197 to 190. "People thought it was a publicity stunt and that Turk was in on it, but I don't know," Leafs teammate Joe Klukay says. "Smythe had Turk run up and down the stairs at the rink every day, and that didn't look like too much fun."

Nutrition and exercise tips arrived from fans across the country, and Broda's battle of the bulge even drew headlines on the society pages. He missed only one game before making the required weight.

Broda, whose nickname came from his unusual build—a large upper body offset by spindly lower limbs—which caused friends to label him "turkey legs," was adamant that his stocky frame didn't hinder him from stopping the puck. One day after practice, a determined Broda challenged teammate Max Bentley, thought to be the NHL's fastest skater, to a race and beat the flashy speedster.

No one disputed that hockey's fabulous fat man carried on an intense love affair with the nightlife. "He never seemed to have any money," Liscombe says. "Every day, he'd be borrowing 10 bucks off somebody."

But there never was any question as to whether Broda carried his weight when the games mattered most. Montreal's Bill Durnan is considered the dominant goalie of Broda's era, but put their numbers side by side and a significant difference emerges. Durnan won six Vezina Trophies and two Stanley Cups; Broda won two Vezinas and five Cups. His regular-season goals-against average was 2.53. In the playoffs, it dropped to 1.98.

"He was one of the best money players ever," former Boston center Milt Schmidt says. "He always did play real well during the playoffs."

The postseason was serious business to Broda. On game day he'd arrive early at the rink to take a nap in the dressing room. Before one key contest he was perturbed to discover some scrubs, extra bodies called up from the minors for playoff insurance, playing cards in his impromptu bedroom. He ordered them to leave and when they refused, he smashed every lightbulb with his pillow, shrouding their game in darkness.

The way he performed on the ice, you'd have thought he'd taken the same pillow to the red light behind his cage.

"Turk had a different attitude toward the game than most goalies and I think that's why he was so good in playoffs," Klukay says. "He was a happy-go-lucky guy. If things didn't go his way, he'd just say, 'I'll have to try to do the opposite the next game.' And that's what he did. Turk was Turk, and we loved him for it."

Broda Was a Winner Because . . . He played in eight Stanley Cup finals, winning five times. He posted 13 shutouts and a 1.98 goals-against average in 101 playoff games.

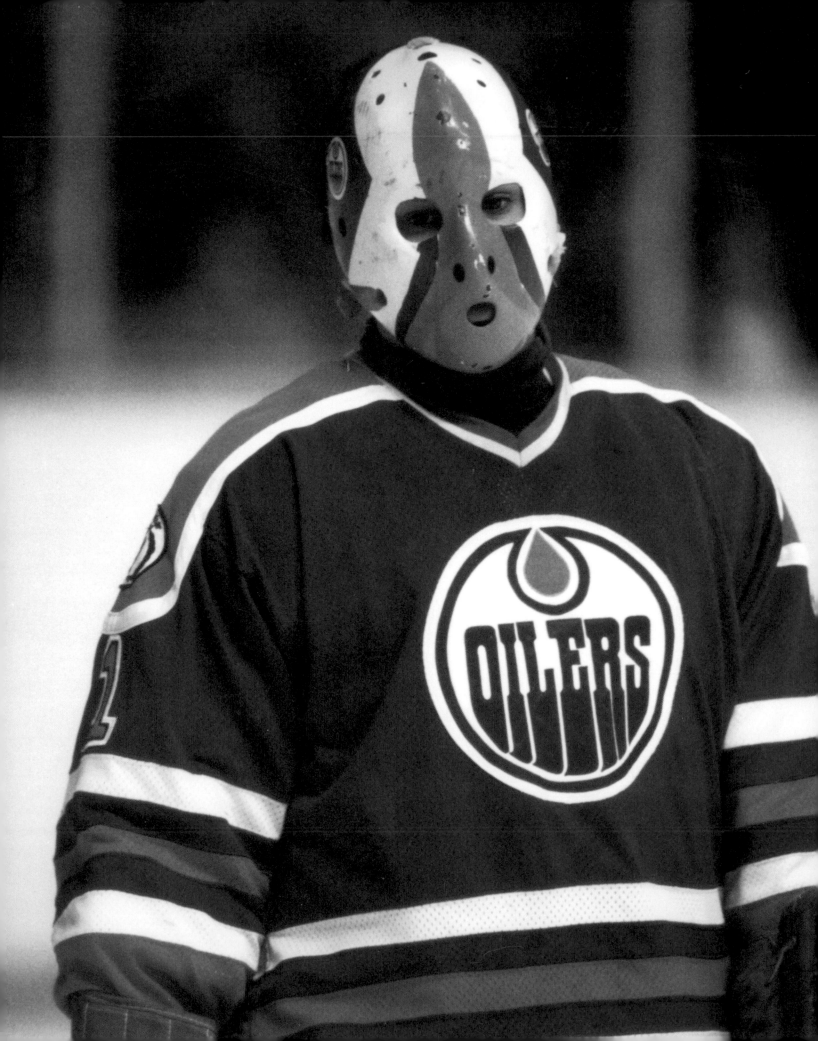

12 | GRANT FUHR

BORN: Spruce Grove, Alberta, September 28, 1962		
SHOT: Right	HEIGHT: 5'10"	WEIGHT: 201 lbs.
Stanley Cups: 5		Vezina Trophies: 1
Jennings Trophies: 1		NHL First All-Star Team: 1
NHL Second All-Star Team: 1		NHL All-Star Games: 6

NOTABLE ACHIEVEMENTS: Named 1987 Canada Cup All-Star; played in Rendezvous 1987; second all-time among goalies in Stanley Cup games played, wins, and minutes; led the NHL in shutouts, 1987–88; posted an NHL-record 23-game unbeaten streak by a rookie goalie in 1981–82; fifth all-time in games played by an NHL goalie; played NHL-record 79 games in 1995–96, including 76 in a row, also a single-season mark.

Johnny Bower's Commentary on Fuhr

"He was a hard-working goaltender who was well liked by all of his teammates. He played a style similar to Glenn Hall and Tony Esposito in that he was a stand-up goaltender who was very effective in the butterfly. The Leafs sent me out to find a goaltender in 1981 and I went out west to watch Fuhr play. I must have seen him play almost a dozen games before sending in my report to my supervisors. I told them that he was a solid goaltender who was quick and talented. I wasn't sure that he could step into the NHL right from the juniors, but I felt that he could make it with some seasoning. He was my number one choice. But the organization felt that we couldn't draft a black player at the time. I told the team that we'd regret it if we didn't choose him and I stand by that to this day!"

Second Opinion: Los Angeles Kings General Manager Dave Taylor on Fuhr

"What I remember about Grant is that if the Oilers were ahead 5–2, you might get the third and fourth goal against him. But you would never get the fifth. He had the ability to shut it down when it was necessary; at crucial times he could shut it down. He could jump across the net with half of his body with his glove hand, pads, or blocker. He would lunge across. Most goalies would just reach out with a glove or kick their legs; he would go across with his whole body."

Opponents who were buried by an Edmonton goal barrage in the eighties understood that one key to the shelling was, in fact, the only Oilers player who was no threat to score against them.

"Grant Fuhr was the reason the Oilers could play that wide-open style," says former NHL player Jim Nill. "They knew how good he was—that's why they played the way they did. They knew they could do anything they wanted and he would be back there."

In the mideighties Fuhr was presumed to be the best goaltender in the world. He was almost the perfect blend of temperament and talent. He was ultracompetitive and yet when pressure dripped from the rafters, he always performed as if he was in the midst of a pond hockey game. His style was perfect for a team that often surrendered almost as many prime scoring chances as it generated. Fuhr knew the team's style of play wasn't conducive to him winning the goals-against average title.

"He had the rare ability to give up three or four goals in an 8–4 game and then when the team needed to shut down momentum, he could do that," says former NHL goaltender Darren Pang, now an analyst for ESPN. "He could even give up a bad goal . . . but it was almost as if he would think, 'That didn't happen.' Good goal, bad goal, great save. He was always the same."

Fuhr consistently produced spectacular saves at the best time in the game. When Nill was playing for the Winnipeg Jets, he remembers feeling that though the team had outplayed the Oilers, "We would lose 5–2 because of Fuhr."

Fuhr also had a knack for making spectacular saves that could crush an opponent's spirit.

Under siege from the New Jersey Devils.

"He was like an evolution of guys like Glenn Hall, Roger Crozier, and maybe Tony Esposito in that they were really athletic goaltenders," says Philadelphia coach Ken Hitchcock.

As a teenager, Fuhr was an outstanding baseball catcher, and he now flirts with a pro golf career. To appreciate what kind of athlete he is, consider that he holds the NHL record of 14 assists in a season by a goaltender. That's five more than the second-place total. He finished his career with 46 career assists.

"He really brought an athleticism to the position," Hitchcock says. "He could make some miraculous saves because his hand/eye coordination was above everyone else in the league."

Former NHL goaltender John Davidson, now an ABC analyst, says simply, "Grant's glove hand was unbelievable."

That glove hand had to be exceptional to support Edmonton's open-throttle offense. "The Oilers used to give up as many great scoring chances as any team in the league," says former NHL coach Jacques Demers. "The credit always went to Wayne Gretzky, Mark Messier, Glenn Anderson, Jari Kurri, and company, but Grant Fuhr knew every night that shots were going to come from everywhere. He never got enough credit."

Demers said it wasn't just Fuhr's quickness that made him a dominant player. "He read plays extremely well," Demers says. "He had really good anticipation."

Fuhr's demeanor also seemed to play a role in his success. While most goaltenders are known for intense preparation and moodiness before big games, he always looked like he was on vacation. Instead of getting into a game mode, he liked to play golf on off days. "It clears the head," he would say. "And a clear head makes it easier to play."

He said many times that enjoyment was crucial to success.

"I think having fun prolongs a career," Fuhr says. "You don't wear down as easily."

Teammates knew that Fuhr's relaxed approach wasn't to be interpreted as uncaring. He always wanted to be the best, even if he never showed it. "He's a very proud guy," former Edmonton coach John Muckler says. "He's never going to be number two. He has to be number one."

The most important save of Fuhr's career came in 1990, when he began to pull his life back together after NHL president John Ziegler suspended him 60 games for drug use. The suspension resulted in severe financial hardship for Fuhr. But with the same simplistic approach he used in the goal, he fought his way back. Given that many believed he would never be the same goaltender he had been, it could be considered another miraculous save.

Fuhr attended the famed Betty Ford clinic and another rehab center in Florida before returning to the NHL. By the 1990–91 season, he had reclaimed his position as the Oilers playoff goaltender. Glen Sather, the Oilers general manager at the time, said of Fuhr's comeback: "The pressure of the playoffs, of fighting back from what he was involved in, he took it like a man. It was a Cinderella story."

In discussing his drug problem with *Edmonton Journal* writer Dan Barnes, Fuhr said, "My biggest problem was I wanted to be the way I was in school, just a normal guy. But people didn't look at me like I was just another guy on the street and I had a problem dealing with it. [Drug use] was an escape to get away. I used to run and hide from problems. I led a double life."

Maybe Fuhr was right about fun prolonging careers—he was playing a decade after the Oilers won their last Stanley Cup. He never enjoyed as much success as he had with the Oilers, but he had moments, particularly in one season, when he reminded the hockey world that he was one of the best to ever strap on the pads.

In 1995–96 he set an NHL record when he played in 79 games for the St. Louis Blues. The irony of that effort is that general manager/coach Mike Keenan had suspended him at the start of training camp for showing up at a porky 219 pounds. By the start of the season he was down to 188 and playing some of the best hockey of his career. He won 30 games that season, and posted a 2.87 goals-against average, which was the best of his career to that point.

At the time, Muckler was asked whether he would say that Fuhr was playing as well as he did with the Oilers. Muckler said the comparison was impossible to make.

"Only because you're comparing him to the best goalie in the world," he said. "That's what Grant was back then."

14 | BILLY SMITH

BORN: Perth, Ontario, December 12, 1950		
SHOT: Left	HEIGHT: 5'10"	WEIGHT: 185 lbs.
Stanley Cups: 4		Vezina Trophies: 1
Jennings Trophies: 1		Conn Smythe Trophies: 1
NHL First All-Star Team: 1		NHL All-Star Games: 1

NOTABLE ACHIEVEMENTS: Hall of Famer; selected the All-Star Game MVP in his only appearance; first NHL goalie to be credited with scoring a goal; third all-time in Stanley Cup wins; fifth all-time in Stanley Cup games played and minutes; set Stanley Cup record by being the winning goalie in 19 consecutive playoff series; his No. 31 sweater was retired by the Islanders.

Johnny Bower's Commentary on Smith

"No one would stand in front of the net when Billy Smith was in goal. He could use that stick across your ankles better than anyone I know. And that's because he wanted to win. If I were to have a team of all-time great competitors, Smitty would head it up. He was a big guy that protected his net as if he were protecting his home. And he used his size to his advantage. He took away most of the net when he'd come out to challenge the shooter. But what made him different was the fact that he helped to eliminate the dump-and-chase style of hockey that was necessary when playing the Islanders in the late seventies. You couldn't skate around their defense, so you'd have to dump it in. Problem was Smith could move that puck like no one before him. Billy Smith is a pioneer in the fact that he revolutionized the role of the goaltender forever. When I played, we'd leave the puck for our defense to someone who would move the puck up ice."

Second Opinion: Former NHL player Jim Nill on Smith

"I was with Vancouver when we played the Islanders in the [1982] Stanley Cup final, and Billy Smith was outstanding. Before the series I remember we really wanted to get Smith off his game and we had Tiger Williams. He was going to go right in his crease to do that. But it didn't bother Billy. He just whacked him right back. He was smart and he was focused. He knew when he had to take it and not get a penalty. He had very good positioning. He was never flopping all over the place."

Long after Billy Smith's growl became worse than his bite, the New York Islanders still liked to hang out the "Beware of Dog" sign.

"Not only was Smitty competitive, but he was a lot smarter than people realized," says former Islanders general manager Bill Torrey. "He used the threat of violence and toughness to get other teams thinking. That was part of his style."

In an 18-year NHL career, Smith made just one All-Star team and won only a single Vezina Trophy; yet he's considered one of the more intimidating winners in the league's history. He helped the Islanders win four Stanley Cup championships from 1980 to 1983 on the strength of commando-like toughness and competitiveness.

When Torrey was preparing for the expansion draft, he became fascinated by Smith, and it wasn't because of the goaltender's well-manicured playing style. This was a man whose methods inspired nicknames like "Battling Billy" and "Hatchet Man."

"Early on, he was not a pretty goaltender to watch—he kind of flung himself," Torrey recalls. "But Smitty was so combative and so fearless. Those are the right words."

When the Atlanta Flames and the New York Islanders were preparing for the 1972 NHL expansion draft, it soon became pretty clear that the two best young goaltenders in the minor leagues were Daniel Bouchard and Smith, who was playing for the Los Angeles Kings' American Hockey League affiliate in

Springfield, Massachusetts. Everyone said Bouchard was the best because he was stylish.

Smith, then 21, did play five games for the Kings in 1971–72, and Torrey happened to attend one of his starts against the Montreal Canadiens. What he witnessed convinced him that Smith was the kind of goaltender he wanted for his new team.

"The Canadiens probably won that game 8–2 and probably outshot L.A. 50–15," Torrey recalls. "But I remember in the third period he was kicking them out, and someone ran him in his crease. He dropped his gloves and took on a couple of Canadiens. The fact that he was down six goals didn't matter."

To appreciate Smith's competitiveness, consider that he didn't care if it was friend or foe in front of him when he was trying to see the puck.

"He would use his goalie stick and slash you on the back of the legs to get you out of the way even if you were on his team," says former Islanders defenseman Dave Lewis, now a Detroit Red Wings associate coach. "I got hit a number of times; so did Denis Potvin. You looked at him, and you wanted to hit him, but you would have to go make a play."

Smith's ruthless playoff behavior is legendary, although Torrey believes it has now been exaggerated and that many of Smith's actions were calculated—more for show than effect. That includes his famous slash on Wayne Gretzky.

"If you look close at the Gretzky incident," Torrey says, "he didn't swing very hard, but he made it look like he was going to take his leg off."

The threat of Smitty was sometimes worse than the reality. He learned to use his aura to make opponents worry. "He always had a reputation as a fighter," Torrey says. "But if you look at our championship seasons, Smitty didn't take many penalties."

What has been almost forgotten over time is that Smith actually shared the Islanders goaltending duties with Glenn "Chico" Resch during the regular season. They would also split playoff goaltending. Resch played more games than Smith (45 to 38) in 1979–80, but Torrey and coach Al Arbour decided to go with Smith in the playoffs based on a single factor.

"It was just his strength," Torrey says. "For a man his size, Smitty was incredibly strong. It wasn't an easy decision because Chico had a really good year. But we weren't sure Chico was strong enough."

Former NHL general manager Emile Francis recalls that the difference between Smith in the regular season and in the playoffs was more pronounced than it was with other goaltenders: "He was just average in the regular season, but in the playoffs, he was great."

Tom Laidlaw, a former New York Rangers player, says he never really hated Smith as much as he probably should have.

"You kind of admired the way he played," Laidlaw says. "The bigger the game, the better he played. You could beat him in some games, but you could be sure you weren't going to beat him in the next game."

Lewis says Smith "was always on edge, and the playoffs brought him to a point living on that edge."

"He was out challenging shots," Lewis says. "He wasn't afraid to leave the crease. He would fight. I remember one regular-season game where he and [Edmonton's] Dave Semenko tied up. We were all thinking, 'Oh, my God.' Dave Semenko hit him so hard that his helmet went up four feet in the air. He showed up. He scrapped. He did it all."

Smith played more than 50 games in a season only one time during his career. "The thing with Smitty was that his intensity was so great and for him to carry that over 80 games was almost impossible," Torrey says. "You never spoke to him on a day of the game. He would start getting ready the moment he got up. Once the game was over, it was like he came out of a trance."

Smith Was a Winner Because . . .

He always cranked up his intensity level in the postseason, as evidenced by his four championship rings.

Although competitiveness was his trademark, Smith had some style distinctions. He liked to swing his stick along the ice surface when the other players were moving out.

"He was also one of the first to go with the bigger catcher's glove and the bigger arms on his jersey," recalls former NHL goaltender John Davidson.

Smith was also an endearing character to his teammates, who have fond memories of his oddness and his malapropisms. He was extremely picky about how his equipment was set up around his stall.

"He would have his goalie stick leaning against the wall and, if anyone touched that goalie stick, he would go nuts," Lewis says. "He would lose it. It was taboo. Game day he was really focused."

A few times when Smith wasn't playing, he brought a cushion to use on the bench. He also brought popcorn to eat during the game.

"There always seemed to be a different set of rules for Bill," Lewis says. "At least that's how I remember it. [Arbour] knew how to treat Bill."

Smith never quite mastered figures of speech. For example, he would say "get on my good eye" instead of "get on my good side."

When a player would get words tangled up, teammates would say he had "Smittyness" or had uttered a "Smittyism."

But that's not what Torrey will remember about Smith. Says Torrey: "All I know is that if we went to war, I would want Smitty in the trenches with me."

21 | MARTIN BRODEUR

BORN: Montreal, Quebec, May 6, 1972

SHOOTS: Left	**HEIGHT:** 6'2"	**WEIGHT:** 205 lbs.
Stanley Cups: 2		Calder Trophies: 1
Jennings Trophies: 2		NHL Second All-Star Team: 2
NHL All-Star Games: 6		

NOTABLE ACHIEVEMENTS: Youngest NHL goalie to reach the 300-win mark; along with dad Denis (1956), became the only father/son goalies to win medals in the Olympics; one of two goalies with Stanley Cup/Olympic gold medal double (with Ed Belfour); selected to NHL All-Rookie team, 1993–94; scored a goal in 1997 playoffs; posted four shutouts in the 2000–01 playoffs; owns 14 career playoff shutouts; shares the NHL record of three 40-win seasons (with Terry Sawchuk and Jacques Plante); one of three NHL goalies with seven consecutive 30-win seasons (with Tony Esposito and Patrick Roy); one of only eight NHL goalies to post three shutouts in one Stanley Cup series (with Clint Benedict, Davey Kerr, Turk Broda, Frank McCool, Felix Potvin, Brent Johnson, and Patrick Lalime); had 10 shutouts in 1996–97 and 1997–98, making him the first goalie to hit double digits in consecutive seasons since Bernie Parent (1973–74, 1974–75); played an NHL-record 4,433 minutes in 1995–96.

Johnny Bower's Commentary on Brodeur

"Martin Brodeur is one of my favorite goaltenders to watch. He plays a style that is the closest to that of a traditional stand-up tender. That is why Martin is so tough to beat in clutch games. His style hardly ever puts him in a position where he can't make a save. He has the second quickest catching hand to that of Patrick Roy, but is a much better puckhandler. He's like Eddie Giacomin in that he's a thinking goaltender who can read the play. That's why he generally takes few risks when handling the puck. He'll make the smartest play—whether that's clearing the puck off of the glass or playing it up the boards. With him in goal, it's as if they brought back the rover position in the defensive zone."

Second Opinion: ABC Analyst John Davidson on Brodeur

"Brodeur has three different shots with the puck. He has that down to a science. I did a television spot for ABC and he showed me three different wrist shots he uses to get the puck out of the zone, depending on the situation. He has a high flip shot, the hard wrist shot, etc. He looks at who's coming at him, where the puck is, and makes a decision about which one to use. He's a tremendous goalie at stopping the puck where there are scrambles and battles. Physically he is very strong. He can battle through traffic to get to where he needs to get. When you interview him, you think here's this marshmallow. Wrong. People look at him and think because he is such a great guy that he's not competitive. If they think that, they are sadly wrong. As soon as the puck drops, he digs in."

In a profession where tension is a condiment for daily life, Martin Brodeur's ability to disengage from the pressure might be his most important attribute. Twenty-five minutes after he won his first Stanley Cup in 1995, Brodeur literally seemed more interested in horseplay than accepting accolades.

While waiting for a team bus, Brodeur's teammates were all abuzz about his strong play in a major upset of Detroit. But the goalie was busy quizzing a mounted policeman about his steed.

"He's patting the horse on the nose," recalls former NHL player Peter McNab, now a television analyst. "The kid just won the biggest game of his life and he's asking a policeman how much oats the horse eats. I'm thinking, 'OK, OK, the Devils got something special here.'"

Brodeur is undeniably the best puckhandling goaltender of this era, and his overall skill package seems quite complete. But his composure accents his talent and gives his teammates a peace of mind that others don't enjoy.

"With the way he handles the puck, the way he makes saves, it's very comfortable playing in front of Marty," McNab says. "You never see [a teammate] look back to see where a rebound is, lose his man, and then have that man score. They just take care of their man, and Marty takes care of everything else, including clearing the puck out of the zone. He simplifies the game."

Brodeur Is a Winner Because . . .

Whether he's in an NHL rink or an international arena, he's in control of his team's fate.

Brodeur supporters sometimes argue that he has never received enough recognition for his accomplishments. Remember that this is a goaltender who has two Stanley Cup championships and one Olympic gold medal, and who seems almost indestructible. He has averaged better than 70 appearances a season from 1995–96 to 2001–02.

In 2001–02 Devils coach Larry Robinson compared Brodeur's situation to that of Montreal Hall of Famer Ken Dryden.

"A lot of people take [Dryden] for granted by saying he played on great teams," Robinson said. "The last time I looked, the goaltender was part of the team. And the reason they were great teams was because they had great goaltending. And Marty gives [the Devils] great goaltending night in and night out. It's the wins that count."

Brodeur definitely has the wins. He was the youngest goalkeeper to reach 300 wins, needing only 548 games. Only Jacques Plante and Andy Moog required fewer. At his current pace, he will probably be only 32 when he reaches 400 wins. Patrick Roy, Brodeur's idol growing up, was 32 when he reached 400.

Brodeur believes his durability is linked to his demeanor. "I don't get too concerned about the game," he says. "I go out there and really enjoy myself. I don't make it hard on myself. I don't put extra pressure on myself. When you are full of confidence, I think it helps you play a lot of games. You don't feel the pressure. That's when a goalie gets tired—when they feel the pressure."

It's always been said that the 6'2", 205-pound Brodeur is a goaltender in a defenseman's body, and that's how he thinks as well. That's why he doesn't mind playing a lot of games. "If [a goalie] is able to do it, I don't know why you should sit down," he says. "I have a lot of respect for [New Jersey defenseman] Scott Stevens who goes out and plays 82 games the way he does."

Former NHL goalie Darren Pang, now an ESPN analyst, calls Brodeur "the rubber band man."

"Stress isn't part of his demeanor," Pang says. "His body is never tight. He stretches. He stops pucks. He makes it look easy. He doesn't get hurt."

22 | GERRY CHEEVERS

BORN: St. Catharines, Ontario, December 7, 1940

SHOT: Left	HEIGHT: 5'11"	WEIGHT: 185 lbs.
Stanley Cups: 2		NHL All-Star Games: 1

NOTABLE ACHIEVEMENTS: Hall of Famer; posted an NHL-record 32-game unbeaten streak in 1971–72; named the top goalie in American Hockey League, Central Professional Hockey League, and World Hockey Association; played in the 1974 WHA Summit Series vs. the Soviet Union; also played forward in junior and was an excellent puckhandler; twice led the Stanley Cup playoffs in both shutouts and wins; played in four Stanley Cup finals; back-stopped Rochester, New York, to the AHL title, 1964–65; won Memorial Cup with St. Michael's, 1960–61.

Johnny Bower's Commentary on Cheevers

"I roomed with Cheesy when he came into his first training camp. He was a hard worker who asked a lot of questions. He was a guy who would always push himself to improve. I remember that in camp, he'd come up to me wanting to learn how to do the poke check. Being the veteran, I helped him with it, but as the old guy on the team, I was getting a little nervous because he quickly picked up on the nuances of the move. I used to watch him in practice and, after I retired, during games, and I noticed that Gerry would make a little cut in the ice before each period so that he knew where he was on the ice on the short side. That way, he only had to worry about his glove side, not the stick side, when playing the angles."

Second Opinion: Former Teammate Tom Webster on Cheevers

"I got called up to Boston for the playoffs in 1968–69. We were doing shooting drills in practice and I came down the wing and scored. I thought to myself, 'I'm scoring on Gerry Cheevers.' Then I started watching the other guys and they were all scoring on Cheevers. He wasn't stopping anybody. When some of the guys with the heavy shots, like Ken Hodge would come in on him, he'd skate right out of the net. That was just the way Cheesy was. In practice, he was going to do everything in his power to keep from getting hit with the puck. But when it was game time, you knew he was going to do everything in his power to make sure the puck would hit him. His legs, his arms, his head—he didn't care. He'd get something in front of it. And the bigger the game, the better he played."

"Think I'll ever win the Vezina Trophy?" Gerry Cheevers blurted out one day, quizzing the gaggle of reporters in front of his locker.

The assorted gathering looked at their feet, then at each other, before shaking their heads in unison, causing Cheevers' grin to widen.

"Think I care?" he then asked, to which their response was to continue shaking their heads in front of the Boston Bruins netminder.

Other goalies might have been irritated by such acknowledgment of their inability. But to the man they called "Cheesy," it wasn't an insult, but the highest of compliments, because he didn't care about the individual honors bestowed upon athletes. In 13 NHL seasons he never lifted the Vezina; his only personal recognition coming from an appearance in the 1969 NHL All-Star Game. But when all was said and done, you could read Cheevers' name on the Stanley Cup in two places and to him, that was the only recognition worth pursuing.

"Cheesy was a big-money player—one of the greatest," Hall of Famer Milt Schmidt says. "When the need was there to make one big save to save a ballgame, Cheesy was there."

Cheevers was always very aggressive in the net.

Schmidt was coaching the Bruins when Boston claimed Cheevers from the Toronto Maple Leafs in the 1965 NHL intraleague draft. Toronto coach/GM Punch Imlach desperately wanted to keep Cheevers—he tried to hide him on the Leafs' unprotected list by listing him as a forward—but he couldn't fool the Bruins.

"I'm well aware of the fact that in two or three years, or maybe even by next Christmas, people will probably say we made a terrible mistake in letting Cheevers go. But we simply had to protect the two best goalies in the world," Imlach told the *Toronto Telegram*, speaking of Johnny Bower and Terry Sawchuk. That duo combined to win the Leafs a Stanley Cup in 1967, but when the Leafs were drilled in four straight by Cheevers and the Bruins in the first round of the 1969 playoffs, Imlach was out of a job.

Cheevers won his first Stanley Cup in 1969–70 and added another two years later, posting an NHL-record 32-game unbeaten stretch during the 1971–72

season. Cheevers actually played eight games at forward in the junior ranks for St. Michael's, so Imlach wasn't totally lying by listing him at this position. Cheevers used his strong skating and puckhandling skills to play aggressively in the net, challenging shooters, racing well out of his cage in pursuit of pucks. "He was quick, with great hands, and he didn't fall to the ice very much," Schmidt recalls.

Gerry Cheevers Was a Winner Because . . .

He placed the end result ahead of any individual recognition, once suggesting that the only time he cared about shutouts was if his team was up 1–0.

Most remember Cheevers for his one-liners, such as the time someone asked him how it felt to face Bobby Hull's wicked slap shot. "How should I know?" Cheevers responded. "When he shoots, I close my eyes."

Cheevers wrote a 1971 book about his chosen profession, aptly titled *Goaltender*, which he dedicated "to my 26 lodge brothers behind the masks and the two nuts without them." Cheevers kept everyone and everything in stitches, including his mask. He had trainer John "Frosty" Forristall paint mock stitches on the mask whenever Cheevers took a shot to the face.

When chronic knee problems forced Cheevers to retire in 1980, he accepted the position as coach of the Bruins, becoming just the fourth former NHL goaltender to move behind the bench.

He lasted four seasons, suffering 126 losses, but never losing his trademark sense of humor.

"When I took the job as coach of the Bruins, I said, 'Hockey has been my life, so maybe this is life after death,'" Cheevers reasoned. "Well, I found out that coaching is really death after life."

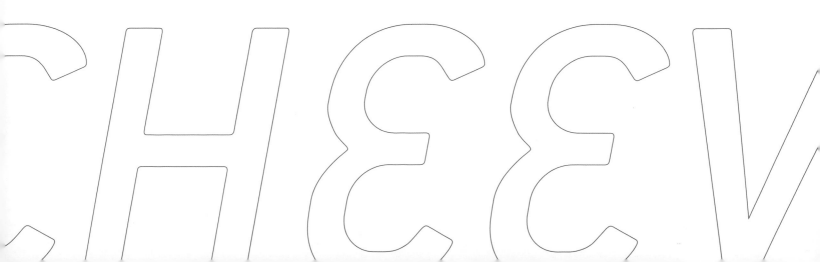

28 | HARRY "HAP" HOLMES

BORN: Aurora, Ontario, February 21, 1892

DIED: June 27, 1941

SHOT: Left	**HEIGHT:** 5'10"	**WEIGHT:** 170 lbs

Stanley Cups: 4	All-Star Selections: 8

NOTABLE ACHIEVEMENTS: Hall of Famer; seven-time Pacific Coast Hockey Association All-Star; Western Canada Hockey League All-Star in 1924–25; backstopped the first U.S.-based Cup winner (1916–17 Seattle Metropolitans), the first NHL Cup winner (1917–18 Toronto Arenas), and the last Cup winner from outside the NHL (1924–25 WCHL Victoria Cougars); led the PCHA in wins three times, in shutouts four times, and in goals-against average five times; led the National Hockey Association in wins once and in shutouts twice; led the WCHL and Western Hockey League in GAA once each; played in five different major pro leagues (NHL, NHA, PCHA, WCHL, and WHL) and reached the Stanley Cup final with clubs from each; American Hockey League goaltending award was named in his honor.

Johnny Bower's Commentary on Holmes

"Reports of the time say that Hap Holmes was highly skilled and consistent, though not spectacular. His nonchalance in the nets led some critics to consider him almost lazy. But easygoing doesn't mean lazy. According to the *Border Cities Star* in 1926, he was cool-headed and modest when he went about the business of making saves."

Second Opinion: The Windsor Star's Vern DeGeer on Holmes

"Bald-headed goalie Hap Holmes was forced to seek cover under a baseball cap in rinks boasting of those old-style hanging galleries. To the customers with a quid of tobacco, capable jaws, and ordinary marksmanship, his shining bald dome presented a tempting target. He first thought of introducing umbrellas into his netminding business, but soon hit on the idea of a peaked cap. 'I swear that some of those fellows used to load their tobacco with bird shot,' Holmes said. 'After a game, my head carried so many lumps, the boys claimed I'd had an attack of chicken pox. My sweater looked as though it had been dragged through a tub of cylinder oil. Those roughnecks became so expert at their business that even a cap didn't save me at times. They used to fire at my neck. I don't think they ever missed.'"

The puck was passed to the slot and directed into the Windsor net by the skate of Cleveland's Gord McFarlane. Referee Mike Rodden immediately waved off the goal, but McFarlane didn't argue. Cleveland fans, though, were of a completely different mind, surging toward the referee as he left the ice.

Cleveland manager Harry "Hap" Holmes, seeing Rodden was in trouble, waded into the mob, dodging a punch from an angry patron. The police apprehended the assailant, but Holmes asked that instead of a trip downtown, they escort the hooligan into the Cleveland dressing room. Inside, Holmes removed his coat and glasses and invited the belligerent fan to take another poke at him. The fellow declined and beat a hasty retreat out an arena exit.

The fan knew two things: you could take a shot at Holmes, but you weren't likely to beat him.

Before he took up behind the bench as a minor league coach, Holmes rated among the winningest goalies in major league hockey history. Wherever Holmes traveled, a famous silver mug seemed sure to follow. He backstopped teams from four different leagues to Stanley Cup success, and each occasion proved a history-making moment in hockey lore. Holmes' run of good fortune commenced in 1913–14, when he took the National Hockey Association's Toronto Blueshirts to the title.

"But for the work of Holmes, who gave one of the best exhibitions of goal-keeping ever witnessed on the local ice, the Westerners would have piled up a substantial lead," the *Manitoba Free Press* reported of his performance in the opener of a three-game Cup final sweep of Victoria.

Hockey was a seller's market back then, with the NHA and the rival Pacific Coast League entering bidding wars for top players. Holmes took the money and ran for the coast, signing with the Seattle Metropolitans. His work paved the way for their 1916–17 Cup triumph over the Montreal Canadiens, making Seattle the first U.S.-based squad to hoist Lord Stanley's mug.

But Holmes was a man who didn't let the moss settle on the soles of his shoes and he was back with Toronto in the winter, suiting up for the Arenas of the newly formed National Hockey League. He led them to the Stanley Cup in an exciting five-game verdict over Vancouver, holding the fort for a 2–1 decision in Game 5.

"[Holmes] was at the top of his form and made stops in all three periods that were little short of marvelous," the Toronto *Globe* reported. "From all angles, the net guardian swept the puck into the corner, kicking away the low ones, jumping into the waist-high shots, and cuffing with hand and glove those shots that were driven at him shoulder high."

Going west again, Holmes took Seattle to successive finals. The 1918–19 series with the Habs was halted because of the worldwide Spanish influenza epidemic. The following spring, the Mets fell in five games to Ottawa. Seattle folded its team in 1924 and Holmes signed up with the Western Canada Hockey League's Victoria Cougars, making his sixth Stanley Cup appearance a success when the Cougars downed the Canadiens in four games. The first Cup champs from the WCHL would also be the last team from outside the NHL to win the storied trophy. The Cougars were back to defend their title the following spring, but were dethroned by the Montreal Maroons in what would be the last inter-league competition for the Stanley Cup.

The western league folded and Holmes returned to the NHL, joining the Detroit Cougars for two seasons before retiring, posting 11 shutouts in his farewell campaign. "He was one of the pioneers of the game," Detroit team-mate Pete Palangio said. "In many ways, he was similar in style to [George] Hainsworth, though Holmes was a much bigger man. He was a stand-up goalie, very solid on his feet, and always seemed to be in position."

Ever prepared to take a shot, as that Cleveland fan discovered.

Holmes Was a Winner Because . . .

Holmes played in seven Stanley Cup finals and won the trophy four times with four different teams from four separate leagues.

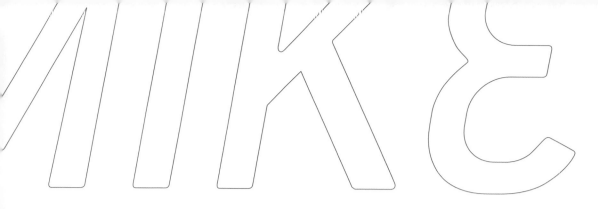

31 | MIKE VERNON

BORN: Calgary, Alberta, February 24, 1963		
SHOT: Left	HEIGHT: 5'9"	WEIGHT: 180 lbs.
Stanley Cups: 2	Conn Smythe Trophies: 1	
William Jennings Trophies: 1	NHL Second All-Star Team: 2	
NHL All-Star Games: 5		

NOTABLE ACHIEVEMENTS: Named the top goaltender in the 1983 Memorial Cup as he led Portland to the title; the winningest goalie in Flames history; earned a silver medal for Canada at the 1991 World Championships; played in the Stanley Cup final as a rookie and appeared in four finals during his career; one of four goalies to beat the Montreal Canadiens in a Cup final series (with Turk Broda, Hap Holmes, and Terry Sawchuk); has posted more than 380 career wins; fourth all-time in Stanley Cup appearances (138) and minutes played (8,214); led the NHL in wins in 1988–89.

Johnny Bower's Commentary on Vernon

"Mike Vernon is the epitome of a great professional goaltender. He's someone who goes to work, does his job quietly, and doesn't quit. He's a steady goaltender who seldom gets rattled on the ice. He's intense but seldom shows emotion on the ice and never shows up his team. Mike is a good angle goaltender who is quick to come out to challenge the shooter. He also has very good lateral movements, which help him on odd-man situations where the defense doesn't take away the pass. Over the years, he has changed his style from being a stand-up goaltender to more of a butterfly goaltender."

Second Opinion: Former Calgary General Manager Cliff Fletcher on Vernon

"When you look at the goaltenders who entered the league in the eighties, he belongs every bit as much in that top category as any of the others, goalies like Grant Fuhr and Patrick Roy. He literally won us the Stanley Cup [in 1988–89]. In the first series that year, we played Vancouver and ended up in overtime in Game 7. Mike made three saves in that overtime [on Stan Smyl, Petri Skriko, and Tony Tanti] that were just miraculous. If it wasn't for Mike Vernon in that game, we would have been finished four weeks before we won the Cup.

Goalies kept pushing the limits on equipment size during the midnineties, allowing smaller goalies to loom larger in the net, while inflating bigger goaltenders to gargantuan dimensions. But Mike Vernon never needed to cheat on the size of his upper-body armor. The chip on his shoulder was enough to deflect any puck.

The little goalie from Calgary with the big attitude took on all comers, turning aside shots with equal aplomb whether they came from a sniper's stick, a journalist's poison pen, or a paying customer's acid tongue. "I've been booed by fans and I've been cheered by them," Vernon says. "I've been praised and crapped on in the papers. I think everyone who plays goal in this league has to learn to deal with that type of thing, because it's part of the game."

The love/hate relationship was probably caused by overfamiliarity. Vernon played his entire amateur hockey career and the first 11 NHL seasons in his hometown of Calgary. "That's a long time to be in one place, even if it is your hometown," Vernon concedes.

He backstopped the Flames to their only Stanley Cup but never seemed capable of winning over Calgary fans. And Vernon being Vernon, he wasn't the type to sit there and quietly take the abuse. "He's a fiery, competitive guy," says ESPN analyst and former NHL goalie Darren Pang. "If you challenge Mike, if you question him, he's going to fight back."

After their 1989 Cup triumph, the Flames were first-round playoff losers for the next four springs, and critics aimed the blame at Vernon. So it almost came as a relief when he was dealt to Detroit in the summer of 1994. "The change did me good," he says.

He took the Wings to their first Stanley Cup final appearance in 29 years in 1995, but when Detroit was abruptly shunted aside by New Jersey in a four-game sweep, Vernon was fingered as the one responsible. "A lot of people gave up on him after that, but I never did," Detroit coach Scotty Bowman says.

Chris Osgood appeared to usurp Vernon's status as number one in the Wings net over the next two seasons. They shared the Jennings Trophy in 1995–96, as Detroit posted an NHL-record 62 wins, but Osgood made the lion's share of the starts. However, as the Wings drove down the stretch toward the 1997 postseason, Vernon began to assert himself and move into the starting role. And when the playoffs began, Bowman put the keys to Detroit's Stanley Cup drive in Vernon's capable hands.

Vernon Was a Winner Because . . .

He won Stanley Cup championships with two teams.

The gamble paid off. Vernon carried the Wings all the way for the first time since 1955, outplaying contemporaries like Grant Fuhr, Patrick Roy, and Ron Hextall, earning the Conn Smythe Trophy as Stanley Cup MVP.

"He was our ace in the hole," Bowman says. "He got hot at the right time. . . . When Mike Vernon was available, I talked to Glenn Hall, who was the goalie coach in Calgary. He told me, 'You'll like him. He's a winner. He plays big in big games.' That was good enough for me."

Vernon's stats don't shine brightly when listed alongside other greats of his era. He garnered just 26 shutouts and his goals-against average hovered near 3.00, but the only factor that ever consumed him was that his team achieved the better result by game's end. "I don't care if it's 2–1 or 9–8, just as long as we get the one on the left side," he says.

32 | RILEY HERN

BORN: St. Mary's, Ontario, December 5, 1880
DIED: June 24, 1929

SHOT: Left	HEIGHT: 5'9"	WEIGHT: 170 lbs.
Stanley Cups: 4		All-Star Selections: 1

NOTABLE ACHIEVEMENTS: Hall of Famer; first pro goalie to win the Stanley Cup; Western Pennsylvania Hockey League All-Star, 1901–02; led league in wins that season; also led Eastern Canada Hockey Association (twice) and National Hockey Association (once) in wins; perfect 10–0 record with Montreal Wanderers in 1906–07; one of only four goalies to win at least four straight Cups (with Jacques Plante, Ken Dryden, and Billy Smith); served as an NHL referee and goal judge; became a prominent Montreal businessman after retirement.

Johnny Bower's Commentary on Hern

"Although it's difficult to know much about Hern's style of play, it's clear that he was one of the best in the world at the turn of the century. You can imagine that a team like the Wanderers would have had their pick of goaltenders. All that is written about Hern suggests he was extremely quick around the net, and was a very smart player. It's funny to read that Hern was fighting for player salary rights 90 years ago. The more things change, the more they remain the same."

Second Opinion: Society for International Hockey Research President Ernie Fitzsimmons on Hern

"Riley Hern was hockey's first truly professional goalie. His reputation was not one of being a great technical goalie, but much like Gerry Cheevers and Grant Fuhr of later eras, he didn't worry about goals-against average. All he did was win, recording a .720 winning percentage."

On the list of premium goalkeepers who have won the Stanley Cup championship, Riley Hern's distinction is that he was the first to be paid to do it.

Or, as one newspaper so aptly reported it, "the first to be paid for his bruises."

With almost 100 years now passed since Hern stood as sentinel for the Montreal Wanderers of the National Hockey Association, it is difficult to unearth the intricacies of his style, and yet it remains obvious that he is deserving of a place among the all-time best. He was the chosen goalkeeper on a Wanderers team that relatively speaking might have been one of the best assemblages of talent ever to win Lord Stanley's chalice.

Hern, who began his career as a forward, played senior hockey for the Stratford Legionaires of the Ontario Hockey League in 1898 and had tours of duty for the Pittsburgh Keystones in the Western Pennsylvania Hockey League and Portage Lakes in the International Hockey League before signing with the Wanderers. He replaced Henri "Doc" Menard, who retired to attend medical school after the 1905–06 season. Given the reputation of the organization, the Wanderers had options and settled on hiring Hern, who had been an IHL All-Star for two seasons.

The Eastern Canada Hockey Association voted on November 25, 1906, to allow professionals to play alongside amateurs for the first time. On December 27, 1906, Hern joined Pud Glass, Hod Stuart, Jack Marshall, and Ernie "Moose" Johnson as the first pros to play in a Stanley Cup game. The Wanderers shellacked the New Glasgow (Nova Scotia) Cubs 10–3 in that contest. Hern and the Wanderers eventually downed the vaunted Ottawa Silver Seven to become Stanley Cup champions.

During his Wanderers career, Hern played behind a defense that, at various times, included Hall of Famers Stuart, Jimmy Gardner, Art Ross, and Lester Patrick. Other Hall of Famers included Johnson, Harry Hyland, Tom Hooper, Marshall, Ernie Russell, and manager Dickie Boon. The Wanderers were a team that brought in the best talent available. After taking down the Ottawa Silver Seven, the Wanderers successfully defended their hold on the Stanley Cup six times in seven challenges over the next three seasons. The only blemish on that run was a loss to the Kenora Thistles in January 1907, although the Wanderers reclaimed the Stanley Cup by defeating Kenora two months later.

Journalistic accounts of the time suggest that the St. Mary's, Ontario, native relied on quickness and composure as his chief strengths. In describing Hern's play in the Wanderers' 7–2 win against Kenora during a Stanley Cup series game on March 26, 1907, the *Manitoba Free Press* wrote: "Hern gave one of the finest exhibitions of goalkeeping ever seen here. He was quick as a flash in getting the puck away. He has undoubtedly given his team a stone wall in net."

Evidence also suggests that Hern was a smart player who relied as much on his intellect as his athleticism. In the December 29, 1908, *Montreal Star*, a reporter offered that "Riley Hern was as careful and painstaking as ever. He treats his goaltending as he does his private business and that is probably the secret to his success."

Hern Was a Winner Because . . .

He backstopped a powerful Montreal Wanderers team.

Hern seemed to have a keen business sense— spending his nonhockey hours organizing other leagues and printing schedules for them. When the NHA and Canadian Hockey Association merged during the 1909–10 season, the *Montreal Star* marveled that Hern had the revised schedule printed and available by the next day.

Rich in business acumen, Hern unofficially could be called the first modern-day player representative. At the very least, he was among the first to speak out publicly for player rights. With two leagues vying for top players, salaries had risen dramatically. When the merger was announced, players feared salary reduction was on the way. They hired a lawyer to represent them. Hern publicly put forth the argument that the merger meant that players were no longer bound by their contracts. Hence, every player would become a free agent.

"If there is peace and a disturbance of our schedule, we will demand higher wages," Hern was quoted as saying in the January 16, 1910, *Montreal Star*.

Hern also owned a clothing store in that era, and his business interests eventually overwhelmed his hockey career. He retired from hockey at 30, although eventually he would still serve the game as an NHL referee and a Montreal goal judge.

During the 1926 Stanley Cup final, in which Montreal Maroons goalie Clint Benedict shut out the Victoria Cougars in the first two games, Hern chided Victoria players about how he could take a nap when he was working behind Benedict because they were never going to beat him.

Naturally this enraged the Cougars, and in particular defenseman Clem Loughlin. Knowing Hern owned Montreal's finest haberdashery, he bet Hern a new topcoat that Victoria would score in Game 3, and he would be the player to get said goal. Believing it to be a safe bet, Hern accepted.

Much to Hern's surprise Loughlin did score in Victoria's 3–2 win. He skated excitedly to Hern's position behind the goal, pounding his chest with his glove while screaming out his coat size. It was the only goal Loughlin ever scored in Stanley Cup play. It was one of the rare times in Hern's career that someone got the better of him.

J S HUTTON

46 | JOHN BOWER "BOWSE" HUTTON

BORN: Ottawa, Ontario, October 24, 1877

DIED: October 27, 1962

SHOT: Left	HEIGHT: Unknown	WEIGHT: Unknown
Stanley Cups: 2		

NOTABLE ACHIEVEMENTS: Hall of Famer; he was 9–1–1 with a 2.09 goals-against average lifetime in Stanley Cup play; only man in history to win the Stanley Cup and the Canadian football and lacrosse titles; led CAHL in wins, 1902–03; career record of 35–9–3; posted an unbeaten 7–0–1 slate in leading Ottawa to 1900–01 Canadian Amateur Hockey League crown; backstopped Ottawa to the Canadian intermediate title, 1898–99.

Johnny Bower's Commentary on Hutton

"Numbers can lie, but in Bowse Hutton's case, they support the revelation that he was the game's first goaltending sensation. Performing at a time when hockey's laws allowed the netminder minimal latitude in thwarting attackers—sprawling on the ice and covering the puck were punishable offenses—and the only equipment advantage provided was a pair of thin cricket pads, Hutton's numbers offer evidence of his athleticism. The gloves he wore were the same style as his teammates', his stick not much wider than theirs, yet Hutton posted a pair of shutouts in Stanley Cup play at a time when double-digit scores were the norm. His goals-against average of 2.62 would not look out of place amid today's oversized puckstoppers and his 9–1–1 slate and 2.09 GAA in Stanley Cup contests display proof of Hutton's value as a money goaltender."

Second Opinion: The Montreal Star's *Baz O'Meara* on Hutton

"He was a gifted goalie in both hockey and lacrosse and a fleet running fullback. He started out as a lacrosse home fielder and dropped back to the nets. On the ice, Hutton was unusual because he used a goal stick with a blade only slightly larger than an ordinary stick. Bowse later became a fine hockey coach, devoting his time to the development of amateur teams and players. He was as modern as the red line in his hockey outlook."

For many legendary puckstoppers, the route traveled to the net isn't paved with great expectations. Often, being placed in goal was a last resort, the bane of the existence of the fat kid, the short kid, the kid who couldn't skate, or, in instances of seniority, the youngest lad on the team.

Such was not the case for John Bower "Bowse" Hutton. An all-around athlete who reached the highest level of competition in three sports, he stood in front of the goal by choice and displayed an unparalleled athleticism, earning him the reputation as the first of the truly outstanding goaltenders.

"Hutton has played lacrosse with the [Ottawa] Capitals, football with the [Ottawa] Rough Riders, and hockey with the Ottawas for half a dozen years," the *Manitoba Free Press* noted in 1904, highlighting Hutton's versatility.

In 1901 Hutton tended goal for the Capitals as they defeated Cornwall, Ontario, to win the Minto Cup as Canadian amateur lacrosse champions in the summer. Strapping on his pads, he was between the posts for the Ottawa Hockey Club, which posted a 7–1 mark to capture the Canadian Amateur Hockey League title. During the fall of 1902, the speedy, powerful fullback helped the Ottawa Rough Riders down Ottawa College 5–0 for the Canadian football championship.

Hutton would win the Stanley Cup twice with the famous Ottawa Silver Seven. It could be said that he was the Bernie Parent of his era, for the Senators were as notorious as they were noteworthy, the Broad Street Bullies of the turn of the century. "Ottawa sticks have a tendency to connect with the anatomy of opponents while avoiding detection by the referee," the *Montreal Star* opined. The *Manitoba Free Press* carried the analogy of the Ottawa roughnecks even further. "It is said that in Ottawa, even the golfers have to wear shin pads," the newspaper suggested.

That comment followed on the heels of a particularly brutal 1904 Stanley Cup series between the Silver Seven and the Winnipeg Rowing Club Oarsmen, which saw seven of nine Winnipeg players require medical attention after what Winnipeg captain Billy Breen described as "the dirtiest game I ever played." The Silver Seven could afford to play with such reckless abandon because they knew they had a rock-solid netminder. "There are few equal to Hutton in goal," the *Montreal Star* said. "In goal, he is a wonder. The way he stops shot after shot brings repeated cheers from the gallery."

Ottawa and Winnipeg split the first two games of a best-of-three set, but Hutton ensured the Cup would remain in Bytown when he closed the door for a 2–0 verdict in the deciding contest. "Hutton perhaps never played a better game in his life," the *Montreal Star* commented. "The Winnipegs found him an absolute stone wall in many a hard attack."

It was the second shutout posted by Hutton in a Stanley Cup–deciding game, leaving Winnipeg manager Pat Manning to applaud the Ottawa netminder. "That Hutton is a great goaltender and saved 20 possible scores," Manning told the *Manitoba Free Press*.

Deciding to exit while on top of the hockey world, Hutton hung up his pads after the 1904 season, finishing his career with a sensational 35–9–3 record and a solid 2.62 goals-against average. He continued to play lacrosse, touring England with the Capitals in 1904 after earning another Minto Cup crown. He also coached junior and senior hockey in Ottawa for several years, earning induction into the Hockey Hall of Fame in 1962.

Hutton Was a Winner Because . . .

He was never on the losing side in the six Stanley Cup series in which he tended goal for the famous Ottawa Silver Seven; he twice posted shutouts in the Cup-deciding game.

47 | PADDY MORAN

BORN: Quebec City, Quebec, March 11, 1877

DIED: January 14, 1966

SHOT: Left	HEIGHT: 5′11″	WEIGHT: 180 lbs.
Stanley Cups: 2		All-Star Selections: 2

NOTABLE ACHIEVEMENTS: Hall of Famer; led the Canadian Amateur Hockey League in wins twice; led the National Hockey Association in wins and shutouts twice each; played for the NHA All-Stars, 1911–12; won the Canadian intermediate title with Quebec Crescents, 1900–01; never played in the NHL but beat the Montreal Canadiens 4–3 while playing for a hastily assembled Quebec team in a February 1918 exhibition game.

Johnny Bower's Commentary on Moran

"No goal crease was painted on the ice when Paddy Moran guarded the net, so he carved out one on his own. The area in front of the goal was his sole domain and those foolish enough to think otherwise paid a toll in the form of welts and lacerations when Moran wielded his trusty goal stick like Paul Bunyan's axe. Moran always had a healthy chew of tobacco stuffed in his cheek while he toiled in front of the cage and another of his favorite tricks was to expectorate a stream of tobacco juice into the eyes of a shooter bearing down on him. He retired in 1917, before hockey's rules allowed goaltenders to drop to their knees in order to make a save. Moran had a stand-up style, and he combined a quick stick with his 5′11″, 180-pound frame—large for that era—to keep the puck out of his goal."

Second Opinion: The Montreal Star on Moran

"There was Moran, however, at the goal of the Quebec team. Moran, who knows every trick of the game and who has been called 'The Invincible.' He saved the situation many times—coolly, surely, and with such *sang froid* as to extract the applause of the now excited crowd. Moran played a fine game for Quebec and was always given a big reception. Though prone to very unsportsmanlike exhibitions of temper, without the services of P. Moran, Esq., the Quebec team would be at a tremendous disadvantage. Moran, moving at eccentric angles, covered every part of the mouth of the yawning net, till finally bones, muscles, and eyesight could not stand it any longer. If Mr. Moran was marked every time he was hit, he would look like the back of a target."

In 1905 the *Montreal Star* asked readers to select an All-Star team from players performing in the Canadian Amateur Hockey League.

"[Paddy] Moran clinched his claim to the title 'King of Goalkeepers,'" the newspaper reported. "Moran was almost the unanimous choice for goalkeeper of the thousands of votes that were cast."

But assessment of Moran's skills was more than just a popularity contest.

Twenty-three years later, New York Rangers manager Lester Patrick reflected on the top goaltenders from his playing days. Patrick knew something about goaltending, later that year climbing from behind the bench to replace his injured goalie Lorne Chabot and lead the Rangers to a 2–1 overtime victory over the Montreal Maroons in Game 2 of the 1928 Stanley Cup finals.

"I would pick Paddy Moran of Quebec and Percy LeSueur of Ottawa for goal," Patrick wrote in his syndicated column. "In their heyday, Moran and LeSueur were two of the smartest goalers I ever saw in action."

Moran's numbers might leave modern fans scratching their heads. He posted a losing record (80–93) and his career goals-against average finished above 5.00. But his story is about perseverance as much as it is about performance.

Seldom the beneficiary of playing behind the more-talented team on the ice, Moran shone, thanks to his superior skills and a surly temperament that ensured no attacker ventured too close to his net. Given the task of protecting the cage, this turn-of-the-century Billy Smith performed on many nights as if he should be locked up in one.

"Paddy Moran was very strong in his work last night, but also very short-tempered," the *Montreal Star* noted after a 1910 game between Quebec and the Montreal Canadiens. "It was due to the referees both being busy watching the play at the Canadiens' end of the rink that he did not get a serious penalty meted out to him when he tried to slash [Henri] Dallaire's head off with one lightning stroke of his hockey blade."

Like Smith, Moran combined his combativeness with a competitiveness that proved equally frustrating to enemy shooters. "A Westmount player became so exasperated at his team's inability to score that he picked up the puck and threw it at the net," the *Montreal Star* reported of Quebec's 17–5 victory over Montreal Westmount on February 18, 1905. "Even then, Moran stopped it."

During this game, Moran became the only Hall of Fame netminder to be beaten by another goalie, when Westmount's Fred Brophy stormed down the ice and lifted a shot past him. That might not be something you'd expect to appear on the résumé of an all-time great goalie, but circumstances explain the entertainment value of the moment.

"The mildest checks with body or stick were treated as flagrant offenses and eventually, there were so few men left on the ice that the two goaltenders began to rush the puck in order to relieve their tired forwards," the *Montreal Star* reported. "In this, Brophy led off, but was unsuccessful. Then Moran retaliated and after narrowly missing the net, he and Brophy sat down together on the ice in the corner. Brophy rushed again and this time scored, while Moran, as well as all the spectators, were convulsed in laughter."

Finally surrounded by competent compatriots, Moran backstopped Quebec to successive Stanley Cup crowns in 1912 and 1913. "He was the most spectacular goalkeeper ever seen," LeSueur wrote in his 1909 *Handbook of Hockey*.

Moran's playing days ended when the National Hockey Association folded after the 1916–17 season and the Quebec franchise opted to take a two-year leave of absence from the newly formed National Hockey League.

"He was an outstanding guardian, a spectacular figure in his cage," wrote *Montreal Star* columnist Baz O'Meara, eulogizing Moran after his 1966 death. "The happiest day of his life was the day he was inducted into the Hockey Hall of Fame."

The happiest day in the life of opposing attackers undoubtedly came when Moran hung up his deft and deadly stick for good.

Moran Was a Winner Because . . .

Even though he was saddled with the difficult task of defending the goal behind inferior teammates, his fans, the media, and fellow players universally regarded him as the best goalie of his era. He took Quebec to back-to-back Stanley Cups.

DOMINIK HASEK

BILL DURNAN

KEN DRYDEN

GEORGE HAINSWORTH

PERFECTIONISTS

FRANK BRIMSEK

JOHNNY BOWER

ALEX CONNELL

ED BELFOUR

DAVEY KERR

MIKE RICHTER

Julian H. Gonzales/Detroit Free Press

5 | DOMINIK HASEK

BORN: Pardubice, Czechoslovakia, January 29, 1965

SHOT: Left	**HEIGHT:** 5'11"	**WEIGHT:** 168 lbs.
Stanley Cups: 1		Hart Trophies: 2
Vezina Trophies: 6		Jennings Trophies: 2
Pearson Awards: 2		NHL All-Star Games: 6
NHL First All-Star Team: 6		

NOTABLE ACHIEVEMENTS: Only goalie to win two Hart Trophies; second to Jacques Plante (seven) in Vezina Trophies; won the Olympic gold medal in 1998, named top goaltender at that tournament; twice named top goalie at the World Championships; three-time Czech player of the year; NHL All-Rookie Team selection, 1991–92; his 13 shutouts in 1997–98 were most in the NHL since Tony Esposito's 15 in 1969–70; his 1.95 goals-against average in 1993–94 was the first in the NHL below 2.00 since Bernie Parent's 1.89 in 1973–74; has played the most NHL games of any European-trained goalie; played in the 1984 Canada Cup at age 19; led the NHL in save percentage seven times; posted a record six shutouts during 2001–02 Stanley Cup playoffs; holds a 2.03 playoff goals-against average.

Johnny Bower's Commentary on Hasek

"He is a goaltender without a style. I honestly don't know how he stops the puck sometimes. It's tough to pick out a weakness in Hasek because this goalie makes the ultimate sacrifice. He is willing to put any part of his body in front of the puck to make the save. I was a stand-up goaltender, so I can't imagine playing the position the way he does. But he is fantastic to watch. If you were to press me for a definition of his style, I'd have to say he's best defined as a true reflex goaltender. He sees the play almost in slow motion in order to make the incredible stops he does. He is one of the best goaltenders of the modern era, both in the NHL and internationally. I think his secret is that he's a very patient goaltender and generally waits for the shooter to make the first move, especially when the shooter gets in close."

Second Opinion: Maple Leafs Forward Gary Roberts on Hasek

"He plays the bottom of the net very well and he doesn't give up on any shots. He makes all the saves that he should make, and that's really all you can ask for from a goaltender. There's no such thing as an easy goal on Dominik Hasek. If he sees the shot, he's going to stop it. The puck almost never gets through him. You have to bear down and keep your concentration throughout when you have a scoring chance against him. You think he's down and out, then he'll kick up a leg, a foot, or a hand—they seem to come out of nowhere—in some unorthodox fashion and make the save."

Up 3–0 on the Chicago Blackhawks in the 1992 Stanley Cup final and comfortably ahead in Game 4, the Pittsburgh Penguins couldn't believe what they were seeing. Chicago coach Mike Keenan was lifting Ed Belfour, his Vezina Trophy–winning goaltender, and sending an unheralded backup into the game.

"There was a lot of confusion on our bench," recalls Barry Smith, an assistant coach with the Penguins that season. "We couldn't understand what Chicago was doing."

"We were all looking at each other, wondering, 'Who is this guy?'" recalls Scotty Bowman, then coach of the Penguins. As the commotion continued, Penguins sniper Jaromir Jagr glided slowly toward the bench, his complexion ghostly, his eyes glazed over, his face frozen in fear. Staring directly at his fellow Penguins, he spoke with terror dripping from his words. "We have to win this game," he said in a pleading tone.

Being a native of the Czech Republic, Jagr was aware of the lore of this masked man. He knew this was Dominik Hasek, and he realized the Penguins were in big trouble.

Pittsburgh hung on to win that game 6–5, and Bowman still gets the shivers when he ponders what might have been. "Hasek was just like he is today," Bowman says. "We couldn't get the puck past him. I'm just glad they didn't decide to put him in for Game 1."

A decade later, Hasek no longer rates as hockey's best-kept secret, but you'll wear out an awful lot of shoe leather seeking out someone who wouldn't rate him the best in the game today. "This guy wins the Vezina every year," says Jim Bedard, a former NHL netminder and the goaltending consultant on Hasek's current team, the Detroit Red Wings. "He's the best in the world, and how are you going to argue with that?"

Hasek Is a Perfectionist Because . . .
He absolutely detests surrendering a goal, even in practice. He will work for hours to hone his craft, keeping teammates on the ice until he is satisfied with his performance.

With six Vezina Trophies and two Hart Trophies as NHL most valuable player to his credit—the latter accomplishment unprecedented among goaltenders—few hockey people are willing to step forward and engage Bedard in debate on this point. "He's the best player in the league, bar none," New York Islanders goaltender Chris Osgood says, an honest assessment, considering he surrendered his job as Detroit's number one puckstopper to Hasek at the start of the 2001–02 campaign.

Adds one NHL scout: "When Hasek's in goal, you could outshoot his team 100–2 and lose 1–0."

Since taking over as the main man in the Buffalo Sabres' goal during the 1993–94 season, Hasek has posted an astonishing .933 save percentage. He led the NHL in save percentage for a record seven consecutive seasons from 1993–94 through 1998–99. In 1997–98, Hasek turned the impressive double of being the NHL's most effective netminder, posting a .932 save percentage, while also being the busiest, facing a league-high 2,149 shots.

All these stops are from a guy the experts insisted would never be able to cut it as an NHL goaltender. Long before he arrived on the NHL stage and earned his reputation as the "Dominator," Hasek was already a legend on the other side of the Atlantic Ocean. He was named the top goaltender in the Czech Republic's Elite League five times while playing for HC Pardubice, his hometown team, and with Dukla Jihlava. On three occasions he was honored as Czech player of the year. On the international stage he was an All-Star selection at the 1983 World Junior Championships and was selected best goaltender at two World Championships. He played for Czechoslovakia in the 1984 Canada Cup at the age of 19 and was already being touted as the heir apparent to Russia's Vladislav Tretiak as the best goalie in Europe.

It would be quite some time, though, before Hasek would earn that reputation in North America. Selected 207th overall by Chicago in the 1983 NHL entry draft, he didn't make it to the Western Hemisphere until the 1990–91 season. He played five games for the Blackhawks that season, posting a 3–0–1 record and a 2.46 goals-against average, spending most of the season with the minor league Indianapolis Ice, where he earned International Hockey League All-Star status.

The next season—the one in which the Penguins got their unnerving introduction—he gained a spot as goaltender on the NHL All-Rookie team. Those close to Hasek quietly saw something in him. They weren't sure what it was, but they knew it worked. "Because he wasn't playing much, he took a lot of extra shots in practice," recalls Chris Chelios, Chicago's captain when Hasek broke into the big leagues. "We just couldn't get the puck by him. He'd always find a way to get something in front of it."

Nevertheless skeptics continued to insist that Hasek's unorthodox, flopping style would be the death of his NHL career and would send him back home with his tail between his legs, the same fate met by every other European goalie who had preceded him to the NHL. Conventional wisdom suggested his way would never work, because nothing appeared to be conventional about Hasek.

"I remember when I first saw him play, I thought, 'Oh God, this can't last,' because he was just flopping around," says television analyst John Davidson, a former NHL goalie. "But you watch him closely, and every move is by design. The man is brilliant. And with his elasticity and his rubberized knee joints, it's a pretty unique style."

Hasek wishes hockey people would have displayed similar flexibility when it came to his puckstopping methodology. His style is difficult to categorize. It's as if some hockey mad scientist took the best qualities of every netminder, put them in a blender, and pureed them into a Franken-goalie. "I'm a butterfly goalie and I have pretty fast legs," is Hasek's own assessment. "It looks maybe unorthodox, but it's a good style."

Part butterfly, part Baryshnikov, and part Gumby, Hasek employs every inch of his body to make saves and isn't above using his head when called upon. "I am not afraid to stop the puck with my head," he says. "I try to do it sometimes even in practice. Not every day, but once in awhile, I say to my teammates, 'Shoot me in my head and I'll try to stop the puck.' Sometimes, if the shot comes at my head, it's an easier save to make with your head."

Goaltending for Hasek is an evening at the improv. He'll throw his paddle aside to snatch the puck up in his blocker, or maybe launch it out of the zone with a Ray Guy–style punt from one of his cumbersome leg pads. He will lie across the goal crease in a swimsuit model–like pose, daring you to go top shelf, then snatch the biscuit up with his lightning-quick glove hand.

His trendsetting ways might never be mimicked, but they're no longer mocked. "I call him a butterfly flopper," says Manny Legace, Hasek's backup in Detroit, pointing toward Hasek's gaunt, rail-thin, 5'11", 168-pound body and shaking his head. Put a pair of work boots on Hasek and you could swing him on the 18th tee at Pebble Beach. "If he turned sideways, you'd lose him, but he looks so huge in net," Legace says.

Reformed in their ways of thinking, goalie gurus now sing the praises of Hasek's methodology, citing how he has revolutionized the way that the puck is parried. "He's changed goaltending totally," Bedard says. "He opened the doors to new ideas and ways of thinking about how the position should be played. He showed that there isn't a certain style you have to play. The bottom line is to stop the puck."

Jim Corsi, Hasek's goalie coach in Buffalo, insists that close analysis of his rubber-rejecting habits display traits commonplace among all legendary net-minders. "The principles of Dominik's style are no different than any other great goaltender," he says. "He's square to the shooter and has both feet in the shooting lane at all times."

It took Hasek three seasons to get the opportunity to prove this to the rest of the NHL. A trade to Buffalo in the summer of 1992 put him into a Sabres uniform. A knee injury to Buffalo's number one netminder, Grant Fuhr, put him in the spotlight, and he took advantage of the opportunity to shine. "When I first came to the NHL, it was frustrating because I never played, so I can't show them that the way I played goal is good enough for the NHL," he says. "I wasn't going to get a chance in Chicago, so going to Buffalo was the best thing that ever happened to me."

Hasek took the NHL by storm during the 1993–94 season. His seven shutouts led the league. His league-leading 1.95 goals-against average was the first in 20 years under 2.00, and it earned him his first Vezina Trophy.

The "Dominator" was born. And his lore only grew. After watching Hasek block pucks for a couple of seasons, no less a source than Wayne Gretzky, the NHL's all-time scoring leader, tabbed him as the man he'd build an NHL fran-chise around. "That Hasek is just unbelievable," Gretzky said.

Hasek's reputation advanced rapidly, and his ability to thwart enemy shoot-ers began to play mental games with hockey's most productive scorers. "You might as well close your eyes and shoot," suggests New York Rangers center Petr Nedved. Adds Legace: "He just stops everything and frustrates guys."

Others agree that Hasek gets inside their heads. "He has an aura about him," Carolina Hurricanes coach Paul Maurice acknowledges. "We'll take shots against every other goalie in the league that we won't take against him."

That aura was most evident during the 1998 Winter Olympics in Nagano, Japan. Putting aside everything and turning the hockey world on its ear, Hasek backstopped the Czech Republic to a stunning gold-medal win as the NHL's best players competed in the Olympics for the first time. He posted an 0.97 GAA and a .961 save percentage for the tournament, allowing only two goals in three medal-round games. In the semifinals against Canada, he blanked the Canadi-ans in a shootout, foiling Eric Lindros, Ray Bourque, Joe Nieuwendyk, Theoren Fleury, and Brendan Shanahan to give the Czechs a one-goal victory. He completely stymied Russia in the gold-medal game, making Petr Svoboda's goal stand up for a 1–0 victory. "We built a team around Dominik Hasek," Czech Republic coach Slavomir Lener said at the time. "That's why we won."

Hasek still gets emotional when talking about the gold medal. "That was my greatest moment," he says. "I was so happy, I saw my whole career flash before my eyes, from the first time my parents took me to a game."

So seldom did opponents see the red light flash behind Hasek that the strat-egy in NHL circles was to avoid meeting up with him in the postseason at all costs. "He has the ability to win a playoff series all on his own," Detroit captain Steve Yzerman says. "Going into the playoffs, all the talk around the league would be that you didn't want to face Hasek in a series."

One year after his Olympic glory, Hasek nearly pulled off another miracle, taking the Sabres—the seventh seed in the NHL's Eastern Conference—to within two victories of the Stanley Cup. Defeat finally arrived in Game 6 with Brett Hull's controversial foot-in-the-crease goal in triple overtime, a tally that appeared to be an infraction of the NHL's rules. "He gives you a chance to win 99.9 percent of the time," says Islanders center Michael Peca, Hasek's former teammate in Buffalo.

Hasek's chance to win came with Detroit in 2001–02, when he posted a record six shutouts as he backstopped the Wings to Stanley Cup glory. "This was my dream," he said after lifting the cherished mug. "Now it's a dream come true." He then retired, bringing his remarkable career to a close on June 25, 2002.

The secret to Hasek's success is really no secret at all. "You never can be completely satisfied," he says, combining his unparalleled ability with a dedication to be better tomorrow than he was today, resulting in a training regimen that is unsurpassed.

"Dominik Hasek's work habits are legendary," Bedard says. "It's the same with Belfour, [Patrick] Roy, or [Martin] Brodeur. These guys are perfectionists. It's more than a job, more than a passion. They live and breathe stopping pucks. Good isn't good enough for them. They have to be the best."

Hockey Night in Canada once put a shot clock on Hasek in a pregame warm-up, and he allowed just three goals on more than 160 shots. In practice he'll chide teammates for not trying hard enough to beat him, imploring them to move in closer and shoot the puck harder. Not that it helps. Earlier in the 2001–02 season at one Red Wings practice, Hasek stopped 31 consecutive shots during a breakaway drill. "It took me two weeks to score a goal on him," complains Detroit winger Tomas Holmstrom.

Hasek shrugs in disbelief when people express amazement at his steely-eyed determination to stop every puck directed his way. "Hockey is supposed to be fun, and for me, fun is stopping every shot," he explains.

He still leaves shooters and critics shaking their heads, still silences doubters in the same confident manner he would stare down Joe Sakic on a breakaway. Asked to assess Hasek's style, St. Louis Blues forward Keith Tkachuk responded with an appropriate, one-word answer. "Whatever," was all he said.

Whatever it is, it certainly worked.

6 | BILL DURNAN

BORN: Toronto, Ontario, January 22, 1916

DIED: October 31, 1972

SHOT: Right	HEIGHT: 6′	WEIGHT: 190 lbs.
Stanley Cups: 2		Vezina Trophies: 6
NHL First All-Star Team: 6		NHL All-Star Games: 3

NOTABLE ACHIEVEMENTS: Hall of Famer; only Jacques Plante won more Vezinas (seven); ambidextrous; had special gloves that operated as both blocker and trapper, allowing him to switch hands; didn't turn pro until the age of 27 and played only seven NHL seasons; led the NHL in goals-against average in six of his seven seasons; won the Allan Cup with Kirkland Lake Blue Devils in 1940; his shutout sequence of 309 minutes, 21 seconds in 1948—49 is fourth longest in NHL history; last NHL goaltender to serve as captain of his team and last NHL goaltender to post four consecutive shutouts.

Johnny Bower's Commentary on Durnan

"I really liked his style because he was one of the best stand-up goaltenders of all time. But that was overshadowed by the fact that he's best remembered for being ambidextrous. Back then, all goaltenders wore what we called 'nets,' or pads that were barely bigger than the width of your shins, and gloves just like the skaters'. As a result, he was able to switch his stick from hand to hand and make glove saves with either his left or right hand, depending on which side of the rink the skater was attacking from."

Second Opinion: Former Maple Leafs Captain Teeder Kennedy on Durnan

"Bill Durnan was the premier goaltender in the regular season at that time in the forties. Turk Broda was the guy you would want in the playoffs—he was the money goalie—but Durnan was the best in the regular season. Durnan was a big man, a stand-up goalie, like most of the goalies of that time. When he went down and was in a kneeling position, he still covered an awful lot of the net. He had a great catching hand. He hardly ever gave up rebounds. The puck would hit those goal pads and he would cover it up with that glove hand really quick. I don't remember anyone ever saying he had a weak spot. He could switch hands at any time, depending on what the situation called for. It wasn't something you would look for, but I remember him doing it often enough."

The tepid target. The reluctant rejecter of rubber. The goaltender who could do it either way, but often appeared to be seeking a way out. This is Bill Durnan's legacy.

Critics obsess about the way he stopped playing, often overlooking the way he stopped the puck. They linger over how the pressure rose to stifle him, not on the way in which he rose to stymie the opposition when the pressure was at its highest. For years hockey history has painted Bill Durnan as a man who entered the nets against his better judgment, someone who'd rather have spent the evening doing anything but what he did best.

Those closest to him—his former teammates—insist this absolutely wasn't the case. "For people to suggest he didn't have nerve, well, that's just not right," says Ken Reardon, Durnan's Montreal Canadiens teammate for five seasons. When Durnan's old compatriots speak of him, they do so with the love that a man would hold in his heart for his own brother.

"All of us looked up to him," Canadiens Hall of Fame legend Hector "Toe" Blake told Red Fisher of the *Montreal Star* upon Durnan's 1972 death. "We looked up to him as a man. Some of us on the team . . . me, Murph [Chamberlain] . . . we were older than he was. But we looked up to him."

"Just a marvelous man," adds Reardon. "If anybody wants to talk to me about Bill Durnan, I've got all day for them."

So why the misconception? Mostly it's a misunderstanding of what Durnan was about, what made him tick. A misinterpretation of the facts.

Was there fear in Durnan's heart? Definitely. But it was the same fright that grips all great goalies. "Goaltenders fear only one thing," fellow Hall of Fame netminder Tony Esposito once explained. "The fear of failure."

Every netminder is deathly afraid of letting his teammates down. This fear certainly gripped Durnan.

"He exhibited a calm and cool presence in front of the rest of us. When he was with us in the dressing room and off the ice, he was an easy-going guy," Reardon recalls. "But we had this anteroom off of the dressing room and during games, the only one allowed in there between periods was Bill. He'd be in there, smoking a cigarette. That was where he found his solace from the game, his solitude."

That, and in his beer. According to teammates, Durnan could put them away at an astounding pace, even for a hockey player. "He had two beers for every one I had," former Montreal center Jimmy Peters Sr. says.

Durnan, it also seemed, owned two Vezina Trophies for every one captured by other netminders. In seven seasons he was named the NHL's top goaltender six times. In league history, only Jacques Plante would win more (seven).

"Durnan, that son of a gun, you couldn't get anything by him," former Detroit Red Wings sniper Carl Liscombe says. "He had eyes like an eagle. He was tall and slim and he'd just take the net away from you. On his worst days he might give you three or four inches to shoot at. When he was on top of his game, it felt like a moral victory if you could hit the post."

At 6′ and 190 pounds, Durnan used his frame to cover much of the goal. "He really knew how to play the angles and make the net look smaller to the shooters," Peters says. "And that was in the day when the equipment didn't make the goalie all that much bigger."

Durnan employed his rapier-quick hands to take away the rest of the net. "My father used to talk about how he had soft hands—soft like a baby," says *Hockey Night in Canada* broadcaster Dick Irvin Jr., whose father coached the Canadiens during Durnan's entire career, from 1943 to 1950.

When people talked in plural about Durnan's hands, it was the proper tense, for he was hockey's only ambidextrous goalie. He wore special gloves, each designed to serve as trapper and blocker. He'd switch his stick to the attacker's strong side on a breakaway and when the puck was in the corner, he always positioned his stick in the hand on that side of the net, employing the lumber to deflect passes aimed for the slot.

Durnan developed this unique trait as a youngster while stopping pucks for Toronto's Westmoreland United Church boys team. He credited his coach, Steve Faulkner, as the one who taught him to use both hands.

"Steve showed me how to switch the stick from one hand to the other," Durnan told the Canadian Press. "It wasn't easy at first, because I was so young, and the stick seemed so heavy. But Steve kept after me, and gradually the stick became lighter and I could switch it automatically. It was a tremendous asset."

Others agreed with that assessment. "It was amazing, the way he'd switch that stick," Reardon says. "The shooters, they didn't know what to do."

Except one. When right hander Gordie Howe broke in on Durnan, the Montreal goalie quickly switched sticks to Howe's strong side. Then the shooter switched his stick to the left and fired the puck past Durnan. Howe was also ambidextrous.

"I never even realized I was doing it," Howe recalls. "I came on right wing. He positioned himself on the post and I switched to my left and had a better angle. That came from when I was a goaltender when I was young. I caught left and that meant I had to shoot left."

On those few occasions that the shooters did discover a way to get the better of Durnan, they had some explaining to do.

"One night we were playing in Montreal and I got one past Durnan," Liscombe recalls. "After the game, we're leaving to head to the train station, and this fellow steps right into my path. It was Durnan. He said to me, 'How'd you score that goal?' I just sort of looked at him and laughed, but he was dead serious. He demanded to know where I'd beaten him, where I found the opening, so that he could make sure it never happened again."

Durnan was methodical and cautious in his preparation. "The day of the game, he wouldn't go to a movie because he was afraid of hurting his eyes," Irvin Jr. says. "He would never catch the puck in practice because he was afraid he would hurt his hands."

Durnan looked upon practice as a necessary evil. "Bill, you'd have to drag him on the ice, but you never had to drag him off the ice," Reardon says.

Unless Durnan was working on some aspect of his game that gave him cause for concern. When a long shot from Toronto's Reg Hamilton hit an ice chip and skipped past him, the goalie spent an hour the next day fielding shots from center. Hamilton's goal was a fluke, a million-to-one shot, but Durnan's obsessiveness made him determined to ensure he'd be prepared the next time he faced such a variable.

"He really studied the position," Reardon says.

Hard luck played a role in keeping Durnan from reaching the NHL until the age of 27. Originally Toronto Maple Leafs property, he missed training camp one year after suffering a knee injury while engaging in horseplay with a friend. A broken leg sidelined him another year, and he was eventually dropped from the Leafs' protected list.

As great a netminder as Durnan was—most from his era willingly label him the best—some feel he was even better while toeing the rubber than he was at stopping rubber.

"He was the best fastball pitcher in Canada," Reardon says. "We had a team in the summer, and I played second base. The ball still hasn't got to me. They couldn't hit Bill. He'd even tell them where he was going to throw it, and they still couldn't touch it."

Durnan was brought to the northern Ontario mining town of Kirkland Lake to pitch for the local team in 1936. Persuaded to play goal in the winter during 1939–40, he carried the Blue Devils to the Allan Cup as senior hockey champions of Canada. That led him to the Montreal Royals of the Quebec Senior League and, after three seasons there, Durnan earned a spot with the Canadiens from a 1943 tryout.

Despite his dominance over the next seven campaigns—in addition to the six Vezinas, he had six first All-Star selections—Durnan was never embraced by Montreal's Francophone supporters. He suffered the same fate as other Torontonians who tended goal for the Habs, such as George Hainsworth and Ken Dryden. They weren't beloved on a scale comparable to French-Canadian netminders, such as Georges Vezina, Jacques Plante, and Patrick Roy. The Canadiens won only two Cups in Durnan's tenure, and the finger of blame was often pointed at him. Fans called for the return of journeyman French Canadian Paul Bibeault, who preceded Durnan between the pipes for the Canadiens.

"The fans were murder," Durnan told Toronto *Globe and Mail* writer Trent Frayne. "Winning is great in Montreal; losing is a federal offense."

Perhaps this attitude helps explain Durnan's sudden and surprising exit from the game. Clipped in the scalp by the skate of Chicago's Jim Conacher late in the 1949–50 season, he never seemed to regain his confidence. During the Stanley Cup semifinals against the New York Rangers, he asked that Montreal coach Dick Irvin Sr. remove him from the nets "for the good of the team."

"It got so bad that I couldn't sleep the night before a game," Durnan said, explaining the tension to the Canadian Press. "I couldn't even keep my meals down. I felt that nothing was worth that agony."

Rookie Gerry McNeil received word in midday that he'd be starting that night, with the Habs facing elimination, and didn't take the news well. Before the game Irvin asked Durnan to take McNeil into his anteroom and try to calm him. "A few minutes later I stepped into the room and what do you think I saw?" Irvin explained to the Canadian Press. "The two of them were in there crying. Yes, crying, and Bill, his voice shaky, his hands trembling uncontrollably, was saying, 'Now Gerry, don't be nervous. Everything will be all right.'"

Durnan never played again. Acclaimed by the majority as the greatest goalie of his era, he left the game as quietly and unceremoniously as he had arrived.

"He was just like a ghost," Reardon says. "Bill would drift in the room and then drift out. You never knew he was there."

7 | KEN DRYDEN

BORN: Hamilton, Ontario, August 8, 1947

SHOT: Left	HEIGHT: 6'4"	WEIGHT: 205 lbs.
Stanley Cups: 6		Vezina Trophies: 5
Conn Smythe Trophies: 1		Calder Trophies: 1
NHL First All-Star Team: 5		NHL Second All-Star Team: 1
NHL All-Star Games: 5		

NOTABLE ACHIEVEMENTS: Hall of Famer; his .743 winning percentage is the best in NHL history; one of only two goalies to win the Stanley Cup before the Calder (with Tony Esposito); three-time NCAA All-American at Cornell; led the NHL in goals-against average four times; his 10 shutouts in 1976–77 was the only double-digit total from 1975 through 1996; one of only six NHL goalies to post multiple 40-win seasons (with Terry Sawchuk, Ed Belfour, Bernie Parent, Martin Brodeur, and Jacques Plante).

Johnny Bower's Commentary on Dryden

"Ken Dryden is one of the top hockey people I have ever met. He was a dynamite stay-at-home goaltender and a thinking man's player. You'd always see him lean on his stick after the whistle. Now we all know that lawyers like to think about what they're going to say before they say it, and when Ken would lean on his stick, I always had the feeling that he was thinking about the players that were on the ice against the Canadiens. He's a very smart man who in my opinion might have walked away from the game too soon. He could have won more awards and championships, but I truly respect him for deciding to leave the game when he did. He had a difficult decision to make. Do I continue to play the game I love and wait another 5 or 10 years to start my legal career, or do I leave now? But what makes Ken Dryden different from anyone else I've met in this game is his compassion for the game and people. When I had a bypass a few years back, he came down to the hospital to spend time with me during recovery. It was so nice to see him there because I know how busy he is [as president of the Toronto Maple Leafs]. But that's the kind of caring person Ken is."

Second Opinion: Former Canadiens Goalie Rogie Vachon on Dryden

"When Ken Dryden came in, the writing was on the wall for me. After we won the Cup, I went in to see [general manager Sam Pollock] and just asked whether we would be sharing the goaltending duties next season. I knew the answer. I don't blame the Canadiens. He was a big guy, and all of a sudden he wins a Cup immediately. He was quick for a big guy. He covered a lot more net. In those days, if you had a goalie who was 6′3″ or 6′4″, normally he was clumsy. Ken Dryden was one of the first big guys who was athletic and fast."

When Ken Dryden was in the net for the Montreal Canadiens, it was his mind over all other matters. He might have been more mentally prepared to play the position than any goaltender who had come before him. His size, his quickness, even his agility were just accessories. "He intellectualized the position of goaltender," says former NHL player Bill Clement. "He approached the position analytically and scientifically. He had studied how to play."

In 1971 the hockey world was flabbergasted that a former college goaltender who seemed more interested in law than hockey could play six games in the regular season for Montreal and then be a difference-maker in the Canadiens' Stanley Cup win. At that time, college hockey players weren't yet being mainstreamed into NHL teams; truthfully, the league wasn't all that accepting of a player like Dryden, who chose to attend law school rather than turn professional after graduation from Cornell the year before. Even after Dryden went 6–0 at the end of the regular season, no one gave him much of a chance in the playoffs, especially in the first round against a Boston Bruins team that had Bobby Orr, Phil Esposito, and a strong ensemble cast.

"There was no description or category that fit Ken Dryden because what he did had never happened before," says former Montreal teammate Larry Pleau. "What do we call him? You can't call him a rookie because he was a rookie the next season. How do you sum up a goalie that wins the Stanley Cup the season before he wins the Calder Trophy as Rookie of the Year?"

At 6'4", Dryden did seem bigger than life upon his arrival in the NHL. Esposito called Dryden a "big giraffe" and a "big octopus." Boston's Derek Sanderson called him the NHL's first "four-story goaltender." His mechanics and unflappable demeanor fascinated most players in the league. Rookies were supposed to be nervous Nellies and prone to panic plays, but Dryden seemed as unchanging as the mask on his face.

Dryden Was a Perfectionist Because . . .

Not surprisingly, given his law degree, he approached goaltending like he was a trial lawyer entering litigation. He was mentally prepared for all possibilities.

Clement laughs when he recalls how instantly dominant Dryden was at the NHL level; weeks before, Clement had faced the so-called rookie in the American Hockey League and came away unimpressed. "I didn't think he could survive in the American League," Clement says.

That theory was based on the fact that Clement, then playing for the Quebec Aces, scored five goals in a weekend against Dryden. "When he won the Cup, I was thinking, 'You got to be kidding me,'" Clement says, chuckling. "I knew he couldn't be any good, because I scored that many goals against him. I never even scored 20 goals in a season until I got to the NHL."

Dryden was studying law at McGill University when he agreed to sign with the Canadiens before the 1970–71 season and play for Les Voyageurs, the Canadiens' Montreal-based affiliate. He had played for the Canadian national team the season before and when that team was disbanded, Canadiens general manager Sam Pollock persuaded him to join the farm team. The deal included a concession that Dryden had to practice only one day per week and that the organization would work around his commitment to studying. He was able to play only five games before Christmas, but after February he was able to play more regularly for Les Voyageurs.

"He could give you the impression that you weren't going to get a good goal against him," says former NHL coach Harry Neale. "If you scored, it was going to be a bad goal, or a deflection. If I thought that and players thought that, he had an advantage."

Eleven months after the Orr-led Bruins won their first Stanley Cup championship, Dryden eliminated them in the first round of the playoffs. There was irony wrapped around the triumph because the Bruins had originally drafted him, but the Canadiens persuaded them to deal Dryden and Alex Campbell for Guy Allen and Paul Reid. Neither Allen nor Reid played in the NHL.

Through the years some critics have tried to explain Dryden's dominance as merely an extension of Montreal's dominance. The argument is that anyone could have looked good playing for the defensively strong Canadiens.

Nonsense, say Canadiens players. Pleau says it was probably more difficult to play for Montreal because opposing teams rarely unleashed a barrage of shots against the team. A Canadiens goaltender might not face any shots for a few minutes and then have to make a big save on a two-on-one break. Most goaltenders have difficulty finding their rhythm in that kind of environment. Dryden had no difficulty staying sharp, even through periods of inactivity.

Pleau marveled at Dryden's concentration. "It was unbelievable," Pleau says. "When the puck left the zone, he relaxed, and then when the puck came in, he could refocus quickly. It was hard to play goal for the Canadiens. You weren't going to face a lot of shots, and you aren't allowed to give up any bad goals. When you can play the way Kenny did and only face 18 shots, that's special concentration."

Dryden was the first NHL goalie to meld size with athleticism.

"Pressure is all relative," Dryden once said. "Everything that is new is a challenge. I don't think there was any greater pressure [in Montreal] than with the Canadian national team."

Dryden's uniqueness extended beyond his goaltending. "He was a genius. He was brilliant," says legendary Montreal *Gazette* sportswriter Red Fisher. "He was by far the best quote in the league, and he was terrific to be around."

In some corners Dryden was considered eccentric, maybe because NHL players weren't accustomed to seeing teammates reading books all the time. They certainly didn't know many teammates who aspired to be an author, as Dryden did. "Some got a little nervous to see him taking notes on the way to his classic book," Fisher recalls.

But the truth is that teammates liked Dryden, who had a terrific sense of humor and accepted their ribbing like every other player. "What's not to like?" Pleau says. "He won games for us. That's what mattered to everyone."

Dryden was not one to spend many hours carousing with teammates, but Fisher insists it wasn't because he was antisocial.

"When he didn't go out with the guys, it wasn't because he didn't like them," Fisher says. "He just didn't want to spend any money. He was tight as a drum. He really saved his pennies. When the guys went out in those days, they would spend $25 on a steak and as much on beer. He wasn't going to do that. Guys would chuckle about it and kid him. But that's where it ended."

Dryden also had other interests, including the culmination of his thoughts on hockey that would eventually become the bestseller *The Game* after his retirement.

Throughout his career Dryden marched to a cadence that only he could hear. As principled as he was talented, he understood his value and his place in the game. When the Canadiens wouldn't pay him what he considered fair value in 1973–74, he retired, at age 26, to become a law clerk for $135 per week. The following season, after the Canadiens struggled without him, the two parties came to terms on a new deal.

But Dryden's career still wouldn't follow a traditional line. He would retire at age 31 when he was still at the top of his game.

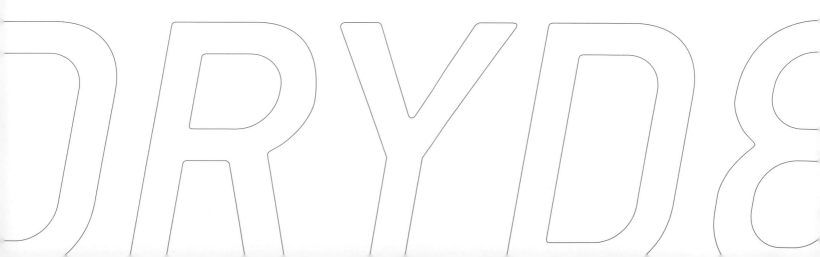

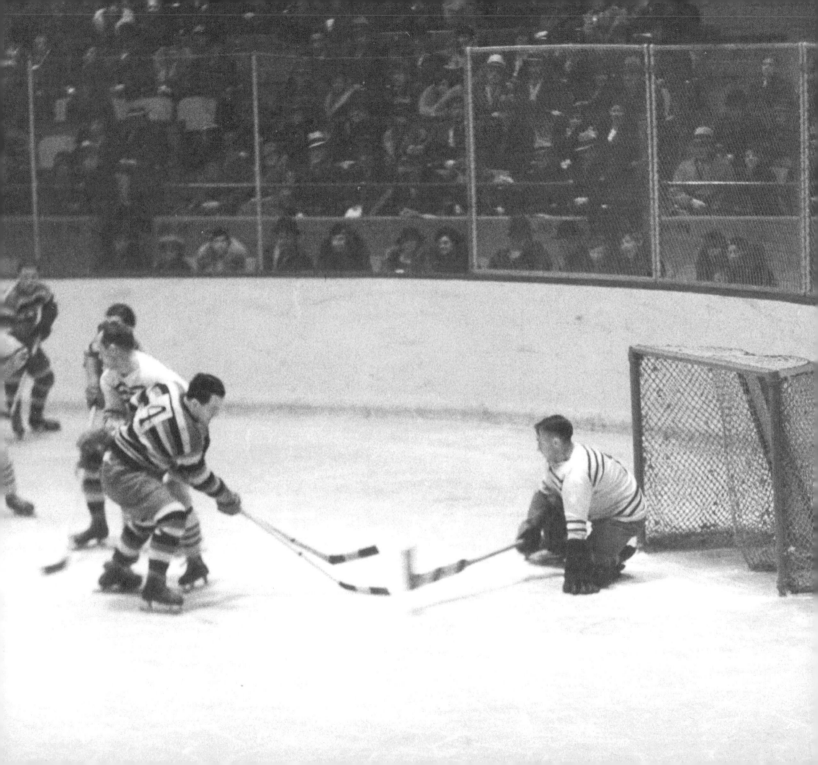

8 | GEORGE HAINSWORTH

BORN: Toronto, Ontario, June 26, 1895

DIED: October 9, 1950

SHOT: Right	HEIGHT: 5'6"	WEIGHT: 150 lbs.
Stanley Cups: 2		Vezina Trophies: 3
NHL All-Star Games: 1		

NOTABLE ACHIEVEMENTS: Hall of Famer; second on all-time shutout list; recorded 22 shutouts and an 0.92 goals-against average with the Montreal Canadiens in 1928–29; won the Vezina Trophy the first three seasons it was awarded; led the NHL in shutouts three times, including three of his first four seasons; one of only four goalies to post 15 or more shutouts in a season (with Tony Esposito, Alex Connell, and Hal Winkler); one of only three NHL goalies to post double digits in shutouts in three successive seasons (with Lorne Chabot and Alex Connell); missed just two games in his first 10 NHL seasons and his first 13 pro campaigns; second-lowest career GAA in NHL history (1.93); posted 104 shutouts in major league hockey; his shutout sequence of 343 minutes, five seconds in 1928–29 is the second longest in NHL history; won the Allan Cup with Kitchener, 1917–18.

Johnny Bower's Commentary on Hainsworth

"George Hainsworth was the last of the old-style stand-up netminders and one of the most nonchalant performers in the history of hockey. He played goal in a fashion that could almost be mistaken for indifference. He was so sound in his technique that he seldom was forced to flop or slide in front of a puck. He made the playoffs in each of his first 10 NHL seasons, but he wasn't one to blow his own horn and was often overlooked when it came time to hand out recognition. When Turk Broda took over for Hainsworth in the Toronto Maple Leafs' goal in 1936, he said he felt as if he were replacing a Toronto institution. George served just as selflessly after his playing days, gaining election as an alderman in Kitchener, Ontario, and working tirelessly on the construction of a new rink in Kitchener."

Second Opinion: Former Canadiens Teammate Pete Palangio on Hainsworth

"He was like a cucumber between the pipes. He was very cool under pressure. He wasn't one of those excitable types. It gave you a lot of confidence as a team playing in front of him, because he was so relaxed back there. He used to feel almost guilty because he didn't make flashy saves, the kind that brought the crowd out of their seats. But that was just George. He was so sound in net that he was never caught out of position, so he didn't need to make the fancy stops. He made them all look so easy. You have to give him credit, because he was honest in assessing himself. He wasn't the type to brag. And he was one of the nicest gentlemen you'd ever want to meet."

All he accomplished during his first five National Hockey League seasons was to win three successive Vezina Trophies, capture back-to-back Stanley Cups, and establish single-season marks for shutouts and goals-against average that have remained on the books for 73 years.

For this, George Hainsworth felt the need to apologize.

If only he were blessed with a flair for the dramatic, Hainsworth might have proved to be the Jerry Seinfeld of his generation—the man who made a show about nothing.

The diminutive puckstopper certainly proved capable of turning nothing into something. It was the show he couldn't come up with. As a stopper, he was second to none. As a showstopper, he left much to be desired. At least that was how he viewed things.

"I'm sorry I can't put on a show like some of the other goalers," Hainsworth lamented in an interview during the 1928–29 season.

In that campaign he recorded 22 shutouts in 44 games and an 0.92 goals-against average, both still NHL single-season standards for a netminder. Hainsworth held the opposition to one goal in an additional 12 games that season and posted a shutout sequence of 343 minutes, five seconds, the second longest in NHL history. He put together a 22-game unbeaten streak (12–0–10) and lost just once in his last 31 games.

Making this feat even more astonishing was the realization that he played much of the season nursing a broken nose, suffered in the warm-up before a game with the New York Americans.

"The Canadiens were tossing pucks at the goaler in practice," explained the *Border Cities Star*. "Hainsworth glanced away for a moment and one of [Aurel] Joliat's sniping drives caught him fairly on the nose. The bridge was shattered, blood poured, his nose puffed up until he was nearly blinded. But he had the injury taped, insisted on playing, and with blood dripping steadily throughout until there was a crimson stain in front of each net, he stood off the Americans, and [the] Canadiens won the game."

Despite his astonishing capability for shutouts, hockey pundits reserved their plaudits for flashier, acrobatic types like Boston's Tiny Thompson, Chicago's Charlie Gardiner, and Roy Worters of the New York Americans, instead of the steady Hainsworth, for whom flamboyance was a foreign object.

"His style has often been his worst enemy," Vern DeGeer wrote in *The Windsor Star* in 1936. And the man known leaguewide as the nonchalant Hainsworth seemed willing to accept his fate as so.

"I can't look excited because I'm not," he said. "I can't dive on easy shots and make them look hard. I guess all I can do is stop pucks."

Like nobody had seen before, as a matter of fact.

"I think he was about the best there was," says former NHL forward Lorne Carr, who faced Hainsworth as an opponent. "I remember when I first started in the league [in 1933], he had quite a reputation. And he'd earned it, because he sure stopped a lot of people in his career."

Carrying a pudgy 150 pounds on his 5′6″ frame, Hainsworth looked nothing like a sensational athlete. His unusual dimensions and diminutive stature gave him an odd-looking disposition. To study pictures of him, it's easy to swear that some trick photographer took a man's head and superimposed it on the body of a little boy.

All of that served to heighten Hainsworth's aura. His physical stature made him look easy to beat, but shooters' psyches took the ultimate beating.

"I really don't know that he had a weakness in his game, at least not one that we were capable of finding out about," former Red Wings right wing Pete Kelly says.

Hainsworth Was a Perfectionist Because . . .

He was a master technician who made stopping the hardest shot appear to be routine work. Also superstitious, he carried a horseshoe in his trunk and wore the same ragged cap in goal for his entire career.

Despite his remarkably successful career, Hainsworth often wished he was more "entertaining" to the fans.

After his hockey days, Hainsworth worked as an inspector in the radio division for Dominion Electrohome Industries, and he brought a similar dedication to duty to his netminding. "He certainly was a pretty steady goaltender and very thorough in his work," Kelly says.

Hainsworth was seldom forced to make spectacular stops, because it was so rare that he'd be caught out of position. "Hainsworth plays goal in a debonair, nonchalant fashion that at times looks to verge on actual carelessness, but isn't," *The Windsor Star* wrote in 1933. "And this isn't done for effect. He makes the tough shots look easy, but that happens to be Hainsworth's style, not a pose."

Born in Toronto, Hainsworth backstopped the Kitchener Greenshirts to an Allan Cup as senior hockey champions of Canada in 1917–18. The Canadiens traded star center Newsy Lalonde to the Saskatoon Sheiks of the Western Canada Hockey League in 1922, where he was named player/manager. Lalonde soon discovered his club lacked a goalkeeper of major league caliber and called his old boss, Leo Dandurand, seeking a lead on a puckstopper.

Dandurand pointed Lalonde toward two options: McGill University's Jack Cameron and Hainsworth. Lalonde chose the latter, signing Hainsworth for two years at $1,600 per season.

It proved to be an astute maneuver. Hainsworth twice got the Sheiks to within one round of the Stanley Cup final and was a league All-Star in 1925–26. But the Western League folded in 1926, and it was time for Lalonde to return the favor.

The Habs were in the market for a goalie after the tragic death of superstar Georges Vezina from tuberculosis, and Lalonde recommended Hainsworth to Dandurand, who purchased his contract for $5,000. Hainsworth proceeded to capture the Vezina Trophy, the award for the NHL's top goalie, named in memory of his predecessor, in each of the first three seasons it was presented.

Nonetheless, Montreal fans were slow to warm to the unspectacular Hainsworth, possibly because he was an English Canadian from hated Toronto. He spoke no French and knew no one in the city, becoming a lonely figure. Even during his 22-shutout campaign, he was booed during Montreal's losses. Eventually, the fans warmed to him, and after Montreal's 1929–30 Cup triumph, one devoted Hainsworth supporter marketed mini-statuettes of the Canadiens' reliable netminder. They sold out almost instantly.

When the Depression hit in the thirties and ticket buyers were harder to come by, the Habs thought a French-Canadian goalie might prove a popular draw and dealt Hainsworth to Toronto in 1933 for Lorne Chabot. "I think this is a nice break," Hainsworth told the Toronto *Globe*. He was right.

The Leafs were Stanley Cup finalists in two of their first three seasons with Hainsworth between the pipes, but failed to lift the grail. But it wasn't the goalie's fault, according to former Toronto defenseman Red Horner.

"We should have won more Cups," notes Horner. The Leafs played in seven finals from 1932 to 1940, but won only one title. "We had a lot of guys who liked to have fun—a lot of teams did—but some of our guys didn't know when to stop. They didn't bear down and concentrate on hockey when it mattered most."

Hainsworth played his final NHL games in 1936–37 at age 41. He posted 94 NHL shutouts, second only to Terry Sawchuk's 103. Factoring in Hainsworth's 10 western whitewashes, he owned more major league zeros than any goalie in the history of the game.

When the show was over, nobody knew more about nothing than George did.

13 | FRANK BRIMSEK

BORN: Eveleth, Minnesota, September 26, 1915

DIED: November 11, 1998

SHOT: Left	HEIGHT: 5'9"	WEIGHT: 170 lbs.
Stanley Cups: 2		Vezina Trophies: 2
Calder Trophies: 1		NHL First All-Star Team: 2
NHL Second All-Star Team: 6		NHL All-Star Games: 3

NOTABLE ACHIEVEMENTS: Hall of Famer, the only American-born netminder enshrined; also inducted into the U.S. Hockey Hall of Fame; led the NHL in wins, shutouts, and goals-against average twice each; only goalie to win Calder and Vezina Trophies and Stanley Cup as a rookie; posted a pair of three-game shutout streaks in his first month as an NHL player, earning the nickname "Mr. Zero."

Johnny Bower's Commentary on Brimsek

"When I was a young whippersnapper growing up in Prince Albert, Saskatch-ewan, I wanted to be Frankie Brimsek. We were one of the few families on my block to have a radio, so on Saturday nights we'd gather around to listen to the hockey game. The highlight for me was when the Leafs played Boston, and Foster Hewitt would go on about the great goaltender from Boston. I would tell my family and friends that someday I was going to be called Mr. Zero, and everyone would laugh at me. But it didn't stop me because I wanted to be just like him, and it helped push me to my goal of being a National League goaltender."

Second Opinion: Former NHL Goaltender Emile Francis on Brimsek

"I just couldn't believe that guys like Brimsek, Mike Karakas, and Sam Lopresti all came out of Eveleth, Minnesota, and all played the same style. Brimsek was more of a stand-up, and he wasn't much bigger than I was [at 5′6″]. We didn't have goaltending coaches back then, and you had to learn by trial and error. Here I was in the National League and I had a problem. We played Boston for the second time and when we passed, I said, 'Can we meet?' He told me to meet him at the Iron Horse [bar] below the Boston Garden. We go way in the corner, and I say, 'I'm getting beat in my kitchen on shots I should never get beat on.' He asked me if I played baseball. I said yes. He said, 'What position?' I told him shortstop and he said, 'That's how you are playing goal. You are coming out too quick and then you have to back up.' He said, 'Slow yourself down coming out.' Then he asked what lie of stick I used and I told him. He told me go to the 13, and you will stand up more and cover more of the net. He was right on the nose. . . . If you asked me who was the best, I would say [Terry] Sawchuk was the best, then Brimsek was next, and the third was [Jacques] Plante."

When Frank Brimsek had the sniffles, a touch of the flu, or a hint of fever, no member of the Boston Bruins would have dared wish him a speedy recovery.

The understanding around the Bruins' dressing room was that the worse Brimsek felt, the better he played. "Any time Brimmy said he felt good, we knew we were in for a bad night," says former Bruins player Milt Schmidt.

Brimsek's regular health woes often provided a sense of comic relief for the Bruins, and even he went along with the gag. Picture him with his head down looking absolutely miserable, and his close friend and teammate Johnny Crawford yelling at him, "Hey, Brimmy what's the matter?"

"Sick," Brimsek would say. "Very sick."

A grinning Crawford would yell, "We are in for a good night tonight, boys."

He would then ask Brimsek why he was sick. "I'm seeing spots in front of my eyes," the goalie would answer.

Brimsek posted six shutouts in his first eight NHL starts.

Crawford would erupt with laughter. "You crazy fool, those aren't spots, those are pucks."

For all of the tomfoolery the Bruins enjoyed during discussions of Brimsek's health, there was serious regard for his ability around the National Hockey League.

"He was a real cool customer," says former Toronto Maple Leafs standout Harry Watson. "I didn't get too many past him. You couldn't get him to make the first move. Never."

Legend has it that Bruins general manager Art Ross, a former Hall of Fame player, invited Brimsek to the rink and took 25 hard shots at him from 10 feet out. The goalie grabbed each shot as easily as if he were pulling cans of corn off the grocer's shelf. That's when Ross supposedly made his decision to sign the 23-year-old and sell Tiny Thompson to the Detroit Red Wings. It was a controversial decision that left many fans irate. Thompson was a popular Boston athlete.

Ironically, the Red Wings had tried to sign Brimsek before that season. "But I wouldn't sign because I didn't like [Detroit general manager] Jack Adams," Brimsek said shortly before he died. "Adams had a bad habit of favoritism, and I wanted no part of that."

Following Thompson in Boston required fortitude because the ousted netminder had won four Vezina Trophies and 252 games in a decade with the Bruins. When Thompson was dealt, Dit Clapper, a longtime Bruins player and close friend of the goalie, threatened to quit.

It didn't help the Bruins' public relations dilemma when Adams called Thompson "the greatest goalie in the world" in Associated Press news reports. Some reporters compared the Thompson trade to the Boston Red Sox's dealing of Babe Ruth to the New York Yankees.

Brimsek recalled years later that the first game he played in Boston Garden was eerily quiet. "I could hear them breathing and could feel their cold eyes on my back," he said.

The Bruins' faithful didn't warm quickly to Brimsek, even when he blanked the Montreal Canadiens 2–0 in his first game on December 1, 1938. But after he posted shutouts in his first four NHL games, it became clear that he could do the job, probably better than Thompson at that stage of his career. It was difficult to argue with Ross' decision when Brimsek won the Vezina Trophy and helped the Bruins win the Stanley Cup in his rookie season. His 23-game winning streak (15–0–8) in 1940–41 still ranks as tied for fourth longest in NHL history.

"He had had fantastic hands and could anticipate just where the puck was going to come," Schmidt says.

After serving with the Coast Guard in World War II, Brimsek came back to the NHL, but the consensus was that he didn't play as well. The media had harsh

WITHOUT FEAR

criticism, which was rather insensitive, given that he was coping with the death of a one-year-old son. According to Schmidt, no one understood that Brimsek's illnesses weren't a laughing matter, either.

"He really wasn't feeling well late in his career," Schmidt says. "He had diabetes, and later in his life he had his leg amputated. Nobody knew anything about it. He kept everything to himself."

To illustrate what kind of man Brimsek was, Schmidt points out that even though Clapper had threatened to quit when Thompson was traded, "Brimsek and Clapper became close friends."

Brimsek Was a Perfectionist Because . . .
He was meticulous about his angles and positioning and was never beaten by his own mental errors.

In fact, when Clapper retired, Brimsek sent a telegram to the Bruins, asking to be traded. He just wanted to be nearer to his Minnesota home. "He liked to hunt and fish," Schmidt says. "He would always find a way to get some fishing in."

The Bruins ended up selling Brimsek to the Chicago Black Hawks for what the media reported to be the highest price ever paid for a player since the Toronto Maple Leafs paid $35,000 to get King Clancy from Ottawa. Brimsek, who became a train engineer after his retirement from hockey, played only one season in Chicago.

Two years before Maurice "Rocket" Richard's death, he said Brimsek was the toughest goaltender he faced: "He was a stand-up goaltender and there didn't seem to be any room to shoot the puck."

In 1966 Brimsek became the first American NHL player to enter the Hall of Fame.

"When Brimmy played with the Boston Bruins, he was in my opinion the best of the goaltenders and that takes in a lot of territory," Schmidt says. "I thought he was better than Sawchuk."

151

18 | JOHNNY BOWER

BORN: Prince Albert, Saskatchewan, November 8, 1924		
SHOT: Left	HEIGHT: 5'11"	WEIGHT: 189 lbs.
Stanley Cups: 4		Vezina Trophies: 2
NHL First All-Star Team: 1		NHL All-Star Games: 4

NOTABLE ACHIEVEMENTS: Hall of Famer; led the NHL in goals-against average four times; a five-time American Hockey League All-Star, three-time AHL MVP, and three-time winner as the AHL's top goalie (Hap Holmes Memorial Trophy) before making the NHL grade for good; all-time wins leader in pro hockey (706); posted 89 shutouts in pro hockey; oldest goalie in Stanley Cup history, at 44 years, four months, and 38 days, with Toronto in 1970; his No. 1 sweater was honored by the Maple Leafs and retired by the AHL Cleveland Barons.

Johnny Bower's Commentary on Himself

"It's kind of funny that everyone remembers me as a stand-up goaltender, but early in my career, I was strictly a reflex goaltender. I used to go down and do the stack-pad save or splits on most shots. Once I arrived in Cleveland, [coach] Bun Cook worked on breaking me of this habit. If I was going to make it in either the American or National League, I had to have more in my arsenal. We worked on standing up, so that I'd be in a better position to stop the rebound. It was this change in style that allowed me to have a successful career in professional hockey. Today goaltenders play the butterfly style, which really hadn't been invented until Glenn Hall came around. The butterfly allows them to get down and take away the bottom of the net. When I was playing I had to rely on making skate saves on low shots. I think the key to success for every goaltender is to learn the basics, such as going up and down, practicing their lateral movements, and working on their angles. Knowing your angles is more than just knowing how to cut down the shooting target for the opposition. It's knowing how to glide out to challenge the shooter to force him to make the first move. It was this skill that made my poke check so lethal. When a player came in too tight, I'd wait for him to move and boom, hit him with the poke check."

Second Opinion: Former Teammate Red Kelly on Bower

"Johnny was a tremendous competitor. He didn't want the puck to go in the net at all, even in practice. Johnny was very solid. He had big arms and big hands and he really covered a lot of that net. He really played the angles well. He knew exactly where he had to be standing in the net to stop you from where you were coming from on the ice. And he had that long poke check. He was really good with that stick, probably the best ever at the poke check. In those days goalies tended to be loners more than anything else. Bower was usually one of the guys. He liked to be part of the group. He was more talkative, more outgoing than the majority of the goalies I played with."

All goaltenders are possessors of unique, individual quirks. Glenn Hall never fished the puck out of his net when a goal was scored. Arturs Irbe repairs his own equipment. But Johnny Bower was the owner of the strangest offbeat netminding nuance of all.

At a time when most people simply referred to Cleveland as the "Mistake by the Lake," Bower was certain that the city was nirvana. Long before Drew Carey arrived on the scene to sing Cleveland's praises, Bower filled the role.

Bower played there for nine minor pro seasons with the American Hockey League's Barons and still holds Cleveland close to his heart. When the New York Rangers came calling after trading for him in the summer of 1953, he politely said, "No thank you," to the NHL.

Bower snares a shot as teammate Red Kelly watches.

Flabbergasted, Rangers general manager Murray "Muzz" Patrick set out in search of Bower, which, in the warmer months, was no mean feat. Patrick flew to Saskatoon, then made the long drive northward in his rented car to the minuscule Saskatchewan resort town of Waskesiu, where Bower's Big Boy held forth as the best burger joint in the burg.

Patrick arrived during the lunch rush, finding Bower busy at the grill. As the crowds thinned, Bower threw a patty on the fire for Patrick. While he flipped the burger, Patrick flipped figures in his direction. "I didn't want to go," Bower said. "I was happy in Cleveland."

Sometime between the entrée and dessert, they cooked up a deal. Patrick paid the check; Bower signed his first NHL contract.

Born John Bower, he was adopted by a Ukrainian family named Kishkan. He returned to his birth name when he was of legal age, but his name change led to confusion over his date of birth. For years, the debate about Bower's age was as timeless and ageless as he himself appeared to be while he was winning titles with the Toronto Maple Leafs.

First, though, he would open on Broadway. Gump Worsley won the Calder Trophy as the NHL's top rookie in 1952–53, but when the paunchy netminder showed up for training camp next fall, he lost his job to the determined Bower.

"The year Johnny Bower played in New York, he had the best record since Davey Kerr in 1940," Rangers Hall of Fame defenseman Harry Howell recalls. "But he was gone the next year, because Gumper was younger."

"I had a really good year for the New York Rangers, a 2.60 average with a last-place club," Bower says. "We didn't have a very good team. There were players going up and down all season long. It was so disorganized in New York. It seemed like they had a different coach every year."

Bower's Manhattan memories soured him on the NHL. He was 34 when Toronto claimed him in the 1958 intraleague draft. Back with Cleveland, he again felt no desire to leave, but Barons owner Jim Hendy persuaded him to go. "He felt Toronto was rebuilding, it was a good chance for me, and besides, they only wanted me for two or three years," Bower recalls.

Those two or three years turned into twelve, followed by fourteen more as an assistant coach and scout. Bower still calls the Toronto area home. He won four Stanley Cups and two Vezina Trophies, all the while defying Father Time. He was 45 when he played his farewell NHL game.

"[Toronto coach/general manager Punch] Imlach told me once, 'Johnny, you can play until you're 50 years old, if you keep playing the way you are,'"

Bower's unsurpassed agility and athleticism allowed him to play in the NHL until he was 45.

Bower says. "Actually, we always knew what my age was. It just became a big joke, because I looked so much older than the rest of the guys."

What was never a laughing matter to Bower was his work ethic. A master craftsman between the pipes, he detested being beaten, even during simple practice drills. "I've never seen a goalie work so hard in practice," Leafs teammate Ron Ellis says. "Johnny would be totally despondent if he gave up a goal."

For Bower, this attitude was the only approach he saw as being effective. "I always felt that the way you played in practice was the way you were going to play in the game," he says. "I never liked to let my teammates get any goals on me in practice. I felt I had to stop every puck that I could. That was my job."

Bower would dare his teammates to beat him, even placing wagers on the outcome of their showdowns. "We'd play for milkshakes," he says. "I must have won hundreds of milkshakes from those guys, but they never paid up. That just made me try even harder not to let them have any goals."

Bower Was a Perfectionist Because . . .

His diligent dedication to duty and to physical fitness allowed him to remain a top-flight NHL netminder into his midforties. He detested being beaten by a puck, even while doing drills.

It also led his teammates to engage in nefarious methods of getting the puck past the ancient stone wall in the net. Among the most determined to get Bower's goat was his closest friend, Leafs captain George Armstrong.

Ellis recalled one infamous Armstrong trick that he kept up his sleeve for days when Bower was being particularly stingy. "George Armstrong used to hide in the corner when we were doing breakaway drills," Ellis says. "Chief would wait until the shooter was just about to let it go, then he'd slide another puck right through Johnny's field of vision, just to mess with him."

But when the game was on the line, they never messed with the man who seldom missed. Bower fondly recalls all four of his Stanley Cup triumphs, but the last one, in 1967, is the one he's most asked about. Toronto won that spring with the oldest championship team in NHL history, an average age of 31.4 years.

"We had eight or nine guys who were over the hump," Bower says. "A lot of guys were playing hurt, but I think what kept us going was most of us knew it was our last chance. If we didn't do it that year, we'd probably never win another Stanley Cup."

The reason why they did it was simple—the two old coots in the net.

Bower, 42, and Terry Sawchuk, 37, refused to surrender. Bower's save percentage was .951, while Sawchuk kicked out pucks at a .933 clip.

Bower remains a Toronto icon, on par with the CN Tower and the city's trendy theater district. But he still loves Cleveland, and Cleveland still loves him. Just last season, the AHL Barons honored him by retiring Bower's No. 1 sweater.

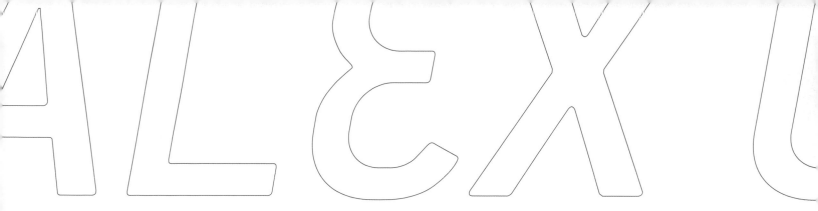

23 | ALEX
CONNELL

> **BORN:** Ottawa, Ontario, February 8, 1902
>
> **DIED:** May 10, 1958
>
> | **SHOT:** Right | **HEIGHT:** 5′9″ | **WEIGHT:** 150 lbs. |
> | --- | --- | --- |
> | Stanley Cups: 2 | | |
>
> **NOTABLE ACHIEVEMENTS:** Hall of Famer; posted the lowest career goals-against average in NHL history (1.91); led the NHL in shutouts four times, including three of his first four seasons; sixth on all-time shutout list; posted an NHL-record shutout streak of 461 minutes, 29 seconds with Ottawa in 1927–28; one of only four goalies to post 15 or more shutouts in a season (with Tony Esposito, George Hainsworth, and Hal Winkler); one of only three NHL goalies to post double digits in shutouts in three successive seasons (with Lorne Chabot and George Hainsworth); worked as a firefighter in the off-season; didn't play goal until he was a teenager.

Johnny Bower's Commentary on Connell

"Alex Connell is considered one of the greatest money goaltenders of all time. It was no wonder he was so great under pressure, since Alex worked in the summer months as a firefighter. Stopping pucks and putting out fires—now that's a man without fear. He came back to the NHL when hockey people thought him washed up. A slim man who never tended goal without his trademark black cap, Connell was one of the earliest angle goalies and he was nearly impossible to beat on a breakaway. He was known as the shutout goalie and led the league in this department four times, once posting six of them in a row, an NHL record. He finished his career with 81 shutouts, but because he played behind so many weak clubs, never won the Vezina or was recognized as an All-Star."

Second Opinion: Hall of Famer King Clancy on Connell, from a 1986 Interview with Karl-Eric Reif and Jeff Z. Klein

"Alex Connell, to me, was the sharpest of all—I mean of all the goalkeepers who played in Ottawa. He could play the angles like there was no tomorrow. He wasn't a good skater; in fact, he was one of the poorest skaters of them all, but damn it, he could sure cut down those angles. He'd give you nothing to shoot at. And one on one, he was terrific, too. He was the best goalie I ever played with."

He sat contentedly in the corner of the Montreal Maroons dressing room, a smile cracking wearily across his tired face, tears trickling slowly downward from his eyes. A few minutes earlier, after the final seconds ticked off the clock, Alex Connell bounded from his goal and leaped into the arms of teammate Lionel Conacher. Soon, rejoicing gave way to reflection. Conacher, puffing on his pipe, came over to pat his netminder on the back. Coach Tommy Gorman gave Connell a playful peck on the cheek. A few feet away, the cause for their joy, the Stanley Cup, was stationed in the middle of the floor.

Connell's serenity at this time of tremendous accomplishment was entirely understandable, for the veteran goalie had turned sport's most challenging trick. He had come back and he had come out on top.

For eight seasons Connell held forth as the goalie for the Ottawa Senators, and hockey people rated him among the elite at the position. But early in the 1932–33 season, after allowing four goals in a game against the New York Rangers, Ottawa coach Cy Denneny lifted Connell in the second period in favor of Bill Beveridge. Connell shook Beveridge's hand as he entered the game, then skated off the ice, stopping to speak with the coach in Patrick Roy fashion. "Your move was the height of stupidity," he told him, according to the Toronto *Globe*.

Connell never wore Senators colors again.

He'd won a Stanley Cup with Ottawa in 1926–27 and posted an NHL-record shutout sequence of 461 minutes, 29 seconds in the Senators' goal in 1927–28, recording six consecutive shutouts. As the NHL grew, small-market Ottawa couldn't keep up financially, forcing the team to sell many of its stars to survive, but Connell's work in the nets kept the team competitive.

"With a good team in front of him, he would still be among the sport's best, but it has been the irony of fate that this stellar athlete should have been forced to play for mediocre aggregations," the Toronto *Globe* wrote in 1933.

Enjoying retirement, Connell played two periods for the New York Americans in a March 15, 1934, game at Ottawa, filling in for an injured Roy Worters, earning a 3–2 victory and opening the eyes of Gorman.

Connell Was a Perfectionist Because...

His tidy work in the nets allowed him to set an NHL record by posting six consecutive shutouts in 1927–28.

Gorman, at one time Ottawa's hockey guru, coached Chicago to the 1933–34 Stanley Cup, only to be unceremoniously fired by eccentric Black Hawks owner Major Frederic McLaughlin. Quickly hired by the Maroons, Gorman, a defensive wizard who always built teams from the goal out, knew the guardian he wanted behind his team.

Critics scoffed at the notion that Connell, nearly two years removed from serious NHL work, was the answer, but he would have the last laugh. The Maroons finished second to Toronto during the 1934–35 campaign, 11 points behind the Leafs, and were heavy underdogs when they met in the best-of-five Stanley Cup final. After a 3–2 upset win in the opener, Connell—known as the "Ottawa Fireman" because he worked as secretary of the city's fire department from 1921 to 1950—doused the Leafs in Game 2. Toronto held a 44–18 edge in shots, but Montreal skated off with a 3–1 win.

"I remember Connell as putting on the greatest goalkeeping performance in the history of hockey," Gorman told the Toronto *Globe*.

A 4–1 Maroons victory completed the stunning sweep. "Alex Connell has the courage of a lion," NHL referee Mike Rodden wrote in the Toronto *Globe*. "He came back where others would have feared to tread. His comeback rivals fiction, a Merriwell act."

Connell didn't lose a game that spring, posting a 1.12 goals-against average. His career GAA for the playoffs was a paltry 1.19 and his regular-season GAA of 1.91 is the lowest in NHL history, even though he posted a winning record in just three of his last eight seasons.

"He astounded National League fans by his ability," wrote Rodden.

In the end, Connell had good reason to smile.

27 | ED BELFOUR

BORN: Carman, Manitoba, April 21, 1965		
SHOOTS: Left	**HEIGHT:** 5'11"	**WEIGHT:** 192 lbs.
Stanley Cups: 1	Vezina Trophies: 2	
Calder Trophies: 1	Jennings Trophies: 4	
NHL First All-Star Team: 2	NHL Second All-Star Team: 1	
NHL All-Star Games: 5		

NOTABLE ACHIEVEMENTS: Named to the NCAA All-Tournament team, 1987; named the International Hockey League's top rookie, 1987–88; has posted seven 30-win seasons and 364 career wins; led the NHL in wins and goals-against average as a rookie; one of only four goalies to win the Calder/Vezina double as a rookie (with Frank Brimsek, Tony Esposito, and Tom Barrasso); led the NHL in shutouts, 1991–92 through 1994–95; twice led the Stanley Cup playoffs in shutouts and three times in GAA; was never drafted, signing with Chicago as a free agent; NHL All-Rookie team selection, 1990–91; one of only six NHL goalies to post multiple 40-win seasons (with Terry Sawchuk, Martin Brodeur, Bernie Parent, Ken Dryden, and Jacques Plante); one of only two goalies with Stanley Cup/Olympic gold medal double to his credit (with Brodeur); played a record-tying 1,544 minutes in 1998–99 Stanley Cup playoffs (tied with Kirk McLean, 1994); ranks third all time in Stanley Cup minutes played (8,639).

Johnny Bower's Commentary on Belfour

"Ed has had a great career with Chicago and Dallas, even though he's a bit of a hothead and gets a little carried away at times. But when he's on the ice, he makes the big saves when he has to. Belfour is a butterfly goaltender in its truest sense. He goes down in the spread eagle but is big enough to take away the top shelf. What I like about him is the quickness of his feet. He can get back up in time to be square to the shooter for the second shot."

Second Opinion: Former Teammate Darren Pang on Belfour

"He is married to the position of goaltender. Handling the puck is definitely one of his strong suits. He doesn't make bad decisions with the puck. He can read the play. He knows when to leave it for his defensemen and when to send it to his forwards. He has a good grasp of being a forward. He's a good left wing. In terms of his personality, he's not an outgoing person. He doesn't go out of his way to have conversations. He's never going to be a people person. But he also minds his own business. And players like that."

Eddie the Eagle wouldn't know what it's like to have the wind beneath his wings. For the vast majority of his hockey career, Ed Belfour must have felt as if he were trying to soar against gale-force headwinds. The hockey world didn't begin to acknowledge his place among the elite goaltenders until late in his career—and then only begrudgingly. He didn't even make his Carman, Manitoba, high school team until he was a senior, and he had no scholarship offers after playing junior hockey. He was a walk-on at the University of North Dakota and then led the school to a national championship. Even after he signed as a free agent with Chicago and won NHL Rookie of the Year, the hockey world seemed to want to view him as a temporary wonder. It wasn't until he won the Stanley Cup with the Dallas Stars in 1999 that Belfour finally received his due.

Says Stars center Mike Modano, "In the nineties, he's been one of the better goalies in the league. It's just unfortunate that he doesn't get the respect he deserves. A lot has to do with our location down here."

But some of it has to do with Belfour's personality. Even in a profession where eccentricity is part of the job description, he comes across as quirkier than most. He is comically fastidious about his equipment. This is an athlete who once spent six hours sharpening his skates. He has been known to have a chef and a masseur. As much as teammates respect Belfour's focus, they view him as different.

The irony, of course, is that the very traits that make him seem odd are the attributes that have allowed him to become superior at his craft. In the nineties, Belfour won 304 games, and only Patrick Roy had more (317). Belfour's extreme focus on goaltending was what allowed him to challenge Roy.

"His routine to focus is down to the last seconds," says former Dallas coach Ken Hitchcock. "It's not the focus during a game. With Eddie, it's focus during the day and during the season. He is very articulate in his preparation. He is very focused in the timing of his sequence of events. That's how he trains."

Belfour won the Calder/Vezina Trophy combo with Chicago.

"He epitomizes the term *battler*," says former NHL player Peter McNab, now a television analyst in Colorado. "You can't define his style. As unorthodox as Dominik Hasek is and as much of a technician as Patrick Roy is, all you can say about Belfour is that he is a battler. When he won that Cup, that justified saying he is great."

Belfour's intensity level, especially early in his career, was volcanic, but he seemed to find the proper balance between competitiveness and explosiveness once he arrived in Dallas. Belfour's goaltending master is former Soviet national team standout Vladislav Tretiak, who was Belfour's goaltending coach when he played for the Blackhawks. "I think he talks to him a lot more than people know—a lot more," Hitchcock says.

Although Belfour has only one Stanley Cup championship, his playoff mystique is noteworthy. Belfour joined Jacques Plante, Turk Broda, and Ken Dryden as the only goaltenders in NHL history to post goals-against average below 2.00 in three consecutive playoff seasons. "[With Belfour] you have a goaltender in net who is always going to be there," says former Dallas teammate Guy Carbonneau. "He's not going to be up and down—extraordinary one game and average the next."

His image was certainly hurt when he was arrested for creating a disturbance at a Dallas hotel. He also once left the Stars team briefly after a few weeks of butting heads with Hitchcock. But despite Belfour's reputation as a loner, there is evidence to support that this isn't the case. Two seasons ago, on a road trip to Toronto, he rented out Maple Leaf Gardens and invited friends from Dallas, Chicago, his summer home in Michigan, and his native Manitoba to come to the arena for the mother of all pickup games. Belfour played forward.

Belfour Is a Perfectionist Because . . .

His game preparation might be the yardstick by which other goaltenders should be judged. His focus is legendary. No one wants to approach Ed Belfour on a game day.

35 | DAVEY KERR

BORN: Toronto, Ontario, January 11, 1910

DIED: May 11, 1978

SHOT: Right	HEIGHT: 5'10"	WEIGHT: 160 lbs.
Stanley Cups: 1		Vezina Trophies: 1
NHL First All-Star Team: 1		NHL Second All-Star Team: 1

NOTABLE ACHIEVEMENTS: One of only eight NHL goalies to post three shutouts in one Stanley Cup series (with Clint Benedict, Martin Brodeur, Turk Broda, Frank McCool, Felix Potvin, Brent Johnson, and Patrick Lalime); posted four shutouts in the 1936–37 Stanley Cup playoffs; led the NHL in shutouts twice and in wins once; featured on the March 14, 1938, cover of *Time* magazine; won the Allan Cup with Montreal AAA in 1930–31; entered the Canadian Armed Forces after the 1940–41 season and never played hockey again.

Johnny Bower's Commentary on Kerr

"Davey Kerr retired before my time, but those who knew him said he was a very dependable goaltender. He was very cool under pressure, and that was as important back then as it is today. He was known as an angle goaltender, and he apparently was very good at positioning his defensemen to help him get a clear view of the shot."

Second Opinion: NHL Historian John Halligan on Kerr

"Besides being a Stanley Cup winner and the recipient of the Vezina Trophy in the same season [1939–40], Davey Kerr has a distinction that no other hockey player—forward, defenseman, or goaltender—can ever take away from him. Davey Kerr was the very first hockey player to appear on the cover of *Time* magazine. The date was March 14, 1938, and it was an accomplishment no other hockey player would manage until Maurice "Rocket" Richard did it some 20 years later. The accompanying article was a somewhat disjointed treatise that sought to explain hockey itself, through the eyes of the New York Rangers, to the magazine's readership. And there on the cover, looking more than a little out of place, was hawk-eyed Davey Kerr in a painting specially commissioned by *Time* by the artist S. J. Wolff. 'The guys ribbed me a lot about that magazine,' Kerr recalled years later. 'Cec Dillon in particular. Cec was pictured inside and said he should have been on the cover, since he was better looking than me. He admitted that I was better looking than [racehorses] Seabiscuit, War Admiral, and Man o' War, whose photos happened to be on the same page that the hockey article began.'"

Davey Kerr's legacy might have been more glorious had he not been offended by the New York Rangers' heavy-handed contract negotiation tactics.

Kerr was 31 and in the prime of his career, just one year removed from a Vezina Trophy and the Stanley Cup championship, when he retired from the NHL after the 1940–41 season.

"He was pretty well fed up with things when he left," says his son, David Kerr Jr. "Even after he retired, the Canadiens wanted him, but he just refused to come back."

According to Kerr's son, his father and Rangers general manager Lester Patrick had butted heads on contract matters throughout his career, but the final battle came after the 1939–40 Stanley Cup championship season. As it was explained to Kerr Jr., the Rangers had a $77,000 budget for players and that was split among all the players. The average was $4,500 per player, although some received a little more and some received a little less.

"Lester and my father didn't get along at all," Kerr Jr. says. "The only way to get more money was to get some bonuses for winning the regular season or the Vezina Trophy and so forth. With those bonuses, he made $10,000, and Lester didn't want to give him that the next season. Finally he told Patrick to give him $10,000 because he wanted to get out of the game and make some real money. He said he would put in one more year."

Kerr made good on his promise, leaving the game to enter the hotel and bar business as an owner. Using his NHL name, he was quite successful in those endeavors, but his early departure might have cost him in terms of his permanent place in the game. Kerr isn't in the Hall of Fame, even though he posted a 2.15 regular-season goals-against average and 1.74 playoff goals-against average.

"He was a steady type of goaltender," says Clint Smith, who played with Kerr on the 1940 championship team. "He was a very great angle player. He studied the game well. He knew every shooter. He had a book on everybody."

He was a perfectionist in how he wanted his teammates to perform. According to a 1957 *New York Times* article, he would tell his defensemen that if they kept players outside a certain radius, then it would be Kerr's fault if they scored.

Kerr Was a Perfectionist Because . . .

He was so good at playing the angles that he could have been a geometry teacher.

"And if we got too close to [Kerr]," former teammate Muzz Patrick told *The New York Times*, "[he'd] slash us on the ankle with [his] stick. Some of the worst cracks I ever got in hockey, I got from him."

In that same article, Kerr talked about pressure: "The last few years I was with the Rangers, I used to take a wine cocktail before my dinner to relax me. But I think it's like any other job. You can't let it get to you."

Kerr was known as a smart goaltender who always tried to use the rules to his advantage. Growing up, the younger Kerr always heard the story about how his father had his pads custom made to go above his knees. His father desired that extra room to give him a place to drop the puck when he wanted to stop play. As it was explained to him, the NHL rules at the time required goalkeepers not to stop play by simply catching the puck. According to the Kerr family legend, the NHL changed the rule after his father figured out a way to beat it. However, Kerr Jr. has never been able to confirm that. "My mother used to say that Dad would have made a fortune if he had patented those pads," Kerr Jr. says.

Clearly Kerr's tiff with Patrick was rooted in a management/employee feud. Kerr wasn't viewed as a difficult man to get along with. "Wonderful fellow," Smith says. "Well liked by all of the players. He was a real gentleman. He had a little trouble with his contract, and Davey was very frugal. But I also think he quit because he wanted to be home more."

Kerr played every game of the last five seasons he was in the game, and twice led the NHL in shutouts in that span. He finished with 51 shutouts and averaged one shutout about every 8.4 games.

"He was a good angle goaltender, cut off all the angles," Smith says. "I don't put him in the same class as Tiny Thompson or [Bill] Durnan, but he was a great goaltender."

Kerr died in 1978 at age 68, and throughout his life, he wasn't inclined to discuss his career much, even with his family. "He didn't speak of these things," his son says. "He didn't like to talk about it. He liked the people he played with and stayed friends with them through the years."

But Kerr was able to read his father's view of the hockey establishment. "He used to say strong backs, weak minds," he says. "It left a pretty sour aftertaste."

37 | MIKE RICHTER

BORN: Abington, Pennsylvania, September 22, 1966

SHOOTS: Left	**HEIGHT:** 5'11"	**WEIGHT:** 185 lbs.
Stanley Cups: 1		NHL All-Star Games: 3

NOTABLE ACHIEVEMENTS: Posted a record-tying four shutouts in 1993–94 Stanley Cup playoffs as he led the New York Rangers to their first Stanley Cup in 54 seasons; named MVP of the 1996 World Cup as he backstopped the USA to an upset of Canada; won MVP award at the 1994 All-Star Game, the first goaltender honored in eight years; named the Western Collegiate Hockey Association's top freshman at Wisconsin in 1985–86; played for the USA in three Olympics; led the NHL in wins (42) in 1993–94; has led the Stanley Cup playoffs in shutouts three times.

Johnny Bower's Commentary on Richter

"Playing goal in New York City is arguably the toughest position in all sports. When you play well in a Rangers jersey, you're the greatest goaltender ever. When you struggle, you're just a bum! They're such good hockey fans in New York, but they will ride the players like you wouldn't believe. Fortunately for Mike, they don't have the balcony at the modern Garden, where the fans could sit and throw items on the ice. One time after I gave up a bad goal, a fan threw a rotting fish wrapped in newspaper at me. Talk about the odor! I tried to hide in the net, but that only made things worse. That's why I admire Mike Richter."

Second Opinion: 2002 U.S. Olympic Assistant GM Larry Pleau on Richter

"The way he handles himself is very impressive. He is well prepared, and he's in great shape. He has proved himself a winner, and I don't think there is anyone better with his pads and feet. His ability to stretch in the crease and get to the low shot is tremendous."

Richter Is a Perfectionist Because . . .

If stopping breakaways is the essence of goaltending, then he is better prepared than most NHL goaltenders. He works diligently to prepare himself for one-on-one encounters.

Practicality dictates that a goalie unable to kneel could have no prayer of being the starter at the Olympics six months up the road. But even after New York Rangers netminder Mike Richter had major knee surgeries in back-to-back seasons, it was impossible to eliminate him for consideration for the U.S. starter's job at the 2002 Games in Salt Lake City.

"When I called to talk to him about his rehabilitation schedule and the outlook, I remember he kept telling me, 'Don't sell me short, don't sell me short,'" recalls U.S. coach Herb Brooks. "He kept telling me, 'I will be there. Somehow, I will get there.'"

No one ever rules out Richter when it comes to hockey, and particularly international hockey. While Frank Brimsek is considered the best American goaltender in hockey history, Richter is probably the most respected U.S. goalie of the past half century. Not only was he able to make the U.S. team in 2002, he played superbly to help the Americans win the silver medal—the first piece of Olympic jewelry for U.S. hockey since the "Miracle on Ice" in 1980.

Richter was a popular choice with the U.S. players, many of whom had scrapped alongside him in 1996 when he helped lift the USA to victory in the World Cup. The Americans had to win two games in Montreal, a Canadian hockey Mecca, and Richter's play earned him the Most Valuable Player award. He is a three-time U.S. Olympian, and even as a teenager he helped the USA win the bronze medal at the World Junior Championships, a tournament that traditionally is unkind to American teams.

"He's a great east/west goaltender, and there is a lot of east/west play in the international game," Brooks says.

Richter's other advantage is his knack for stopping breakaways. Thanks to a blend of quickness and instincts, he has stopped 12 of 13 penalty shots in his career, and it's estimated that his efficiency could be as high as 90 percent for thwarting players who are in alone on him.

"Just ask Pavel Bure," former NHL goaltender John Davidson says. "Some of the greatest match-ups you will ever see have to be him and Pavel. Bure must have 15 breakaways against him in his career, and Richter has stopped most of them."

Included in those classic battles was Richter's save against Bure on a penalty shot in Game 4 of the 1994 Stanley Cup final. The Rangers were trailing 2–1 early in the second period. If Bure had scored, it could have given the Vancouver Canucks the game and tied the series. Instead, the Rangers fed off the save and rallied for a 4–2 win and a 3–1 series lead.

"Mike has the ability to back up at the same speed as the shooters," Davidson says. "If you are going fast, he backs up fast. He's such a good skater. He can beat you to the goal post if you try to go around him."

His career with the Rangers hasn't always been joyful. In the 1992 playoffs he gave up a 65-foot goal to Ron Francis that clearly turned that series in the Pittsburgh Penguins' favor. In 1992–93 Rangers coach Roger Neilson lost confidence in him, and Richter even spent some time in the minors.

On the night the Rangers won, coach Mike Keenan told the media: "[Richter] is one of the stories within the story. Michael's rise to the top of the league, to the top of his game, was epitomized on the last save [against Bure] he made in the final moments of Game 7. It's been a long road to come from the hardships he suffered to where he is now."

TERRY SAWCHUK

GEORGES VEZINA

BERNIE PARENT

CHARLIE GARDINER

TRAGIC HEROES

AL ROLLINS

LORNE CHABOT

ROGER CROZIER

CHUCK RAYNER

MIKE KARAKAS

NORMIE SMITH

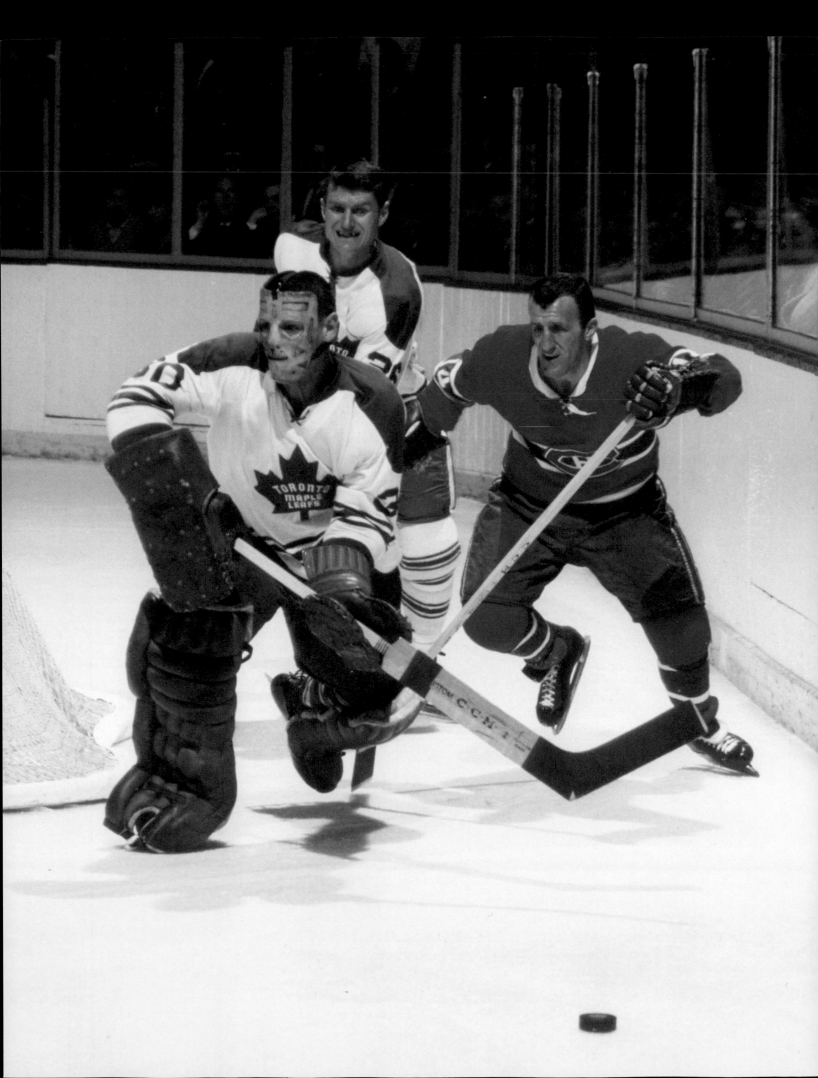

2 | TERRY SAWCHUK

BORN: Winnipeg, Manitoba, December 28, 1929

DIED: May 31, 1970

SHOT: Left	HEIGHT: 5'11"	WEIGHT: 195 lbs.
Stanley Cups: 4	Vezina Trophies: 4	
Calder Trophies: 1	Lester Patrick Trophies: 1	
NHL First All-Star Team: 3	NHL Second All-Star Team: 4	
NHL All-Star Games: 11		

NOTABLE ACHIEVEMENTS: Hall of Famer; the NHL's all-time leader in shutouts (103), games (971), and minutes played (57,194); second in career wins (447) and tied for second in single-season wins (44, twice); shares the NHL record for most 40-win seasons, (three, with Martin Brodeur and Jacques Plante); one of only three NHL goalies to play 900 games (with Patrick Roy and Glenn Hall); named Rookie of the Year in NHL, American Hockey League, and United States Hockey League; second-youngest NHL goalie to win 300 games (behind Brodeur); one of only six NHL goalies to post multiple 40-win seasons (with Brodeur, Ed Belfour, Bernie Parent, Ken Dryden, and Plante); shares NHL record for most seasons played by a goalie (21, with Gump Worsley); his No. 1 sweater was retired by the Red Wings.

Johnny Bower's Commentary on Terry Sawchuk

"Terry Sawchuk is the greatest goaltender ever. When we picked him up in 1965, I told everyone that we were going to win another Stanley Cup, and we did in 1967. But Terry was also one of the most unique people I've ever met in the game. He was probably the worst practice goaltender ever in the history of the National Hockey League, but that's because he focused his efforts on games. He was the kind of player who went through the motions in practice and warm-up but, come game time, there was none better. There would be times when I'd get pulled and he'd come in without a warm-up and be stellar. One of Terry's strengths was his crouch; it was one of the best that I'd ever witnessed. He remained square to the shooter as much as possible, but cheated on rushes in that he wasn't the quickest goalie to come out and cut down the angle. But his cat-like reflexes were what allowed him to stay a little deeper in the net."

Second Opinion: Former Detroit Coach Jimmy Skinner on Sawchuk

"I saw a lot of the greats—[Jacques] Plante, [Bill] Durnan, [Gump] Worsley—but to my mind, I haven't seen anyone better than Sawchuk. Reflexes, angles, he had it all and he also had a lot of guts. He'd always say to the guys, 'Get me a couple and we'll win.' And he meant it. He didn't say it in a bragging kind of way. He was just that confident. He was a very low-key guy. And he could be very moody and surly when he was playing. He didn't talk much. You really had to get to know him to get him to talk. He was in the crouch, but he never left his feet. You wouldn't see him go down so quickly like the goalies do today. He was always injured, but even toward the end when he was over the hill and playing with the Rangers, he was still outstanding. He was the best."

Looking back on the moment, with 35 years of reflection to alter his perception, Ron Ellis remains unwavering. He still calls it "the most courageous goaltending performance I've ever seen."

The Toronto Maple Leafs—hockey's version of the over-the-hill gang, with two players past 40, seven over 35, and 12 past 30, with an average age of 31.4 years—were up against it. They were facing the NHL's best team, the Chicago Black Hawks, in the opening round of the 1967 playoffs, the first stop en route to an improbable Stanley Cup.

Seeking to decipher a way to silence Chicago's lethally potent offense, which had produced an NHL-record 264 goals and featured the banana blades and boomerang shots of Bobby Hull and Stan Mikita, the Leafs looked to be between a rock and a hard place. That was exactly how the Hawks came to feel, however, every time Terry Sawchuk stoned them.

"The way Terry stood up and challenged Hull and Mikita in that series, it was truly amazing to witness," says Ellis, a right wing on that Leafs team. "He wore these battered old shoulder pads, the same ones he'd used since junior, and they were in tatters. And his chest protector was nothing more than a piece of felt. But he'd charge out there, absolutely fearless, and just keep putting his body in the way of those shots. I can only imagine the pain he must have endured."

In Game 5 of the series, many in the Chicago Stadium's capacity crowd imagined that Sawchuk no longer felt the pain. They were certain he was dead.

Sawchuk Was a Tragic Hero Because . . .

No goalie accomplished more and endured more pain. He overcame family tragedy, illness, fractures, and lacerations to post an NHL-record 103 shutouts.

Toronto and Chicago split the first four games, but when Chicago captured Game 4 by a 4–3 count on Maple Leaf Gardens ice, Toronto coach/general manager George "Punch" Imlach opted to go to veteran Johnny Bower for his first start of the series in Game 5. Bower, who'd been out with a broken finger, looked rusty from the layoff. With the score deadlocked at 2–2 through 20 minutes of play, Imlach consulted with assistant GM King Clancy and told Sawchuk to get ready, because he'd be taking over to start the second period.

Almost immediately after the opening faceoff, Hull got loose down the left wing, burst into the clear, and struck the puck forcefully with the curved blade of his stick, unloading one of his 100-mph slap shots. The searing orb caught Sawchuk flush on the left shoulder, glanced off his forehead, then catapulted into the crowd. He slumped to the ice, lying there motionless. A hush fell over the crowd. Hull, who'd always lived with the terrorizing notion that his powerful blasts might someday kill a netminder, fretted that he was living out his worst fear. But just when it looked like Sawchuk's next stop would be six feet under, he rose up and stopped the Hawks 36 more times over the two periods, leading Toronto to a 4–2 win.

"It woke me up, I guess," Sawchuk told *The Windsor Star*'s Jack Dulmage of Hull's howitzer, which left his entire shoulder a hideous yellow and blue hue.

It also got the attention of Sawchuk's Toronto teammates. And their never-ending awe. "When that series was over, Terry's entire upper body was just black and blue," Ellis says. "I've never seen anything like it. And I've never seen anyone display as much courage under fire."

For 21 NHL seasons, Sawchuk was the NHL version of a goaltending Timex, the reason they coined the phrase, "No pain, no gain." He took a beating, but was seldom beaten. While putting his body in harm's way he suffered punctured lungs, ruptured discs, a blocked intestine, a ruptured spleen, infectious mononucleosis, severed hand tendons, a broken instep, a dislocated elbow that never healed properly, leaving one arm shorter than the other, a twice-broken nose, and 600 stitches.

Sawchuk once checked himself out of a hospital to play a Stanley Cup game. "I'm one big aching bruise," he once lamented. "I spend my summers in the hospital."

He spent the hockey season making opponents feel ill. Sawchuk broke into the NHL during the 1949–50 season, going 4–3 in seven games for the Detroit Red Wings. He posted one shutout and impressed Jack Adams so much that Detroit's general manager cast goalie Harry Lumley adrift in the summer, dealing the veteran to Chicago, even though he had just carried the Wings to the Stanley Cup.

Adams believed he had a superstar in waiting. And he was right. Sawchuk won the Calder Trophy as the NHL's top rookie in 1950–51, missing out on the Vezina Trophy by one goal. On the way to the NHL he'd already been named the top rookie in both the United States Hockey League and the American Hockey League. Sawchuk posted a 1.99 goals-against average that first season, and it would be his highest mark during the first five seasons of his career. Sawchuk is the only goalie in NHL history to record a GAA under 2.00 in each of his first five seasons, and he recorded 56 shutouts and 195 wins over that span, leading the league in victories each year.

"He was a wide-body frame," recalls Red Kelly, Sawchuk's teammate in Detroit and Toronto. "He stood up. You didn't see a lot of the goal when you were coming in, trying to put that puck past him. He sure could cover the net. He never went down a lot. When he went down, he got up quickly. He always crouched low to see that puck coming through."

The Sawchuk crouch revolutionized goaltending. Glenn Hall, a netminder with Detroit's junior affiliate across the Detroit River in Windsor, Ontario, often snuck across the Canada/U.S. border to catch Sawchuk in action at the Olympia. He developed his own netminding style, the butterfly, from watching Sawchuk perform. "I tried to copy his style, to use that low crouch which he played," says Hall, himself a Hall of Fame netminder.

The crouch was developed out of necessity. When Sawchuk's arm injury, suffered while playing baseball as a child, left his catching arm shorter than his stick-hand arm, he had to crouch to compensate for the disability. "He had to stay down low, or he couldn't completely cover that side of the net," says former Red Wings forward Carl Liscombe, who played against Sawchuk in the AHL.

That injury was among the many maladies—both physical and emotional— that would torment Sawchuk throughout his life. His brother, Roger, died from pneumonia when Terry was a baby, and an older brother, Mike, also a goalie,

Sawchuk fearlessly stood up to NHL snipers like Bobby Hull.

suffered a fatal heart attack at age 17. Terry, seven years younger, began organized hockey the following year, playing goal and donning Mike's pads. Tragedy brought him to the net and it would eventually remove him from the crease as well.

In his second full NHL season Sawchuk led the league with a record 44 wins, 12 shutouts, and a 1.90 GAA, but that was just the appetizer. In the playoffs he posted eight straight wins, four shutouts, an astonishing 0.63 goals-against average, and a brilliant .977 save percentage. The red light never went on behind him in four games at the Olympia, and his four shutouts tied a Stanley Cup record. "You couldn't put a pea by him," recalls Detroit center Alex Delvecchio.

Adams told Sawchuk that he was the greatest goalie in the world. Then he told him to shape up or ship out. "That's when he was big, probably 220 to 230 [pounds], but really agile," Delvecchio says. "Adams told him to get in shape and he lost a lot of weight."

Sawchuk reported to training camp in the fall of 1952 down to a gaunt 169 pounds. "When he was young, he was roly-poly and they got on him about being too heavy," Kelly says. "They tried to get him to bring his weight down."

Adds Delvecchio: "Once he came back in training camp, he looked like he was sick. I think it just turned him around a little bit, and I don't think he was quite as sharp the next couple of years."

Sawchuk went from fighting the battle of the bulge to battling to maintain his weight. "He got sick and he couldn't get the weight back," Kelly says.

Detroit still won two more Stanley Cups backed by Sawchuk's netminding, but Adams knew Hall was ready for the big leagues and surprisingly dealt his All-Star goalie to Boston in the summer of 1955.

Things went from bad to worse in Boston, when during his second season as a Bruin, Sawchuk tired easily, and no amount of rest seemed to help. In December of 1956 he was diagnosed with mononucleosis. After a two-week rest he foolishly returned to the nets. By mid-January, on the verge of mental and physical breakdown, he announced his retirement.

"Boston didn't believe that he was sick," longtime friend and teammate Marcel Pronovost says. "That hurt him. It crushed him emotionally. He was never the same after that."

Sawchuk ended his retirement when the Wings acquired him from Boston in 1957, and he wore the winged wheel for the next seven seasons.

Over the years his insecurities grew, as did his moodiness. Sawchuk was a complex, paradoxical man, capable of unique kindness and horrible abuse.

"He liked to present himself as this moody, aloof person, because then people would leave him alone," Pronovost says. "One time a young boy got hit with a puck during a game. They brought him into the dressing room afterward and Terry got his stick signed by all the players and gave it to the boy. Then he turned to me and said, 'If you tell the press about this, I'll kill you.' That's the way he was."

A brilliant netminder who appeared to be able to stop everything except misfortune, Sawchuk struggled with his self-esteem. Out of the goal, he was out of his element and constantly fretted about losing his job, allowing these personal demons to possess him. He was a sometimes violent alcoholic and a notorious womanizer. His wife, Pat, filed for divorce four times and finally followed through on the fourth time. Pronovost thinks Sawchuk was his own worst enemy. "He got himself in trouble through his insecurities," he says. "He was always worried about how he would take care of his family when he was done playing. He worried about whether he'd be able to give them all he could."

Detroit wondered whether Sawchuk had given all he had when they left him unprotected in the NHL's intraleague draft. Sawchuck was claimed by Toronto, and the Leafs discovered something was still in Sawchuk's tank. At 37, he teamed with 42-year-old Bower to lead Toronto to that 1967 Stanley Cup. "Johnny and Terry Sawchuk were unbelievable for us in the 1967 playoffs," Ellis says. "We had no right winning that Cup and we all know why we won it—those two guys in the nets."

After that miraculous season, Sawchuk's career floundered. He went to Los Angeles in the NHL expansion draft, back to the Red Wings for a year, then to the New York Rangers in 1969, where he posted his record 103rd and final NHL shutout. "One hundred and three shutouts—that's incredible," New York Islanders goalie Chris Osgood says. "That's like a player scoring 1,000 goals."

After the season, Sawchuk scuffled with Rangers teammate Ron Stewart during an argument over who would clean the rented home they shared. Sawchuk fell on Stewart's knee and paid for the toll years of hard drinking had exacted from his liver. He underwent three surgeries, first to remove his gall bladder, then to alleviate internal bleeding from his damaged liver. But at 9:50 A.M. on April 31, 1970, Sawchuk, 40, died in his sleep from a pulmonary embolism, death caused when a blood clot traveled through his veins and clogged a pulmonary artery.

Pronovost was at a Sunday afternoon barbecue with his first wife, Cindy, and some friends when word of Sawchuk's death arrived by phone. "I had tears in my eyes," he says. "I was shocked."

But deep down in his heart, Pronovost was forced to acknowledge that Sawchuk's tragic demise wasn't entirely a surprise. "The way he lived his life, it seemed like he was asking for it."

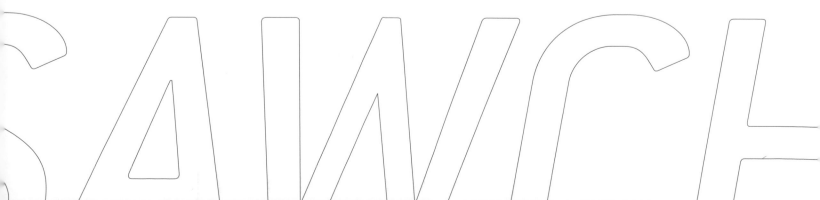

9 | GEORGES VEZINA

BORN: Chicoutimi, Quebec, January 21, 1887

DIED: March 27, 1926

SHOT: Left	HEIGHT: 5'6"	WEIGHT: 185 lbs.
Stanley Cups: 2		

NOTABLE ACHIEVEMENTS: Hall of Famer, one of the original 12 players elected in 1945; played 15 consecutive seasons (367 games) in the Canadiens' net; his 1.97 goals-against average in 1923–24 was first below 2.00 in NHL history; posted the first shutout in NHL history and was the NHL shutout leader twice; led the NHL in goals-against average three times; played in five Stanley Cup finals; the Vezina Trophy was named in his honor; the Quebec Senior League also honored its top netminder with a Vezina Trophy.

Johnny Bower's Commentary on Vezina

"Vezina handled his goal stick with the sterling touch of a Ty Cobb, batting pucks away from his net with supreme confidence and ease. Vezina developed the knack for being able to angle shots into the crowd, deflecting them from danger while keeping rinkside fans on their toes. The myths that have been purported about Vezina over the years—that he was the father of 22 children and seldom spoke because he hadn't mastered the English language—simply aren't true. Vezina had two sons and was fluent in English and French. His quiet nature stemmed from a publicity-shy personality. There were no myths about his puckstopping ability. He blocked shots with the speed and agility of a cat."

Second Opinion: The Ottawa Citizen on Vezina's Retirement

"Georges Vezina, noble Roman of the gate, has passed out of hockey. The tributes that go with him—so richly deserved—are worthy of notice, for they show, no matter what unfairness may sometimes lurk in the roar of the crowd, it is the true sportsman that makes the most appeal. Vezina's is a spirit that is needed in hockey, a man whose word was as good as his bond. 'If there was any argument over a goal around his net, then ask George,' NHL referee Cooper Smeaton said. 'If it was a goal, Georges would say, "Yes." If it was not a goal, he would say, "No."' Whatever he said, you knew that it was straight."

In the movie *Pride of the Yankees*, when Gary Cooper, portraying Lou Gehrig, finally cracks the lineup, launching his record stretch of 2,130 consecutive games, he trips and falls over a stack of bats while heading from the dugout to the diamond. He gets up and dusts himself off as if nothing happened. "What are we going to have to do, kill you to get you out of the lineup?" queries a Yankee teammate.

If you accept that the Montreal Canadiens are hockey's version of the Bronx Bombers and that Howie Morenz was the Habitants' Babe Ruth, then you must acknowledge that Georges Vezina was the Gehrig of the Canadiens. From the moment he first took up position in front of the Habs' goal until the day his career was tragically cut short, Vezina was ever present in the Montreal starting lineup, sharing with Gehrig a quiet, dignified demeanor and a matchless ability.

"I doubt if hockey will ever know his like again," Canadiens manager Leo Dandurand told the Canadian Press when tuberculosis forced Vezina's 1925 retirement from the game. "He has been a credit to professional sport. A great athlete and gentleman. Quiet to taciturnity, he let his deeds speak for him."

Vezina played 367 consecutive games in Montreal's net; his introduction to the big leagues was remarkably similar to Gehrig's emergence. Gehrig came to the Yankees from Columbia University, not exactly a hotbed of baseball talent. The Canadiens stumbled onto Vezina while participating in barnstorming tours of tiny Quebec towns. Chicoutimi was a regular stop during these exhibitions, which were designed as fund-raising promotional tools. But in Chicoutimi, the Canadiens continually ran into a stumbling block.

"There were at least three games in Chicoutimi between the Canadiens and the Chicoutimi team," says A. J. Vezina, the great-great-nephew of Georges Vezina. "And each time, Chicoutimi won, thanks to Georges' goaltending."

On their third visit the Habs were blanked by the lanky custodian and set out to persuade Vezina to become one of them. In 1910 Montreal offered a contract to Georges.

He posted the NHA's best goals-against average in three of his first four seasons. Montreal was a first-place club by 1913–14 and Stanley Cup champions for the first time two years later. "Vezina, in goal for the locals, was a mainstay," the *Winnipeg Free Press* noted in its coverage of Montreal's final Cup success over the Portland Rosebuds. "Vezina shoved aside numerous shots that appeared likely to be sure counters."

That sort of goaltending excellence became commonplace whenever Vezina was on duty between the posts. His ease of manner while partaking in the most demanding occupation in professional sports caused people to label Vezina the "Chicoutimi Cucumber."

"His coolness under fire, his immovability, were known wherever hockey is played," Dandurand said. "He has a calmness not of this world," author Ron McAllister noted in a biography of Vezina.

The Canadiens were a team in transition during the early twenties. Veterans Newsy Lalonde, Didier Pitre, and Louis Berlinquette were moved out, as Dandurand gambled on a youthful forward line for the 1923–24 campaign consisting of rookie Morenz and second-year men Aurel Joliat and Billy Boucher. In what might correctly be labeled as the first instance in NHL history of a goalie carrying a team to greatness on his shoulders, Vezina proved to be the glue that held the club together until they jelled. At midseason of the 24-game campaign, Montreal was a mediocre 4–8, despite Vezina's solid 2.31 GAA. At the end of the regular season, Montreal had improved to 13–11, good enough for second place and a playoff spot, while Vezina's 1.97 GAA was the first under 2.00 in league history.

In the playoff opener against favored Ottawa, Vezina turned aside 78 shots for a 1–0 shutout victory, posting a sensational 1.00 GAA while leading Montreal to the Stanley Cup.

Montreal's big-time goalie never took a liking to the big city. His family stayed in a hotel during hockey season, always returning to Chicoutimi for the summer, where Vezina often entertained his teammates at his hunting lodge northwest of that city. "Vezina and I were close friends," Dandurand said. "While quiet, he was very observant and a great lover of nature. Some of my happiest hours were spent shooting and fishing with him in the woods near Chicoutimi."

When Vezina reported to training camp in the fall of 1925 it was clear to Dandurand that something was amiss. His face was gaunt, his movements laborious, but as was his nature, Vezina didn't complain and went about the business of blocking pucks as if nothing was wrong. Just to be safe, Dandurand signed Alphonse "Frenchy" Lacroix, goalie for the 1924 U.S. Olympic team, to serve as Vezina's spare.

Vezina Was a Tragic Hero Because . . .

From the moment he was signed by the Montreal Canadiens in 1910 through his final start in 1925, he persevered through fractures, lacerations, and abrasions to play 367 consecutive games until tuberculosis claimed his life at age 39.

The Canadiens opened the 1925–26 season November 28, playing host to the Pittsburgh Pirates. It was only Pittsburgh's second NHL game, but it would be Vezina's last. Despite a 102° temperature, he stopped everything during the scoreless first period, but collapsed in the dressing room during the intermission, having suffered an arterial hemorrhage.

Vezina steadied himself and insisted on returning to his net. Moments before referee Cooper Smeaton dropped the puck to commence the period, Vezina slumped to the ice in front of his cage, blood dribbling from the corner of his mouth. He had to be carried from the ice and Lacroix took over in goal.

Doctors eventually informed Vezina, who had lost 30 pounds since the start of training camp, that he was dying of tuberculosis. He went to the Forum to break the sad news to Dandurand, insisting that no one else be told. Upon his arrival, trainer Eddie Dufour began laying out Vezina's gear, assuming the netminder was back to assume his position, a ruse the goalie intended to continue.

"Perhaps they will play better if they think I am coming on," Vezina told Dandurand.

"It was his last act of devotion to the club," Dandurand explained.

Vezina sat briefly in the corner amid his equipment, tears trickling down his cheeks. He gathered up one souvenir—his sweater from the 1924 Cup victory—and took the train home to die.

"He suffered a horrible death," A. J. Vezina says. Every day after they finished school, George's sons J.J. and Marcel would rush to the hospital to visit. "It was a terrible thing they saw," A. J. Vezina says. "It took him five months to die."

The end came March 27, 1926. The 10,000 fans at the Montreal Maroons/Ottawa playoff at the Forum that night held a moment of silence in Vezina's memory. The arena band played "Nearer My God to Thee."

The following season the Canadiens donated the Vezina Trophy to professional hockey; today it continues to honor netminding excellence in the NHL.

"Hockey fans whose memory serves them could compile a long list of great goalkeepers, and the name of Georges Vezina would occupy a place near the top of all lists," the Toronto *Globe* noted in Vezina's obituary.

Seventy-six years after Vezina's passing, those words still ring true.

Vezina played 367 consecutive games in the Montreal Canadiens' goal.

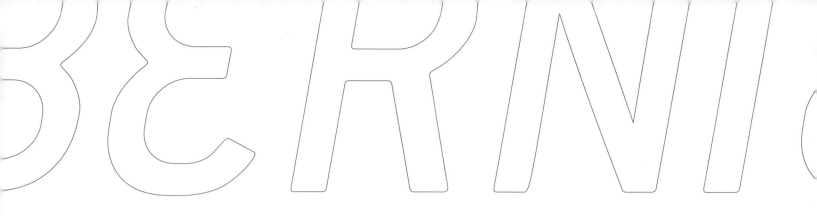

10 | BERNIE PARENT

BORN: Montreal, Quebec, April 3, 1945

SHOT: Left	HEIGHT: 5′10″	WEIGHT: 180 lbs.
Stanley Cups: 2		Vezina Trophies: 2
Conn Smythe Trophies: 2		NHL First All-Star Team: 2
NHL All-Star Games: 5		

NOTABLE ACHIEVEMENTS: Hall of Famer; only goalie to win back-to-back Conn Smythe Trophies; posted an NHL-record 47 wins in 1973–74; one of only seven NHL goalies to hit double digits in shutouts in consecutive seasons (with Alex Connell, Lorne Chabot, George Hainsworth, Terry Sawchuk, Harry Lumley, and Martin Brodeur); led the NHL in shutouts three times; led the NHL in goals-against average twice; posted four shutouts in the 1974–75 playoffs; first player ever signed by the World Hockey Association; one of only six NHL goalies to post multiple 40-win seasons (with Sawchuk, Ed Belfour, Brodeur, Ken Dryden, and Jacques Plante); his No. 1 sweater was retired by the Flyers; won the 1964–65 Memorial Cup with the Niagara Falls Flyers.

Johnny Bower's Commentary on Parent

"My former teammate Bernie Parent is a classic. Not only was he a tough-as-nails goaltender on the ice, he was the team joker. He would keep the guys loose and alive in the dressing room by cracking jokes and pulling pranks. I'm not sure if it was the jokes or his delivery in his broken English that kept us laughing and loose, but he had a real gift in that way. Bernie had two things going for him. He had good quick hands and he played angles well. He wouldn't race out to the shooter, rather he'd coolly edge out to cut down the angle. Before the shooter knew it, he would run out of real estate. By the time the shooter was ready to let the shot go, there wasn't much of the net exposed. He basically said to the shooter, 'Go ahead, try to beat me. You're not going to score.'"

Second Opinion: Former NHL Goalie and Executive Emile Francis on Parent

"Jacques Plante helped Bernie Parent. Even though Plante was living in Switzerland, the Flyers brought him in on occasion to help Parent. And Parent did many things that were reminiscent of Jacques Plante. The way he stood up. The way he played his angles. The way he positioned himself on faceoffs. The way he played the puck behind the net. He had much the same demeanor as Jacques Plante. Those two years in the playoffs, they can say what they want, but there is no way the Flyers would ever have won the Stanley Cup without [Parent]. In those two years, Parent was as good as any goaltender I've ever seen in the playoffs.

The incessant, love-laden chants of "Bernie, Bernie, Bernie" echoed off the walls of Philadelphia's Spectrum. Bumper stickers proclaimed, "Only God saves more than Bernie Parent." The City of Brotherly Love embraced Bernie Parent. But it was a relationship that got off to a rocky start.

Parent and Doug Favell were the goalies Philadelphia plucked from the established clubs when the Flyers entered the league via the 1967 NHL expansion draft.

Parent and Favell backstopped Philadelphia to a first-place finish in 1967–68, but the story of the early years of Flyers hockey was one of disappointment and playoff letdown. In their first five seasons, the Flyers never captured a playoff series, winning just three postseason games in that span. Seeking to shake things up, Philadelphia dealt Parent to the Leafs, handing Favell the No. 1 job. But the Flyers were swept by Chicago that spring and missed the playoffs completely in 1971–72 when Favell let in a long shot by Buffalo's Gerry Meehan in the dying seconds of the last regular-season game.

The Flyers were under the direction of coach Fred Shero by this time and were building a physically intimidating team with an emphasis on a strong defensive system. One piece was missing from the puzzle—a front-line netminder—and the Flyers realized they'd discarded the necessary piece two years earlier.

Fortunately for them, that piece was on the auction block. After two years in Toronto, Parent jumped to the rival World Hockey Association but sought a return to the NHL after one season of broken promises and rubber paychecks. The Flyers brokered a deal with the Leafs to acquire Parent's NHL rights, dealing Favell to Toronto, a move that didn't sit well with the Philadelphia faithful.

Favell was a popular Flyer. Parent paid an early price for costing the team a fan favorite. "My first game was an exhibition game against the New York Rangers and they scored seven goals on me in 12 minutes," Parent recalls. "You better believe I heard it."

It wasn't long before the victories began to pile up and the tide turned. Parent blanked Toronto 2–0 in the season opener and followed up with a 6–0 whitewash of the New York Islanders. He'd posted six shutouts by Christmas, and it was clear the Flyers were a team to be reckoned with.

"I didn't know how much I'd missed Philadelphia and the league," says Parent, who was rejuvenated by his return. "But I thank God for the time I spent in Toronto, because I played with Jacques Plante and I learned so much about goalkeeping from him. He taught me a lot of tricks."

Parent won the Vezina Trophy in 1973–74, posting a 1.89 goals-against average. He'd be the last NHL goalie to garner a GAA under 2.00 for 20 seasons, and his 12 shutouts were the most collected by a netminder in 18 years. "Any way you looked at it, if you tried to measure up against Parent in that era, you came up short," says ESPN analyst Bill Clement, a former teammate. "I tell people for at least three years and possibly four, Bernie Parent was easily the best player in the world."

And he was about to inspire the Flyers to become the best team in the NHL.

Reaching the Stanley Cup finals for the first time in their history, the Flyers weren't expected to beat the mighty Boston Bruins machine led by Bobby Orr and Phil Esposito. But Parent had other ideas and with every sparkling stop, he installed that belief system within his teammates.

"We knew Bernie would make the first save," former Flyers defenseman Andre "Moose" Dupont says. "He was the best goaltender in the league at the time. Going in against Boston, for sure that gave us so much confidence. And with the type of defense we played in front of him—we were pretty tough— the rebounds, there were not too many."

No goaltender in the league controlled rebounds better than Parent. He stood up and challenged the shooters, rarely presenting an opening to them. "He was so patient, that was probably his best quality," Dupont says. "He didn't ever make the first move. He'd wait the shooters out. So many times, when guys would come in on him on a breakaway, they would end up shooting it right at Bernie, because he just didn't give them anything."

In the decisive sixth game of that 1974 final, Parent made Rick MacLeish's first-period goal stand up, stopping 30 shots for a 1–0 victory. "It was easy to play goal behind a team that gives you only five or six tough saves to make in a game," Parent says, downplaying his accomplishment. "Most nights, I could have taken a deck of cards out there with me."

Parent Was a Tragic Hero Because . . .

He was unanimously rated the game's best goalie in the midseventies, but a back injury slowed him; then an eye injury ended his career in 1979.

He leaves the superlatives to his Flyers mates, who, unlike Parent, rarely stop when discussing his greatness. "If you look at that era, [Ken] Dryden was coming, but if you said, 'Who do you want in goal in a seven-game series, Dryden or Parent?' it would be Bernie Parent," Clement says.

Another Cup followed in 1974–75, again a six-game triumph, this time at the expense of Buffalo. When the Cup was there to be won, Parent was once again impenetrable, posting a 2–0 win in the clincher. He won the Conn Smythe Trophy as playoff MVP for the second consecutive spring.

Even opponents marveled at Parent's puckstopping capabilities. "There was a year or two when he was invincible," former New York Islanders GM Bill Torrey says. "He never got the credit. It was always the Broad Street Bullies or Bobby Clarke. He never got the credit for how important he was to that team."

After backstopping the Niagara Falls Flyers to the 1964–65 Memorial Cup as junior champions of Canada, Parent made his NHL debut the following season with the Bruins, turning heads while toiling behind a last-place team.

Toronto Maple Leafs assistant coach Rick Ley was Parent's teammate in Niagara Falls and Toronto and wonders what might have been had Leafs owner Harold Ballard anted up the cash to keep Parent from jumping to the WHA. "You think about some of the additions to the hockey club in the next few years," says Ley, pointing out the likes of future Hall of Famers Darryl Sittler, Lanny McDonald, and Borje Salming. "You wonder where that would have taken us in the future."

The future took Parent back to Philly, where his talent was equaled by his ability to easily deal with the stress of his position. "Bernie talked about the pressure, but it never seemed to bother him," former Flyers GM Keith Allen says.

Often he'd laugh in the midst of the most significant games. Clement recalls how Parent would call him to the net during stoppages for impromptu chat sessions: "He would lean over to me and say, 'Hey, Billy, how's she going?' And he would laugh. I think part of it was to relax me, part of it was to break the tension, and part of it was to relax himself. And part of it was his sense of humor. In the middle of the heat of battle he would do this. . . . That's a great memory."

Parent is the only NHL player to win back-to-back Conn Smythe Trophies as Stanley Cup MVP.

Almost as quickly as he rose to the top, Parent's career was a memory. A back injury slowed him after the 1974–75 season. Just as he seemed to be regaining his All-Star form, Parent was clipped in the right eye by the stick of New York Rangers forward Don Maloney during a February 17, 1979, game, forcing him to leave the game for good.

The Flyers retired Parent's No. 1 sweater on October 11, 1979, the first goalie to be so honored. Just like that it was over; but the memories of Parent's legend linger. "He was a great goalie," Ley says. "I'd still say he was as good as any of them in the game today."

17 | CHARLIE GARDINER

BORN: Edinburgh, Scotland, December 31, 1904

DIED: June 13, 1934

SHOT: Right	HEIGHT: 6′	WEIGHT: 176 lbs.
Stanley Cups: 1		Vezina Trophies: 2
NHL First All-Star Team: 3		NHL Second All-Star Team: 1
NHL All-Star Games: 1		

NOTABLE ACHIEVEMENTS: Hall of Famer; led the NHL twice in shutouts and once in goals-against average; led the playoffs three times in shutouts; posted a career 1.43 goals-against average in Stanley Cup play; missed just four games in six seasons and was on a 298-consecutive-game streak at the time of his death; won just 13 of his first 84 decisions playing for the woeful Black Hawks, despite a 2.31 GAA; the only goaltender to captain a Stanley Cup winner in NHL history.

Johnny Bower's Commentary on Gardiner

"Among the first southpaw netminders, Charlie Gardiner was his era's Dominik Hasek. Gardiner's unmatched goaltending skills allowed the mediocre Black Hawks to rise to great heights. In an era when netminding was a paint-by-numbers process—stand-up was the only style considered to be in vogue—Gardiner's colorful methods went beyond the lines. Gardiner allowed that his acrobatic style evolved as a youngster as he tried to keep his hands and feet from becoming frostbitten in the below-zero temperatures on the frozen ponds of Winnipeg. Using whatever means necessary to block the puck, Gardiner hurled himself recklessly into the path of opposing shooters, kicked out drives with his lightning-fast legs, and deftly blocked shots with both stick and glove hand. Occasionally, he'd discard his paddle to scoop up the puck in his gloved hands. He possessed tremendous patience between the pipes and seldom made the first move. Genial in disposition, Gardiner was nonetheless a tremendous competitor and leader."

Second Opinion: Former Referee Mike Rodden on Gardiner

"Charlie Gardiner was one of the greatest players and sportsmen hockey ever produced. He loved battles of wits and strategy. Throughout the years, possibly only [Georges] Vezina and Roy Worters ever really rated in the same class as the curly-headed star. Ever smiling, affable, a keen but fair competitor, Gardiner never deliberately fouled an opponent. Opponents admired and respected him. Gardiner gloried in outguessing attackers after the latter had beaten the Chicago defense. On such occasions he looked them coolly in the eye, made them make their moves first, and then astounded them by making remarkable saves. He was ambitious to stop every puck aimed in his direction, but he was ever-willing to give a successful attacker credit for beating him. He could pick a puck out of the strings with the same nonchalance and goodwill with which he made the stops."

The Chicago Black Hawks were nursing a one-goal lead late in a game at Chicago Stadium against the powerful New York Rangers when New York right wing Bill Cook burst past the Chicago defense and bore down on goalie Charlie Gardiner. Cook, a deadly sniper and a two-time NHL scoring champion, was the last player the home crowd wanted to see loose on a breakaway, but Gardiner did not share their fears. He steadied himself between the pipes, his smile widening as Cook drew closer. Cook made his move, shooting for an open corner, and could only watch helplessly as the goalie snaked out a leg to foil his scoring bid, laughing as he cleared the puck to safety.

"Tough luck," Gardiner said, still grinning at Cook. "But be sure to come around and try again."

Such was the jovial nature of Gardiner, considered by many NHL players who skated in the thirties to be the greatest netminder ever to strap on a pair of pads. "He was the hardest netman I ever tried to outguess," Montreal Canadiens superstar Howie Morenz told the Canadian Press.

Gardiner captained Chicago to the 1934 Stanley Cup.

As friendly as he was fabulous, Gardiner was driven to save every shot. His Chicago teammates would often scream in frustration at their inability to beat him in practice, but Gardiner never allowed his determination to affect his deportment. "No matter how tough the going was, Chuck was always a cheery soul and a real inspiration to the team in front of him," NHL president Frank Calder told *The Windsor Star*.

Gardiner Was a Tragic Hero Because . . .

Ignoring a painful tonsil infection that spread through his body, Gardiner led Chicago to the 1933–34 Stanley Cup, but died two months later at the age of 29 from a brain hemorrhage.

Born in Edinburgh, Scotland, in 1904, Gardiner and his family moved to Canada when he was six, settling in Winnipeg. Taking to hockey, he ended up in goal because of his poor skating ability. But Gardiner quickly established that he'd found his calling and was performing in the intermediate ranks by the age of 14. Turning pro with Winnipeg of the American Hockey Association in 1926–27, he had six shutouts and a .938 save percentage, catching the attention of the Black Hawks, who purchased his contract.

Playing for the Black Hawks was a netminder's nightmare. Billed as the NHL's goalless wonders, during the 1928–29 season Chicago scored only 33 times in 44 games and was shut out in an NHL-record eight consecutive games. Despite posting a 1.85 goals-against average that season, Gardiner recorded a paltry seven victories, was constantly booed by Chicago fans, and was ready to give up the game until he was counseled otherwise by Chicago star Duke Keats.

"I was very close to Chuck," Keats told *The Windsor Star*. "He was one of the greatest goalies that ever lived."

Gardiner played the game with passion but never allowed that passion to consume him. Suffering through an 11–3 rout in Toronto, an excited Maple Leafs fan doffed his derby and tossed it on the ice. Gardiner scooped up the expensive hat and plopped it on his head, wearing it for the remainder of the contest. But this outwardly personable nature disguised an inner fire that was stoked by competition. He took defeat especially hard. He wept openly after allowing 12 goals in an intermediate game. When his Winnipeg Selkirks were beaten in the Manitoba senior playoffs, Gardiner, who had performed brilliantly in defeat, took back alleys home to avoid crossing paths with spectators.

Chicago's defensive system during Gardiner's era was described as "backchecking and a prayer, or two prayers," and he was the answer to those prayers. He backstopped the Black Hawks to the 1930–31 Stanley Cup final, where Chicago was edged by the Montreal Canadiens in a five-game series, earning the first of four NHL All-Star Team selections that season. He brought the Black Hawks back to the final three seasons later as team captain, winning his second Vezina Trophy in the process.

WITHOUT FEAR

"It is my one ambition to win the Stanley Cup," he told *The Windsor Star*. That ambition was about to come true, as the Black Hawks downed Detroit in a four-game final series. "Gardiner was without doubt, the greatest single factor in the winning of the Cup," Chicago manager Tommy Gorman said.

As that season progressed, however, friends and teammates began to sense that Gardiner was a changed man. His trademark smile often deserted him and he was prone to fits of temper. During Detroit's 5–2 win in Game 3 of the Cup final, Gardiner skated to the Chicago bench after the fourth Red Wings goal and argued with teammate Johnny Gottselig, waving a threatening fist in his direction.

He recovered his composure and posted a 1–0 shutout in the decisive fourth game, decided when Harold "Mush" March scored after 30:05 minutes of overtime. "It was probably the best game of his eventful career," Chicago defenseman Lionel Conacher told *The Windsor Star*. And the last.

To pay off a preplayoff bet, Black Hawks defenseman Roger Jenkins playfully carted Gardiner through Chicago's business district in a wheelbarrow. "He was the greatest goalkeeper in the world," Jenkins recounted to *The Windsor Star*.

A few days later, Gardiner returned to Winnipeg, where he ran a sporting goods business. Preparing to leave for a singing lesson—he was the owner of a rich, baritone voice—he collapsed and was rushed to the hospital. Comatose, he died June 13, 1934, at the age of 29, from a brain hemorrhage. "This condition originated from a tonsillar infection," Dr. W. G. McIntosh, who attended to Gardiner at Winnipeg's St. Boniface Hospital, explained to the Canadian Press. "Uremic convulsions developed and from this condition, the hemorrhage resulted."

It was only at this point that Gardiner's teammates became fully aware of the serious nature of the ailment he'd hidden from them all season. That he had gamely battled through the pain without complaint was no surprise to anyone in NHL circles. "I came to know him well and to appreciate the sterling qualities that made up his character," Calder said. "Hockey fans the continent over admired him much for his skill and more for his courage."

Gardiner defied the NHL's best shooters. He defied the Chicago fans who rained down verbal abuse upon him, oblivious to his brilliance. But as great as he was, he wasn't capable of making a death-defying save. Yet his legend lives on.

"You can't say enough regarding Charlie's ability," fellow netminder Roy Worters told the Toronto *Globe*. "He was tops, the greatest of them all."

30 | AL ROLLINS

BORN: Vanguard, Saskatchewan, October 9, 1926

DIED: July 27, 1996

SHOT: Left	HEIGHT: 6'2"	WEIGHT: 175 lbs.
Stanley Cups: 1		Vezina Trophies: 1
Hart Trophies: 1		NHL All-Star Games: 1

NOTABLE ACHIEVEMENTS: Led the NHL in wins and goals-against average, 1950–51; won the Hart Trophy with a Chicago team that missed the playoffs; won the Allan Cup in 1947–48 and again in 1965–66, coming out of a three-year retirement; picked up by Toronto after six minor pro seasons when Toronto GM Conn Smythe decided goalie Turk Broda was too fat; shared netminding duties with Broda in 1950–51 in the first season-long two-goalie system in NHL history; his 47 losses in 1953–54 are the second most in an NHL season.

Johnny Bower's Commentary on Rollins

"In 1949 Al and I split the duties as the goaltenders in Cleveland. We picked him up just before the season started, and I was relegated to the backup role because of his play. He was very much the opposite of Terry Sawchuk in that he was the hardest-working player in both games and practice. Nothing got under his skin more than giving up a goal that he knew he could stop. His work ethic and size allowed Al to make sensational saves look easy."

Second Opinion: Former NHL Player Joe Klukay on Rollins

"Al was the exact opposite of Turk [Broda] in terms of personality. I wouldn't say he was moody but it seemed that way because Turk was so easy-going. But he was a good goaltender, no doubt about that."

Al Rollins' strength as a goaltender was the ability to maintain focus and efficiency even when logic would have expected him to wilt under the pressure.

This is a man who was able to win the Hart Trophy with a 12–47–7 record, and who also had to measure up to public scrutiny when Toronto general manager Conn Smythe decreed that popular Turk Broda was too portly to be effective. Rollins was brought in to replace the legend. In his first full NHL season, Rollins played the majority of Toronto games in 1950–51 and won the Vezina Trophy. Rollins and Broda combined in the playoffs to lead the Maple Leafs to the Stanley Cup championship, but Rollins was 3–0 in the finals with a 1.55 goals-against average.

"I think it was tough on him, following Turk in Toronto, but that would have been a tough act for any goalie to follow," says Harry Watson, a member of the 1950–51 championship team. "Turk was good, but Al was great." Rollins has become a forgotten man, primarily because he had to follow the crowd-pleasing Broda in Toronto and then ended up with the Chicago Black Hawks, a franchise that symbolized futility in that era.

When Rollins won the MVP acclaim in 1953–54, he posted a 3.23 goals-against average and it could have easily been five goals per game had he not played brilliantly. Forward/defenseman Tommy Anderson (Brooklyn, 1942) is the only other NHL player from a last-place team to win the Hart Trophy.

Rollins was 6'2", and lean. He looked like a slender skyscraper in the net.

He had his flaws, though. "Goals through the five hole were really rare," Toronto's Teeder Kennedy says. "The only goalie I remember who had a bit of a problem with the five hole was Al Rollins."

Rollins became the Leafs' number one netminder in 1951–52, but the following summer he was traded in the deal that brought Harry Lumley to Toronto. Rollins' goals-against average had risen about a half of a goal (1.77 to

Rollins Was a Tragic Hero Because . . .

He never had the right circumstances

to allow his talents to be recognized.

Rollins won the Hart Trophy with a Chicago team that finished in last place.

2.22) in his first two seasons with the Leafs, and the theory was that he wasn't the same goaltender without Broda pushing him for playing time.

At only 26 it appeared Rollins was headed for a lengthy NHL career, especially after he was able to lead Chicago into the playoffs in 1952–53, and took the eventual Stanley Cup champion Montreal Canadiens to seven games in the semifinals. But that was his last trip to the playoffs, and after five consecutive losing seasons with the Black Hawks, he retired.

Nothing illustrated Rollins' talent more than his ability to win an Allan Cup playing for the Drumheller Miners just before his 40th birthday in 1966. "A goalie doesn't really mature until he's 30," Rollins told the Canadian Press during that Allan Cup run. "Goalkeeping doesn't depend on speed so much as playing the angles. That comes with experience."

Rollins' legacy is as a goaltender whose talent seemed to always fall below the hockey world's radar.

"He was from Saskatchewan, and they even forgot about him," says former NHL goaltender Emile Francis, a Saskatchewan native. "He just got inducted into the Hall of Fame a couple of years ago and he's been dead since 1996."

But Francis, who played junior hockey against him, hasn't forgotten him. "Let me say this," he says. "He would have no trouble playing in the NHL today."

34 | LORNE CHABOT

BORN: Montreal, Quebec, October 5, 1900

DIED: October 10, 1946

SHOT: Left	HEIGHT: 6'1"	WEIGHT: 185 lbs.
Stanley Cups: 2		Vezina Trophies: 1

NOTABLE ACHIEVEMENTS: posted a 2–0 shutout of the Montreal Canadiens in his NHL debut; played only one game of minor league hockey in his career; led the NHL in goals-against average in 1934–35; played in three Stanley Cup finals; won back-to-back Allan Cups (1924–25, 1925–26) with Port Arthur, Ontario; eighth on all-time shutout list (73); 2.04 career GAA, 1.54 in playoffs; played in the NHL's two longest games, allowing just one goal in a combined elapsed time of 341 minutes, six seconds, while facing 155 shots.

Johnny Bower's Commentary on Chabot

"Certainly viewed as one of the legendary goaltenders of hockey history. If a goalie is to be judged by how brilliantly he performs in important games, Chabot measured up to any of his eras. He was said to be a smart goaltender with good quickness. It's clear that the fact that he spent his career shuffling between teams probably hurt his Hall of Fame candidacy. It's difficult to understand why he was traded so often, especially given how respected he was. When he was ill at the end of his career, reportedly all of his NHL friends paid their respects."

Second Opinion: Former Detroit Red Wings Player Pete Kelly on Chabot

"He was a very good goalkeeper. I remember seeing him quite a bit while I was playing amateur in Montreal. He'd always cheat a bit toward the far side of the net. [He would] give you a little room on the short side and try to convince you to sneak one in on the near post."

It wasn't a quest to be razor sharp that prompted Lorne Chabot to routinely insist upon shaving before taking the ice for every National Hockey League game he played.

Chabot preferred a close shave because he believed stitches would go in easier and were less likely to cause a lasting scar on a smooth face.

That logic makes sense for a goaltender who was known for having bad luck throughout his NHL career. A case can be made that Chabot (pronounced Cha-BO) is among the most underrated goaltenders in NHL history, and that he might be the best goaltender who didn't make the Hall of Fame.

To appreciate the black cloud that hung over Chabot's career, consider:

- He was a member of the 1927–28 championship New York Rangers team, but a Nels Stewart shot struck him in the eye in Game 2 of the final. The fact that 48-year-old manager Lester Patrick replaced him in goal in that game is now legendary. No one remembers who replaced Patrick.
- Chabot helped Toronto win a Cup in 1931–32 and helped them reach the final in 1932–33, but he was traded to Montreal because they wanted a French-Canadian goaltender.
- After one season with the Habs, he was dealt to Chicago as a replacement for Charlie Gardiner, who had died suddenly after leading the Black Hawks to the Stanley Cup. It was an impossible assignment, given the circumstances, yet Chabot managed to win over the fans by capturing the Vezina Trophy. But if Chabot thought his luck had finally changed, he was wrong. The following season he suffered a knee injury and the Black Hawks decided to keep his replacement, Mike Karakas.

- In 1936 he was with the Montreal Maroons and surrendered a goal to Mud Bruneteau in the longest game in NHL history as his team lost the series to the Detroit Red Wings. The Maroons cut him after the season.

When Chabot's career was over, he had 201 wins, 73 shutouts, and a sparkling 1.54 goals-against average. He was also the winning goaltender in the second-longest game ever played—Toronto's 1–0 win against Boston in 1933 that was only settled after 104:46 minutes of overtime. Yet there is a sense that Chabot's career was somewhat disappointing. Much had been expected of him when the Rangers signed him in 1926 after he had led Port Arthur to back-to-back Allan Cups in 1924–25 and 1925–26.

One theory is that he never truly recovered from the eye injury he suffered in the 1928 final. At first doctors had feared he might lose his eyesight. The theory is that Patrick traded him for that reason.

Former Montreal Canadiens and *Hockey Night in Canada* broadcaster Dick Irvin Jr., whose father coached Chabot in Toronto, views him as one of the most underrated goaltenders of all time.

Chabot Was a Tragic Hero Because . . .

He died at a very young age without ever garnering the full respect due him.

"His record is just excellent," Irvin says. "He was one of my dad's favorite guys. When a coach wins his first Stanley Cup, he tends to think fondly of the goaltender."

The lack of respect Chabot endured reached comical proportions when he was with the Rangers and a public relations person with too much time and creativity hypothesized that if the team changed Lorne Chabot's name to "Leopold Chabotzky," the team might start drawing more Jewish fans. The Rangers actually billed him as the first Jewish star and some newspapers actually began using Chabotzky instead of Chabot. Said a report in *The Windsor Star*, "It looks as if the French Canadian is going to change his nationality whether he wishes to or not, though it is known that Chabot resents the effort to have him sail under any name but his own."

The last bit of bad luck Chabot endured was far more serious. He died at age 46 of osteoarthritis and progressive nephritis. His kidneys and body simply shut down. He was bedridden for the last year of his life.

36 | ROGER CROZIER

BORN: Bracebridge, Ontario, March 16, 1942
DIED: January 11, 1996

SHOT: Right	HEIGHT: 5′8″	WEIGHT: 165 lbs.
Vezina Trophies: 1		Calder Trophies: 1
Conn Smythe Trophies: 1		NHL First All-Star Team: 1

NOTABLE ACHIEVEMENTS: Won Harry "Hap" Holmes Award for lowest American Hockey League goals-against average, 1963–64; named AHL's top rookie that season; named NHL's top rookie the following season; led NHL in shutouts in his first two full seasons (1964–65, 1965–66); led NHL with 40 wins in 1964–65; won inaugural Conn Smythe Trophy as playoff MVP; the first of four to win the Conn Smythe Trophy while playing for runner-up teams (with Glenn Hall, Reggie Leach, and Ron Hextall); played in the 1975 Stanley Cup final with the Buffalo Sabres; the NHL's award for save percentage leader is named after him.

Johnny Bower's Commentary on Crozier

"Roger was an average-size goalie but he was all heart. He would have had a Hall of Fame career had illness not cut it short. He would come way out of the

213

crease to take away the net. He was so quick that he'd move right back in and then if need be back out again to take away the corners. I think that Roger's record speaks for itself, in that he won the Hap Holmes, Calder, and Conn Smythe Trophies in three consecutive years [1964–66]."

Second Opinion: Former NHL Goaltender Jim Rutherford on Crozier

"He is very similar to [Montreal Canadiens goalie] Jose Theodore: quick, small goaltenders with a great glove hand. Roger was a lot more spectacular than Theodore. There was a lot of talk in those days about Roger's nervousness and what he went through before and after a game, but he was a great goaltender. And he was a great guy. I remember I spent one training camp with him and he was great to me. Just a first-class man."

The late Roger Crozier literally couldn't stomach success, through no fault of his own. He spent his entire NHL career trying to stop pucks while dealing with serious health issues that included an ulcer and pancreatitis. In his first full NHL season with the Detroit Red Wings in 1964–65, he led the league in shutouts and came within a pair of goals against of besting Johnny Bower and Terry Sawchuk for the Vezina Trophy. At that time he joined Sawchuk and Frank Brimsek as the only NHL players to win the Calder Trophy and make the All-Star team in the same rookie season. Like Glenn Hall he could look like an octopus in the net, with his arms and legs flailing about. The great Maurice "Rocket" Richard once said that Crozier "probably has the best reflexes in hockey."

Says former Detroit defenseman Bill Gadsby: "He would have one arm on the crossbar and his leg sticking way out over there and the other hand would be stretched out. I used to sit on the bench and think, 'How in the heck did he get that one?' His glove would never be where you thought it should be. I've seen him with his elbow on the crossbar, and he would just be hanging there. But he always managed to stop the puck." With his catching glove on his right hand, Crozier always appeared to be even more unorthodox than he was. He would show open net and then take it away with the quickness and magic of his glove hand.

When Crozier won the Conn Smythe Trophy while playing for the losing team in the 1966 Stanley Cup final, it seemed as if he was on the road to greatness. But analysis of Crozier's career today now centers on the hypothetical question of what he might have been able to accomplish had he been blessed with good health. "His stomach problems were far more serious than any of us knew in Detroit," Gadsby says.

While many players struggled to keep weight off, Crozier always fought to keep weight on his 5'8" frame in his early days with the Red Wings. Because his illness would limit what he could eat, his weight would sometimes dip below 160. It also didn't help that he was a fretter and prone to self-doubt. At age 25 he announced his retirement, saying he had "lost his confidence" after losing three consecutive games. He went home to his native Bracebridge, Ontario, where he worked as a carpenter. Crozier would return to the sport four months later, but that sabbatical established a reputation for nervousness that he was never able to shake.

Crozier Was a Tragic Hero Because...

Health problems kept him from reaching his potential.

Crozier was never able to achieve the superstardom that was expected of him. He was dealt to the Buffalo Sabres in 1970 and, by the time he retired in 1977, he had been hospitalized more than 30 times because of his pancreatitis.

Dave Dryden, Crozier's goaltending partner in Buffalo, told writer Jon Trontz: "I did get a kick out of his philosophy. He was always saying when he was up in Bracebridge, on the roof of a cottage and hammering a nail, that there aren't 15,000 people booing if he bends one. If you bend a nail, you bend a nail. He would hint that he couldn't take the pressure."

Despite the torturous ordeal Crozier went through while playing, teammates remember that he was a fun-loving guy who enjoyed team pranks and jokes. Crozier, who died in 1996, could laugh in the face of constant pain. Even though his achievements pale in comparison to some of the legends of the game, hockey aficionados still view him as a true goaltending great.

215

38 | CHUCK RAYNER

BORN: Sutherland, Saskatchewan, August 11, 1920

SHOT: Left	**HEIGHT:** 5′11″	**WEIGHT:** 190 lbs.
Hart Trophies: 1		NHL Second All-Star Team: 3
NHL All-Star Games: 3		

NOTABLE ACHIEVEMENTS: Hall of Famer; won the Hart Trophy and backstopped the heavy underdog New York Rangers to Game 7 of the 1950 Stanley Cup final against Detroit; never played again in NHL playoffs; last goalie in the history of the New York/Brooklyn Americans; led the NHL with five shutouts in 1946–47; a Memorial Cup finalist with Kenora, 1939–40; great puckhandler who scored two goals in exhibition games; experimented with a Plexiglas face mask in practice; played with James "Sugar Jim" Henry on the Rangers in one of the first two-goalie systems.

Johnny Bower's Commentary on Rayner

"I owe a lot of my success to Prince Charlie. Chuck was the person who taught me the poke check while I was with the Rangers in 1953–54. We'd work on the move every day after practice for 10 minutes until I was able to do the poke check. Chuck was one of the best puckhandlers and most aggressive goaltenders in the NHL at the time. He knew that I wasn't the greatest puckhandler and told me that if I wanted to stick in the NHL that I would have to learn how to take the puck from the opposing forwards. The key to a successful poke check is timing. So Chuck would lay five pucks in front of the net and force me to poke them to him. We'd repeat this drill every day until I got the move down pat. I really appreciate what he did for me in my career."

Second Opinion: Former Detroit Red Wings Great Gordie Howe on Rayner

"He was from Saskatoon, and I had been in his house. I know him well. One night in New York I was chasing a record and I was after a hat trick. There's a faceoff in the Rangers' zone. Charlie Rayner winked at me and pointed to the top corner. Delvecchio won the faceoff and I slapped the damn thing and he plucked it out of midair. He looked at me and said, 'Harder.' He sucked me right in. He was really funny. He was a big man. When you threw it in the corner, he would just go out and get the puck. He really forced us to change the way we came into the zone. No one else other than Jacques Plante later on was doing that."

Chuck Rayner's love affair with the art of goaltending didn't mean he was married to the idea that a goalie should stay home in his crease. Although Jacques Plante is often credited with being the first wandering goaltender, most players in that era view Rayner as the goalie who was the most adventuresome.

"When I broke in, I remember I was shocked that Rayner would bring the puck almost to your end," says former NHL goaltender Emile Francis. "He could handle the puck better than some of the players he played with."

Rayner laughingly says that during his playing days, if he saw the puck, "I figured it was mine."

He says his wanderlust came with the full blessing of New York Rangers general manager Frank Boucher, who believed the goalie was helping the defense and offense. "A lot of times I would get up pretty close to our blue line and forward the pass to one of our people," Rayner recalls.

Having played for Eddie Shore in Springfield, Massachusetts, Rayner was schooled in the importance of goaltenders being strong skaters. "He always told me you have to have balance on your skates," he says. "And you would just find yourself moving out to get the puck."

Rayner began to believe he was going to score a goal in the NHL. He did score when he was playing for the Royal Canadian Army team—and not into an empty net. He saw a loose puck during a goalmouth scramble, seized control, skated the length of the ice, and flipped a shot past the stunned netminder.

Remember this was the forties, when most goalkeepers could barely backhand the puck to the boards.

"I got to the blue line in Toronto one night and I just missed the net by two inches," Rayner recalls. "Another time we had a big row against the Chicago Black Hawks and we were three-on-three. The puck hit me in the chest and bounced in front, so I went after it and got all the way through to their blue line until Max Bentley got me right there."

The highlight of Rayner's career was probably the 1949–50 season, when he helped the Rangers make an unlikely run to the Stanley Cup final. He played

Seldom tethered to his net, Rayner frequently vacated his goal crease to play the puck.

so brilliantly that the highly favored Red Wings needed double overtime to beat him in Game 7.

"We had to win a game in Chicago just to get into the playoffs," Rayner recalls. "And when we left for Montreal, we were told to pack one shirt because we would be home in a hurry."

Rayner surrendered seven goals in five games against the Canadiens, and shut out Montreal 3–0 in the deciding game. That was the series that drove Montreal goaltender Bill Durnan to quit.

With a circus scheduled for Madison Square Garden, the Rangers had no home ice for the final. Five games were played in Detroit and two were played in Toronto. Just forcing the Red Wings to a seventh game under those conditions makes Rayner's goaltending accomplishment one of the best of all time.

"The best individual goaltending I ever witnessed was Bernie Parent in the playoffs [in 1974 and 1975] and the next best goalkeeping was Chuck Rayner in the 1950 playoffs," says Francis, who was in the Rangers' organization at the time. "Rayner was the MVP of the regular season and as far I was concerned, he was the MVP of the playoffs."

Rayner was highly respected around the league, and not just for that particular season.

"He battled all the time," says former teammate Harry Howell, who came to the Rangers in 1952–53. "He was just diving and ducking all over the place. He'd end up getting stitched between periods. He was a target because he was so big."

Teammates looked up to Rayner because playing with him was like having a coach on the ice. Former Rangers player Dean Prentice remembers that the goalie used to counsel him and Andy Bathgate about shooting.

"I learned more about scoring goals from a goalie than I did from anybody else," Prentice recalls. "Charlie would take us down to one net and have us shoot pucks at him. He'd show us where to shoot them, where goalies hated to have the puck shot."

In terms of style, Howell compares Rayner to Terry Sawchuk. "He'd get down low, look between the legs of the defenseman and the forwards who were trying to screen him," Howell recalls. "And when you're down there that low, you are going to get a few pucks around the ears."

Rayner used his stick very effectively. "He was the best poke-checking goaltender I had ever seen, and if he missed you with his stick, he was so big he would knock you ass-over-teakettle with his body," Francis says.

Teeder Kennedy was even more animated when describing Rayner's poke checking: "You would be going in on Charlie and that stick would come out like a serpent's tongue, and you would be on your fanny in no time."

Francis believes Rayner's aggressiveness shortened his career because spilled forwards were constantly crashing into him.

Rayner left the game with as much humility as he had when he joined the Rangers. Too many goalmouth scrambles and pileups had left one knee severely damaged. He had injured the other one trying to compensate.

"I felt that I was letting the club down," recalls Rayner. "I went to [GM] Frank Boucher and said, 'I'm just not playing as well as I would like to play.'"

Boucher wouldn't accept Rayner's attempt to retire. "I stayed on a couple of games, but I could see it was getting weaker and I had to quit," Rayner says. "I didn't want to quit, but I had to."

He wouldn't accept anything less than his best. "I would have loved to be on a Stanley Cup team, but I have no complaints," he says. "I feel the Rangers treated me right, and I don't think I have anything to complain about."

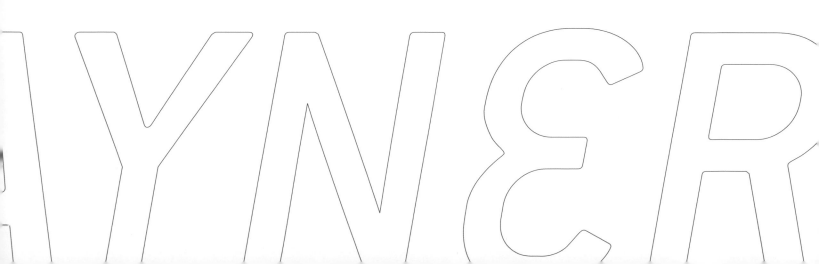

42 | MIKE KARAKAS

BORN: Aurora, Minnesota, December 12, 1911

DIED: May 2, 1992

SHOT: Left	HEIGHT: 5'11"	WEIGHT: 147 lbs.
Stanley Cups: 1		Calder Trophies: 1
NHL Second All-Star Team: 1		

NOTABLE ACHIEVEMENTS: Led the NHL in wins twice; NHL's first U.S.-born and -trained goalie; an All-Star in American Hockey Association and American Hockey League; played in two Stanley Cup finals; an original inductee to the U.S. Hall of Fame in 1973; won the Stanley Cup in 1937–38 with Chicago while playing with a broken toe.

Johnny Bower's Commentary on Karakas

"Karakas was an adventurous netminder who would roam halfway to the blue line to knock away a puck. He relied heavily on a first-rate glove hand. He was considered very acrobatic in that era."

Second Opinion: Former Teammate Clint Smith on Karakas

"He was what we called a jumping jack goaltender. Some nights, he was really hard to beat and some nights, footballs could have gotten past him. Mike was very solid. He was here, there, and everywhere, but he was fast and he could get away with it. He seemed different from most of us. We were all Canadians, and he was an American. He was bit louder than we were."

Karakas Was a Tragic Hero Because . . .

He ended up playing in the minors during the prime of his career because of contract disputes.

In the nineties the province of Quebec became known as the cradle of NHL goaltenders. In the late thirties and forties, that title belonged to Eveleth, Minnesota, a small mining community about 60 miles from Duluth and 100 miles from the Canadian border. During an era when the NHL was almost exclusively an all-Canadian club, Eveleth natives Mike Karakas and Frank Brimsek owned two of the six number one goaltender berths. When Karakas departed Chicago, another Eveleth native, Sam LoPresti, moved in.

Although Brimsek is considered to be the best of the trio, Karakas was the trailblazer and had already won a Stanley Cup championship (with the Chicago Black Hawks in 1937–38) before Brimsek had even reached the NHL.

Karakas and Brimsek had been batterymates for the Eveleth High School baseball team, with Brimsek the hard-throwing pitcher and Karakas the iron-willed catcher. That might explain Karakas' style. "He had a tremendously quick glove hand," says Pete Palangio, who played with him on the 1937–38 championship team. "He had a stand-up style, very steady and reliable."

In reviewing Karakas' accomplishments from a historical perspective, it is tricky to assess his true place among elite-level goalkeepers because he never had the luxury of playing with a truly excellent team. The Black Hawks posted an embarrassing 14–25–9 record in the 1937–38 regular season before vaulting to the championship, largely on the shoulders of Karakas, who was 6–2 in the postseason with a 1.71 goals-against average and two shutouts. "He was acrobatic," says former Chicago teammate Vic Heylinger. "He always took care of himself. He was always in great condition."

At age 24, Karakas had received his first shot at the NHL in 1935–36 only because Lorne Chabot was injured. When Karakas posted four wins, including three shutouts, in his first four games, the Black Hawks decided to keep him. Chabot eventually was traded to the Montreal Maroons.

Former NHL goaltender Emile Francis recalls that Karakas used to bend over in goal like a shortstop. Says Francis: "He was a very determined goalkeeper. He was big for his time. I saw Karakas get hurt and come back and play. He was tough."

When Chicago won the 1938 Stanley Cup the team was coached by American Bill Stewart. He had great respect for Karakas, according to Stewart's grandson Paul Stewart, who is an NHL referee. "He was very tough. Once when he broke his toe, they cut out part of the boot and fitted him with a special sidecar on the boot and he played. After they won the Stanley Cup, Karakas asked for a $500 raise and ownership balked. He left. It was that kind of independent spirit that made him unique."

44 | NORMIE SMITH

BORN: Toronto, Ontario, March 18, 1908

DIED: February 2, 1988

SHOT: Left	HEIGHT: 5'7"	WEIGHT: 165 lbs.
Stanley Cups: 2		Vezina Trophies: 1

NOTABLE ACHIEVEMENTS: Recorded a Stanley Cup–record shutout sequence of 248 minutes, 32 seconds during the first three games of the 1935–36 playoffs, his first three Stanley Cup appearances; the only goalie to post shutouts in each of his first two Stanley Cup games; won an International Hockey League title with Windsor, 1930–31; led the NHL in wins twice, in shutouts once, and in goals-against average once.

Johnny Bower's Commentary on Smith

"The fact that his playoff-shutout-minutes record has stood for 76 years testifies to what kind of goaltender Smith was. He was reported to be a reflex goaltender who challenged shooters. And I always liked goaltenders who came out and made the shooter beat them. All goalies played stand-up style in those years, but he was known to use some acrobatics. The Toronto *Globe and Mail* once described him as a 'jumping, kicking, catching, and sprawling' netminder."

Second Opinion: Former Minor League Goaltender Charlie Teno on Smith

"Clint Benedict was playing goal for Windsor [of the International Hockey League in 1930–31]. He got hurt and was going to be out for the season. So they called me and asked me to sign with them. I turned them down. So Windsor went out and got Normie Smith from the Montreal Amateur Athletic Association. I saw Normie play a lot of years. He was a great goaltender, really quick on his feet. Well, don't you know, Windsor wins the championship that year with Normie in goal and he ends up with the Montreal Maroons the next season. He finds his way to the Red Wings a few years later. Let me tell you, I was kicking myself watching Normie play goal in Detroit and thinking about how it could have been me. But years later Normie got sent to the minors and Detroit promoted my brother, Harvey, to replace him. I guess you can say that when it came to Normie's career, the Teno brothers opened and closed the door."

Fire hydrant–sized Detroit Red Wings netminder Normie Smith was 5'7", 165 pounds on his tallest and heaviest days, and yet he must have seemed like a monstrous presence to the Montreal Maroons on March 24, 1936, when he was flawless in the longest playoff game ever played.

Using sugar dunked in brandy to keep his energy level high, Smith posted 90 saves in a 1–0 win against the Maroons that wasn't decided until 21-year-old Modere "Mud" Bruneteau scored at 4:46 of the sixth overtime. Playing his first NHL playoff game, Smith stood in the goal for almost six full hours. The contest ended at 2:25 A.M.

"He seemed to play his best in big games," says Pete Kelly, who played with Smith on the 1935–36 and 1936–37 Detroit championship teams.

Considered reliable and efficient, Smith always seemed to have the proper temperament for the playoffs. He was virtually unflappable; he didn't come unhinged by pressure. "He was a very, very consistent goalie," Kelly says. "Not flashy, mind you, but very steady. He played a big part in both of our Cup wins."

According to Kelly, Smith was the perfect fit for a Red Wings team that lacked superstars.

"He was a quiet guy but he was always in good spirits," Kelly says. "I think that was the strength of those Detroit teams. We had real harmony amongst all the players—a family feeling. There were no petty jealousies. We had a lot of good players, but it was a team effort that won it for us."

That wee hour triumph came against the defending Stanley Cup champion Maroons in the best-of-five semifinals. Smith needed five more wins to win the

Cup and went 5–1 over the next six games to achieve that. He posted a 1.34 goals-against average.

Detroit coach Jack Adams didn't gush about Smith—once telling the Toronto *Globe and Mail* that Smith was the "third-best goalie" in the six-team league behind Tiny Thompson and Wilf Cude.

But when Smith also made 36 saves to post a 3–0 shutout over the Maroons in Game 2 of the semifinal, the Canadian Press reported that Adams put his arm around Smith and said, "By gosh, Normie, that's the best game I've ever seen you play."

This came three days after Smith's 90-save game. His first NHL playoff games established a postseason record of 248:32 minutes of shutout hockey.

Stories in that era always pointed to Smith being pudgy, even though he wasn't a large guy. It might be stretching it to say he was 5'7" because when Emile Francis showed up at Red Wings' training camp after Smith's retirement, Detroit officials called Smith to borrow his equipment. It was a perfect fit for Francis, who was 5'6", 145 pounds.

The Red Wings beat Toronto in the 1936 final, and the Maple Leafs left with plenty of respect for Smith.

Even after they beat him 4–3 in Game 3, Toronto's Harvey Jackson told the media, "That bird Normie Smith robbed me more times than any goaltender I ever fired at. I thought I had him beaten at least four times. But he got his arm to the puck and knocked it over the net."

Despite helping Detroit win two Stanley Cup championships, Smith never completely won over Adams. When Adams had the opportunity to acquire Thompson for Smith, 30, and $15,000 in cash, he made the deal.

Smith's former Detroit teammate, Carl Liscombe, says, "[When the trade was done], Normie said he wasn't going and retired." He wasn't willing to play for Boston's farm team—which is what they would have wanted, with Frank Brimsek in place there.

Smith Was a Tragic Hero Because . . .

He was 30 and in the prime of his career when he was traded by Detroit's Jack Adams, who never had a great fondness for him. Knowing Frank Brimsek was the guy in Boston, Smith retired.

229

TRAGIC HEROES

SMITH

GUMP WORSLEY

TOM BARRASSO

HARRY LUMLEY

ROY WORTERS

UNDERAPPRECIATED PLAYERS

ROGIE VACHON

ED GIACOMIN

CURTIS JOSEPH

CHRIS OSGOOD

BILL RANFORD

JOHN VANBIESBROUCK

19 | GUMP WORSLEY

BORN: Montreal, Quebec, May 14, 1929

SHOT: Left	**HEIGHT:** 5'7"	**WEIGHT:** 180 lbs.

Stanley Cups: 4	Vezina Trophies: 2
Calder Trophies: 1	NHL First All-Star Team: 1
NHL Second All-Star Team: 1	NHL All-Star Games: 4

NOTABLE ACHIEVEMENTS: Hall of Famer; led the NHL with .929 save percentage for the New York Rangers in 1957–58; faced the most shots per game of any NHL goalie six times between 1954–55 and 1962–63; lost an NHL-record 352 games; Western Hockey League MVP in 1953–54; shares the NHL record for most seasons played by a goalie (21, with Terry Sawchuk); didn't don a mask until his final season; won four Stanley Cups, even though his teams never advanced past the first round of the playoffs during his first 10 seasons.

Johnny Bower's Commentary on Worsley

"Gump is one of the funniest men you'll ever meet. He was a short little goaltender who was ferocious on the ice. He was a good stand-up goaltender, not so much out of choice but out of necessity. What I remember most about him is the way that he used to slap the puck up into the stands when he would get frustrated. Of course that was back in the days when you wouldn't get a delay of game penalty for it. I first met Gump in New York in 1953–54. That year I won the Rangers' starting job from him because he came to camp a little out of shape. I played every game that season with the Rangers and posted a solid goals-against average, despite the fact that we had a losing record. My problem was that in the off-season, I was feeling a little cocky and came into camp the next year out of shape. Gumper came into camp fit and took the job back from me."

Second Opinion: Hall of Fame Defenseman Harry Howell on Worsley

"He was quite a character. When they asked him, 'Which team gives you the most trouble?' he'd say, 'The Rangers,' just to rub it in a little bit. But we did struggle. The Gumper was a great competitor. Gumper was a bit of a flopper. He stopped a lot of them lying on his back and he'd get them by putting his hand or his leg up. He was a little unorthodox, not really the stand-up kind of guy, because he was a little round. He stopped the puck any way he could and he did a darn good job at it. Going to Montreal was a fresh life for him. We were hardly ever a playoff team and he goes right to the Stanley Cup champions. I think they grew to appreciate him when he went to Montreal, because he won a couple of Vezina Trophies and a couple of Stanley Cups. You have to be a pretty good goaltender to get into that class."

Mickey Redmond was a rookie right winger with the Montreal Canadiens who possessed a potent shot and a powerful will to be noticed. But when he nearly left an impression on the forehead of Montreal netminder Lorne "Gump" Worsley, his blast almost cost Redmond more than a chance at NHL glory. "I whizzed a shot past his head in practice," Redmond recalls. "The next thing I knew, here comes Gumper's stick at me, just like a helicopter blade. Then he charged out of the net toward me, grabbed my sweater, and said, 'Thanks, kid. You just gave me an excuse to leave practice early.'"

Redmond learned his first lesson about Worsley—the man was a puckstopping contradiction in terms.

Take whatever means necessary to keep the puck from entering his net in a game? No problem. Do likewise during practice? No way. Stand in the path of Bobby Hull's 100-mph slap shot without the benefit of facial protection? Consider it done. Step through a gateway and onto an airplane for a flight to a road game? You've got to be kidding.

"He never liked to fly," recalls former Canadiens teammate John Ferguson. "One time, we were flying to L.A. We got as far as Chicago and the plane dipped about 10,000 feet. The stewardess broke her back, the serving cart turned over, and some guy was sick in front of us. I was sitting beside Gump. Lorne got off the plane in Chicago and took the train the rest of the way to Los Angeles."

Worsley blamed a flight early in his career in which an engine burst into flames for his fear of flying. As for his fearless nature and willingness to stand bare-faced in the path of oncoming vulcanized rubber—he didn't don a mask until his 25th and final pro season—Worsley, who won four Stanley Cups with Montreal, chalked that up to the gifts provided him by Mother Nature.

"My face is my mask," he liked to say. "Would it have been fair not to give the fans a chance to see my beautiful face? Actually, to tell the truth, I couldn't

A maskless Worsley fearlessly dives in the path of Red Berenson's shot.

see when wearing one. And goaltending is all about confidence. If you don't feel right, you can't be confident."

Worsley donned facial protection—at the insistence of his wife, Doreen—only for the final six weeks of the 1973–74 season with the Minnesota North Stars. Worsley, closing in on his 45th birthday, was planning to retire at season's end and the North Stars weren't going to make the playoffs, so he relented and put on the mask.

Putting things on was nothing new to Worsley, who maintained one of hockey's most predominant funny bones while playing the hockey position most likely to break his bones. Just another one of the Gumper's many contradictions. Even his nickname didn't suit him. He was called Gump because of his facial resemblance to Andy Gump, a tall, lanky comic-strip character from Worsley's youth, but at 5′7″, 180 pounds, Gump wasn't tall or lanky.

"He was portly," Ferguson says. "The goaltenders, they all paddle down now. The Gumper, he could have never gotten the paddle down. It wouldn't have made it past his belly."

Worsley's belly became an issue in New York, where he launched his NHL career with the Rangers in 1952–53. The NHL's top rookie that season, he lost his position the following fall because of his weight, and although he was back on the job a year later, his bulge was the cause of many a battle with Rangers coach Phil Watson.

"He hated Watson with a passion," former Rangers defenseman Bill Gadsby recalls. "He [Watson] called Gump a beer belly one time [in a newspaper]. And we went to Boston the next night and the headlines in the paper were about Gump and Watson having some problems, and Watson saying he had a beer belly."

Bruins fans jumped on this tidbit of information and used it to torment Worsley with a famous line from a Pabst Blue Ribbon ad campaign.

"Even before the game, the crowd started yelling at Gump, 'Hey, Gump, what will you have?' Ten or twelve thousand people were yelling that. Gump was just livid," Gadsby says. "So we get back to New York for practice. Before we go on the ice, Phil was saying a few things and Gump says, 'Can I have the floor?' Watson says, 'What do you want?' And Gump says, 'I'll tell you what I want. That thing in Boston embarrassed me. I don't drink beer. I drink whiskey.'

"Gump was right. I played with him eight years and I never saw him drink beer. He drank whiskey. Not a lot of it, maybe three or four after a game. Just [Seagram's] VO and ginger ale. He says if you want to get a bottle of VO and put it in the dressing room, we will see who can drink it the best. He just kept saying, 'I'm not a beer belly. I drink whiskey.'"

There was no denying Gump had a belly. But the unathletic-looking Worsley was among the game's quickest netminders. He had tremendous reflexes and remarkable agility, especially in practice, where his ability to dodge shots was legendary.

"He was probably the worst practice goalie you'd ever watch," Ferguson says. "When we picked the teams for scrimmages, he'd be the last guy picked. Then he'd get mad and go in the dressing room. We didn't mind, though, because we'd put a player in goal and at least he'd try to stop the shots."

When it mattered, a different Worsley showed up at the rink. "When the games were on, you counted on him," Ferguson says. "He just stopped the puck. It was amazing."

Worsley would often lead the Canadiens to the ice with the chant, "All right, boys, let's win one for the Gumper." He used his edgy sense of humor to deflect the stress of his position.

Worsley Was Underappreciated Because . . .

He toiled for years as the NHL's busiest netminder with the woeful New York Rangers, but it wasn't until a 1963 trade to the contending Montreal Canadiens, where he won four Stanley Cups, that people came to realize his tremendous ability.

While with the Rangers, where he never won a playoff series in 10 seasons, Worsley listed the chicken salad sandwich on the menu of the restaurant he owned as the "Ranger Special." The Gumper was also well known for his practical jokes.

"He was always full of tricks," Ferguson says. "They used to room me with him in the playoffs. We'd go up to the Laurentian Mountains. Ralph Backstrom, who owned a hotel, got 12 dozen golf balls with the name of the hotel put on them while we were there. Gumpy and I went into his room, took 144 golf balls out of the boxes, and threw them all over the floor."

They waited patiently for their teammate and neighbor to return to his room, then laughed uproariously when they heard Backstrom curse as he crashed to the floor. "Then we thought, 'Jeez, what if he broke his leg?'" Ferguson says. They knew Backstrom was OK a few hours later, when an axe came crashing through the door of their room.

Even when the end came, Worsley left them laughing. "I knew it was time to quit when the sons of guys who'd scored on me started scoring on me," he said.

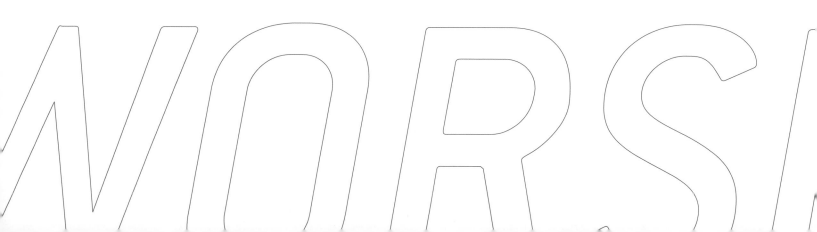

25 | TOM BARRASSO

BORN: Boston, Massachusetts, March 31, 1965

SHOOTS: Right	**HEIGHT:** 6′3″	**WEIGHT:** 211 lbs.

Stanley Cups: 2	Vezina Trophies: 1
Calder Trophies: 1	Jennings Trophies: 1
NHL First All-Star Team: 1	NHL Second All-Star Team: 2
NHL All-Star Games: 1	

NOTABLE ACHIEVEMENTS: Jumped to the NHL directly from the U.S. high school ranks; one of four goaltenders to win Calder/Vezina double as a rookie (with Frank Brimsek, Tony Esposito, and Ed Belfour); his 14-game winning streak in 1992–93 is tied for second best in NHL history; winningest U.S.-born goalie in NHL history (368); first U.S.-born goalie to post 300 NHL wins; selected to the NHL All-Rookie Team in 1983–84; led the NHL in goals-against average and shutouts, 1984–85; his 14 consecutive Stanley Cup wins are a record; first-round draft pick of the Buffalo Sabres; five-time Vezina Trophy finalist.

Johnny Bower's Commentary on Barrasso

"Tom Barrasso has actually become a bit more of a stand-up goalie as his career has gone on, as opposed to more of a butterfly when he first broke into the league. As he's gotten older he can't rely on reflexes alone as much anymore, so we've seen him learn to use his size to his advantage. What really impresses me about Barrasso is that he took time to get away from the game to focus on his family. He has maintained a high standard on the ice while coping with much adversity off of it. For that, he is to be admired."

Second Opinion: Former Sabres Teammate Brent Peterson on Barrasso

"We had the perfect scenario for Barrasso when he came in at 18. We had a veteran team. We had a good defensive team. We had a veteran goalie [Bob Sauve] who could help him out. Scotty [Bowman] also coached a disciplined defensive style. He played very well under that system. He was a big guy and covered a lot of net. Mostly he stayed up, but he would go down sometimes and cover the bottom of the net pretty well. He had a unique style for that era. Back then, not many goalies handled the puck as well as he did. He was very good technically. He was already mature physically and mentally. You have to be a little cocky and confident to play goal, period, never mind an 18-year-old coming into the NHL."

When Tom Barrasso put on a Sabres sweater as an 18-year-old wunderkind, the idea of a player stepping right out of Massachusetts high school competition to play goal in the NHL four months after his senior prom was the sporting world's equivalent of sending a man to Mars. Imagine how out of this world it seemed when Barrasso not only played but also won the Calder and Vezina trophies.

"I don't think he viewed playing against NHL shooters much different than playing high school," says former Sabres public relations director Gerry Helper. Even as a teenager Barrasso had an unwavering belief in his ability to succeed.

General manager Scotty Bowman's decision to draft Barrasso out of Acton-Boxboro High School certainly wasn't shocking because the year before he had taken Phil Housley out of St. Paul High School and the defenseman had instant success. But the idea of using an 18-year-old in goal in an era when the Edmonton Oilers were just starting to crank up their war machine seemed outlandish even for the innovative Bowman.

Barrasso won the Calder and Vezina trophies at the age of 18.

But Helper recalls that Barrasso was different from Housley, even though both were teenagers. "Phil had this 'Gosh, this is cool' attitude, where Tom was very matter-of-fact about who he was and what he was capable of. He handled all the stuff on and off the ice."

As impressive as Barrasso's debut was in Buffalo, he really didn't get his due as a goaltender until he was dealt to the Pittsburgh Penguins. Although the Penguins are rightfully remembered for their offensive might, Barrasso was one of the final pieces of the championship puzzle. In hindsight, he was the ideal goaltender for a run-and-gun team. He had the self-assuredness necessary for a goalie who didn't have much of a chance to post eye-catching numbers.

"They said, 'Don't worry about the goals against—just win,'" Barrasso recalls. "The nice thing about playing for that team was that if you let in a bad goal, it wouldn't cost you the game, like it did when I was in Buffalo." The Penguins don't underestimate Barrasso's contributions to their back-to-back championship runs.

"He made himself look larger than he was," says Chicago Blackhawks winger Steve Thomas. "He plays the shooter big-time and leaves the pass to [be handled by] the defenseman."

Barrasso Is Underappreciated Because . . .

He was never given enough credit for his contributions to the Pittsburgh Penguins' Stanley Cup championships or his status as the winningest American goaltender of all time.

Hurricanes general manager Jim Rutherford liked Barrasso's athleticism so much that he signed him in 2001–02, even though he had been out of hockey for a year. Signed originally as a backup for Arturs Irbe, Barrasso played well enough to challenge him for the number one job, and he made the U.S. Olympic team at age 36. The Hurricanes eventually dealt him to the Maple Leafs, a team looking for playoff insurance when Curtis Joseph was injured.

"He has shown that he has terrific focus," says Rutherford, a former NHL goaltender. "He knows how to prepare himself mentally. And he skates well enough to make his stickhandling even more of a threat."

Barrasso has known many difficult days during his career, but none came close to the ordeal of watching his daughter, Ashley, successfully battle cancer during the prime of his career. He also took off the year before signing with Carolina as she was treated for a recurrence.

Perhaps Barrasso's career would be more revered had he not locked horns with the media for much of it. Ironically, all the traits that allowed him to succeed at such a young age might have undermined his relationship with the press.

The sadness of the friction is that Barrasso is a bright man with good insight into the game. As confident as he was at the time, even he isn't quite sure how he was able navigate so effectively in a new world when he was just 18.

"I don't know how the heck I did it," he says. "[But] I don't think that will be done again."

As the years have gone by, Helper seems to have appreciated the feat more.

"He wins the Vezina and Calder at 18," Helper says, chuckling. "And then he's also on the NHL All-Rookie Team, and you are going, 'Wow, big deal.' You shouldn't think of the All-Rookie team like that, but it seemed like he was beyond that."

St. Louis Blues general manager Larry Pleau also laughs when he thinks about the time scouts were looking at Barrasso in 1983. It was almost as if they couldn't believe their eyes. "He was a huge guy, and people are saying, 'Is he really only 18? Does he have a false birth certificate?'" Pleau says. "It's like when the Russians came over and brought a guy like that, we would always say, 'He's not 18. These guys are probably 21.' . . . He was a confident and cocky kid."

Pleau clearly thinks it is unfair that Barrasso has faced criticism for his personality. "People are upset because he's cocky? Do you think there is any other way to get to that point without being cocky? There is no way. There had to be something special about him."

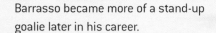

Barrasso became more of a stand-up goalie later in his career.

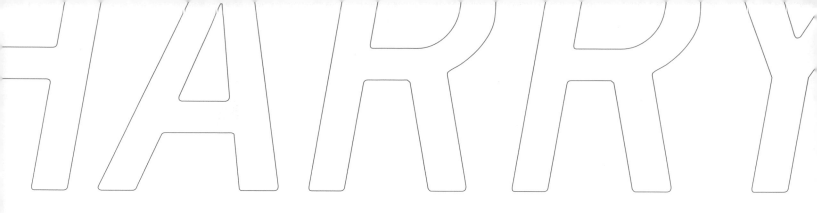

26 | HARRY LUMLEY

BORN: Owen Sound, Ontario, November 11, 1926
DIED: September 13, 1998

SHOT: Left	HEIGHT: 6′	WEIGHT: 195 lbs.
Stanley Cups: 1		Vezina Trophies: 1
NHL First All-Star Team: 2		NHL All-Star Games: 3

NOTABLE ACHIEVEMENTS: Hall of Famer; youngest goalie to appear in an NHL game (17 years, 38 days) and the first NHL teenager to play goal in a Stanley Cup final (18 in 1944–45); played in four Stanley Cup finals, all during his first seven seasons; led the NHL in wins twice, in shutouts three times, and in goals-against average once; his 13 shutouts for Toronto in 1953–54 stand as the club record; his 804 career games played was an NHL mark for goalies when he retired; once scored a goal in an exhibition game.

Johnny Bower's Commentary on Lumley

"Now Harry was a goaltender! He was technically sound and was a great competitor. We all know about Billy Smith taking control of his crease, but in the old days there was nobody who would come around the net when Harry was in goal. He was a big and tough goalie who would move guys from the front of the net himself. He was arguably one of the best big-game goaltenders of his era, but what I remember most about Harry was his pads. When I was playing for the Cleveland Barons I went to visit Pops Kenesky in Hamilton to have a pair of new pads made. Pops showed me a pair of pads that belonged to Harry. Harry was the first goalie to design a pad that was curved so that they formed a bit of a scoop near the toe of the skate. I had always worn straight pads, but because Harry wore them, I took them and wore that pair for years. The curve helps control rebounds and protects the top of the goalie's skates."

Second Opinion: Former Red Wings Defenseman Red Kelly on Lumley

"I always liked Harry. I roomed at Ma Shaw's and Harry was one of the other boarders there. I was a young guy playing in front of him and naturally you're going to make mistakes. But Harry never blamed you for any of them. The other thing about him: when a goal went in, his face was redder than the goal light that went on behind him. He never liked the puck to get by him. He was pretty competitive and he protected his net very well with that big stick of his. And he used to love lobsters. He loved them. He could eat them by the dozen."

On game days during 1949–50 the Detroit Red Wings used to file past goalie Harry Lumley in the dressing room as if they were tiptoeing through a minefield. They understood that if they took one wrong step, he would blow up.

Lumley's dressing stall was adjacent to the dressing room door, and his gear would be laid out in specific fashion near him.

"I have never seen anyone who was so superstitious," recalls former Red Wings great Gordie Howe. "I would come in late and he would be half dressed. If I would just kick his pad a little bit as I went by, he would take everything off again and start over."

Living with Lumley's idiosyncrasies was a small price to pay to have his bullish presence in the net. He was 6′, 195 pounds, and looked like a formidable presence between the pipes. His size actually was his ticket to becoming a goaltender. He was a defenseman at his school in Owen Sound when the team's only goaltender went down. As the team's biggest player he was the logical choice as the replacement. Within four years he was a standout goaltender in junior hockey.

Lumley liked to rub "red hot" liniment oil on himself before a practice and once, after he had lathered his hands with a healthy dose of the goo, he smacked Mr. Hockey on the back. The force of the slap was such that Howe swears he could feel the heat seeping through his pores.

In playful retaliation, Howe played on Lumley's superstitions by knocking down his stick. The goalie pinched him, leaving an ugly bruise. "What I can say about Lumley is that he was a powerful man," Howe says.

Lumley's physical stature also explains why, at 17, he was the youngest man ever to play goal in the NHL. The fact that he was traded a couple of months after winning the Stanley Cup had more to

Lumley Was Underappreciated Because . . .

He probably would have won several more Stanley Cups in Detroit if Terry Sawchuk hadn't arrived.

do with Terry Sawchuk's arrival than any misgivings about Lumley's puckstopping abilities. Although Howe exalts Sawchuk's stature, he says it's quite possible that the Red Wings Cup run in the fifties could have also been accomplished with Lumley as the number one goaltender. "He had quality," Howe says.

But while Sawchuk was emerging, Lumley was serving hard time with the dismal Chicago Black Hawks. It wasn't until he was dealt to the Toronto Maple Leafs in 1952 that he regained his place among the league's best.

He didn't change his preparation rituals when he got to Toronto. "He was a real loner," says former Toronto teammate Harry Watson. "When we came into the dressing room, whether it was before the game or between periods, he didn't want anyone talking to him or anyone near him."

Watson's view was that Lumley's routine went beyond superstition. "He just wanted to be left alone to focus on the game," he says. "Mentally, on game day, he was in the game all the time. [He] was thinking about what he had to do from the moment he got out of bed in the morning. He was very serious about his job."

"Apple Cheeks," as he was nicknamed, was completely different away from the rink.

"He was almost like two completely different guys really," Watson says. "There was Harry the goalie and Harry the guy. He was really a fun guy to be around. He liked to kibitz with other players and he'd always be up to go out for a couple of Kool-Aids."

Having an on and off switch for his competitive juices seemed to work for Lumley, who was respected by friends and foes.

"He was nasty with his stick," says Jimmy Peters, who played with and against Lumley.

Lumley didn't differentiate between friends or enemies when it came to stopping pucks. "He would use the lumber even in practice," Howe says. "He would give it to you if you embarrassed him in practice."

29 | ROY WORTERS

BORN: Toronto, Ontario, October 19, 1900

DIED: November 7, 1957

SHOT: Left	HEIGHT: 5'3"	WEIGHT: 135 lbs.
Vezina Trophies: 1		Hart Trophies: 1
NHL Second All-Star Team: 2		

NOTABLE ACHIEVEMENTS: Hall of Famer; first goalie to win the Hart Trophy, 1928–29; finished as Hart Trophy runner-up in 1927–28; only goalie to win the Vezina Trophy with a team that missed the playoffs; ranks 10th on all-time shutout list; his shutout streak of 324 minutes, 40 seconds in 1930–31 is third longest in NHL history; won back-to-back United States Amateur Hockey Association titles with the Pittsburgh Yellowjackets (1923–24, 1924–25); won the Memorial Cup with the Toronto Parkdale Canoe Club Paddlers (1919–20).

Johnny Bower's Commentary on Worters

"He was the smallest goalie in NHL history, but Roy Worters sure could fill the net. It was the shooters who had trouble filling it behind him with pucks. He was the highest-paid goalie in the NHL in his day and he earned that paycheck. He played for some of the weakest teams in the league, but he'd get them into the playoffs, which explains why he was the first goalie to win the Hart Trophy.

Hockey people from that era put him in the highest class of netminders, right up there with Georges Vezina, Tiny Thompson, and Charlie Gardiner. Worters was an acrobatic goalie. At 5′3″ and barely 135 pounds, he needed quick reflexes to cover the net. He was also the first goalie to effectively use his blocker pad to control the rebounds of shots and steer them to safety away from the front of the net."

Second Opinion: Former Teammate Lorne Carr on Worters

"Roy, he was one of the greats of that time. And he sure liked to have his fun. He and Charlie Conacher were really good friends. They were in business together but on the ice, they really went at it. Charlie came to the Americans late in his career and he had a hell of a shot, maybe the hardest in the game. Every day in practice, he'd come in and let one of those rockets go, and Roy would stop him—get a leg on it, or catch it in his glove. Then he'd show Charlie the puck and just laugh at him. Oh, that made Charlie mad. Roy was a stand-up goalie. He stood up as much as he could. With his size, he had no choice. If he went down, you couldn't find him. He was a battler, a real competitor, even in practice."

New York Americans owner Bill Dwyer handed the contract offer to his netminder. Roy Worters scanned the figures on the page and shook his head. Offers and counteroffers went back and forth but Worters wouldn't budge. Growing weary of the debate, Dwyer relented, presenting Worters with the $8,500 he'd sought from the outset.

When news reached his teammates they were awestruck at Worters' determination, because Dwyer wasn't merely the owner of a hockey team. He was a Prohibition-era bootlegger whose stint on the NHL board of governors was interrupted by a two-year stretch in U.S. federal prison. His business associates included hoods like Legs Diamond, Dutch Schultz, and Owney Madden, the last one once number one with a bullet on the FBI's most wanted list. That Worters didn't back down when confronted by such a shady character exemplified the competitive juices that flowed through this diminutive dynamo who guarded the nets for the Amazing Amerks.

Only 5′3″ and 135 pounds, Worters stood tall in net, which was a good thing, because the teams that stood in front of him rarely did. On many nights this mighty midget performed in a one-man show. During his rookie season of 1925–26 with the Pittsburgh Pirates, Worters made 50 saves in a 1–0 loss to Ottawa and turned aside 70 pucks during a 3–1 setback against the Americans.

He was named to an unofficial NHL All-Star Team selected by league coaches in 1927–28, finishing with a .956 save percentage and as runner-up to Howie Morenz in the Hart Trophy balloting. Moving to the Americans for goalie Joe Miller and the pricey sum of $20,000 the next season, Worters became the first goalie to be honored as NHL MVP. He won the Vezina Trophy in 1930–31 with an Americans club that failed to qualify for postseason play.

Worters performed in only 11 career playoff games, never appearing in a Stanley Cup final. But many hockey people rated him in a class with the best puckstoppers. "He is a marvelous artist in the nets," Charles Hughes, president of the Detroit Cougars, told the *Border Cities Star*.

An artist with no margin for error. Rules of the day called for an automatic goal to be awarded whenever a defender threw his stick in the path of the puck. Worters was victimized three times for goals in this fashion—scoreless ties that went into the books as 1–0 setbacks.

Worters Was Underappreciated Because . . .

He never played for a team that reached the Stanley Cup final. Despite this, he was the first NHL netminder to win the Hart Trophy and won the Vezina Trophy when his team failed to qualify for the playoffs.

During a 1929 playoff set with the New York Rangers, Worters posted a 0.40 goals-against average and lost the series, because the Americans never scored a goal.

He had grown used to winning in the amateur ranks. Worters backstopped the Toronto Parkdale Canoe Club Paddlers to the 1919–20 Memorial Cup and carried the Pittsburgh Yellowjackets to consecutive United States Amateur Hockey Association titles in 1923–24 and 1924–25, posting 17 shutouts and an 0.81 GAA in the latter campaign. A lifelong friend of hockey's Conacher clan—Worters and Charlie Conacher coowned the Conroy Hotel, a popular west-end Toronto watering hole—he was persuaded by Charlie's brother, Lionel, to turn pro when Pittsburgh joined the NHL.

"He could hardly skate to get to the net," former NHL player Clint Smith recalls of Worters. "But once he got to the net, he was fine."

Worters, who took 216 stitches to his face during his career, often left his teammates in stitches with his wicked sense of humor. Spotting heavyweight champ Primo Carnera on the dance floor one night at a New York nightclub, the pint-sized netminder waltzed over and stomped on the foot of the 6'7" slugger, disappearing into the crowd before Carnera could locate his assailant.

Perhaps it was his ability to laugh at life that helped Worters maintain his sanity while defending the goal for so many mediocre teams. "They were a fun-loving bunch," former Americans manager Tommy Gorman told *The Windsor Star* about his team. "And no member of the club had a better time than [Worters] did."

251

33 | ROGIE VACHON

BORN: Palmarolle, Quebec, September 8, 1945

SHOT: Left	HEIGHT: 5'7"	WEIGHT: 170 lbs.
Stanley Cups: 3		Vezina Trophies: 1
NHL Second All-Star Team: 2		NHL All-Star Games: 3

NOTABLE ACHIEVEMENTS: Backstopped Canada to the 1976 Canada Cup title, earning the all-tournament nod in goal; led goalies in wins and goals-against average during the 1967 Stanley Cup playoffs as a 21-year-old rookie; reached the Stanley Cup final in each of his first three seasons; second in Hart Trophy voting, 1974–75; one of the first restricted free agents to sign with another team (the Detroit Red Wings, in 1978); served as coach, general manager, and president of the Los Angeles Kings; first King to have his sweater number (No. 30) retired.

Johnny Bower's Commentary on Rogie Vachon

"That really was something when [Toronto coach] Punch [Imlach] called Rogie Vachon a Junior B goaltender before the 1967 Stanley Cup finals. As soon as I read that in the paper, I thought, 'Oh no, that's the wrong thing to say.' We knew that Montreal wasn't going to give us many opportunities to score, and lo and behold, they spanked us in the first game of the series. Rogie was a solid tender who ended up carving himself a niche in the NHL as one of the stingiest goalies of all time. He was one of those guys who made average teams into very good teams. He was quick as a jackrabbit and showed an ability to get in front of the puck, no matter where he was on the ice."

Second Opinion: Former Teammate Larry Pleau on Vachon

"I played with him as a young kid when he was with the Montreal Junior Canadiens. He wasn't big but was really competitive. He was competitively quick. There are guys who are quick, but not competitively quick. They can't make their quickness work for them. That was the difference in Rogie. You knew that in the course of a season, he was going to win five, six, seven, or more games—just him alone. He was that good of a goalie."

Rogie Vachon had to be content with being a legend in his own time zone. Having spent the prime of his career laboring for the Los Angeles Kings in a precable and pre-ESPN world undoubtedly cost Vachon some richly deserved notice. It might even have cost him a place in the Hall of Fame.

Says former NHL coach Harry Neale: "Vachon was probably a better goalie than most people thought, but you didn't even get the Kings' scores until two days later, and there were certainly no highlights of him playing."

If ESPN had been around then, Vachon would have regularly made the plays of the week with a flamboyant style that was ideal for highlight shows. His glove hand was one of the finest of his generation and his quickness seemed as if it benefited from alien technology. Vachon always made it appear that he was faster than the speed of light. "When I started, there were no masks and you had better be quick to stop the puck or you will end up with a lot of stitches," Vachon jokes.

Neale says Vachon was a difference-maker at a time when NHL games seemed as if they were a continuing series of three-on-two breaks. "You would think you would have him beat and he would somehow get a glove or a stick on it," Neale says.

Vachon is only 5′7″, and his playing weight was 170. "He was a small man, but if you shake hands with him, you will notice he has big hands," says former NHL goaltender John Davidson. "That helped him."

He played in a crouch, much like his idol, Terry Sawchuk. "I was a French-Canadian kid who didn't speak English, and maybe [my idol] should have been Jacques Plante," Vachon says. "But I always liked the name Sawchuk."

Vachon's identity is so closely intertwined with the Kings' logo that it is sometimes forgotten that he was a member of three Stanley Cup championship teams in Montreal. "He was the franchise in Los Angeles," says former Kings player and current Kings general manager Dave Taylor.

Even though Vachon's heroics never appeared until two days later in Eastern time zone papers (or not at all), he would not have traded his seven seasons in Los Angeles for any other venue.

"I felt like I was a pioneer," Vachon says. "When I came [to L.A.], the team was so bad that we were out of the playoffs by Christmas. It was a joke. Then we became more respectable under [coach] Bob Pulford, and one year we outdrew the Los Angeles Lakers. We built the foundation in Los Angeles, and it's still there. I'm very proud of that."

Vachon Was Underappreciated Because . . .

The hockey world never seemed to realize how well he was playing because he spent his prime years outside the Eastern time zone.

The Kings' 105-point season in 1974–75 still stands as a franchise record more than a quarter century later. Vachon had a 2.24 goals-against average that season and was runner-up to Philadelphia's Bernie Parent for the Vezina Trophy. Some thought he should have gotten the Hart Trophy, but it went to the Flyers' Bobby Clarke.

Ironically, Vachon is remembered as much for leaving the team he loved as he was for playing on it. He became the league's first true free agent when he signed with the Red Wings in 1978. "I felt like I had no choice," he says. "The Red Wings got the red carpet out." Detroit offered Vachon a five-year, $2 million deal, while the Kings' three-year deal offer was nowhere near $400,000 per season. Vachon told owner Jack Kent Cooke that he would take less money to play in Los Angeles, but he wanted a five-year deal. "Mr. Cooke was cheap and he didn't want to spend the money," Vachon says. "I felt like I had to go, because I was going to be the best-paid goalie in the league."

In Detroit he never really enjoyed the success he had in L.A. and ended up finishing his career in Boston. He later went back to L.A., joining Kings' management and eventually becoming the team's general manager and president.

As much as he's associated with the Kings, Vachon had his most eye-catching numbers when he was wearing a different sweater. He had a 14–5 playoff record in Montreal, and in Stanley Cup finals he had a 6–3 record and 1.86 goals-against average.

Vachon says his most memorable game was Canada's 5–4 overtime win against the Czech Republic in the 1976 Canada Cup. His glove save against Vladimir Martinec in overtime is overlooked in favor of Darryl Sittler's game-winning goal. Vachon played all seven games in that tournament and gave up just 10 goals.

Anyone who attended Kings games in the seventies remembers the frequent chants of "ROW-Gee, ROW-Gee, ROW-Gee." Recalls Davidson: "Fans could identify with him. You remembered what his stance looked like and what his mask looked like. It was white, with wide-open eyes. It was distinctive, just like him. For a guy who wasn't very big, he played a courageous game."

39 | ED GIACOMIN

BORN: Sudbury, Ontario, June 6, 1939		
SHOT: Left	HEIGHT: 5'11"	WEIGHT: 180 lbs.
Vezina Trophies: 1	NHL First All-Star Team: 2	
NHL Second All-Star Team: 3	NHL All-Star Games: 6	

NOTABLE ACHIEVEMENTS: Hall of Famer; led the NHL in wins, 1966–67 through 1968–69; led the NHL in games played, 1966–67 through 1969–70; led the NHL in shutouts three times; broke into the pro ranks as a trainer and practice goalie with Clinton (Eastern Hockey League); recommended to the team by his older brother, Roly, who was also a goalie; cut when he tried out for junior A at 15 and with the Detroit Red Wings at 18; his No. 1 sweater was retired by the Rangers.

Johnny Bower's Commentary on Giacomin

"Eddie Giacomin is one of the smartest on-ice goaltenders that I have ever seen. Eddie was always able to read the play and was able to headman the puck to his teammates with little difficulty. He was far from what I would consider a puck-handling goaltender, but when he did play the puck, it was tape to tape and the Rangers were able to bust out of their zone. He was a smaller goaltender who played more or less a traditional stand-up style out of necessity, because by standing up, he had a better chance of making the second save if he gave up a rebound. When he had to go down, Giacomin had catlike reflexes and was able to get back up in a matter of mere seconds. He had incredible timing and fast hands and was able to make the most amazing saves, pulling the puck out of thin air sometimes."

Second Opinion: Former Rangers Teammate Pete Stemkowski on Giacomin

"Eddie actually enjoyed playing hockey. A lot of goalkeepers I'd been around were kind of moody. You couldn't talk to them the day of a game. But Eddie always had a big smile on his face. He had a great temperament. If he had a bad game, it wouldn't spill over to the next one. Always worked hard in practice. If someone wanted to stay later and take some extra shots, he would stay. I remember when Detroit claimed him on waivers. We were going to Montreal and somebody noticed that Eddie was not on the plane. Word got out that he was on waivers and had gone to Detroit. It's not often that a tear comes to your eye when you play this game, but there were a few tears from our guys when he came back with Detroit [two days later]. The National Anthem that day was absolutely incredible. I think the singer may have got out three words of the anthem and then it was "Eddie, Eddie, Eddie." You could see he was crying and there was quite a lot of emotion that went through us, too. Not so much that he left the team. That was part of the game. It's just how likeable he was. The loss of him as a friend affected us more so than as a player."

New York Rangers general manager Emile Francis counted on paying a handsome price to acquire Eddie Giacomin from the Providence Reds in 1965. That's why Francis was armed with photographs of his team's best-looking players when he sat across the table from Providence owner Lou Pieri to discuss the potential deal.

Pieri's marketing theory on hockey was that players with matinee-idol looks sold tickets. Apparently, he thought Giacomin's value was tied more to his sex appeal than to his actual performance on the ice. Francis offered goalie Marcel Paile, right wing Sandy McGregor, and defenseman Aldo Guidolin, and Pieri studied the photographs. It wasn't until Francis slid across an eight-by-ten of forward Jim Mikol that the deal was consummated.

"Mikol was a good-looking guy, and Pieri looked at me and said, 'You have yourself a goalkeeper,'" Francis recalls. "Pieri was a bargain hunter."

What Francis had done was bring aboard one of the most popular players in Rangers history, and a future Hall of Famer. Giacomin's flamboyant style seemed to be a perfect fit for Madison Square Garden, where patrons always liked a story line as much as they liked good teams. At a time when goalkeepers were supposed to be tethered to their goal posts, he liked to roam about the ice as if he were a modern-day rover.

Former Rangers publicity director and current NHL historian John Halligan says the team built its marketing around Giacomin.

"Fans loved his style, although he scared the heck out of them when he would skate out to the blue line," Halligan recalls.

Giacomin's athleticism wasn't the only thing that caught the attention of Francis, a former NHL goaltender. "Eddie was playing for a bad team in Providence," he recalls. "But what I liked about him was that he was a competitor. He would be down 5–1, and he would still be trying to help his team. He would be talking it up, helping his teammates."

When he arrived with the Rangers, Giacomin had some flaws. He gave up too many rebounds, according to Francis, and he needed to keep his stick on the ice more. He also wasn't tight enough against the post to survive NHL shooters. But he was considered highly coachable, and by the start of his second season, he could steal a game.

"He turned out to be one of the best goaltenders I ever had at handling the stick and moving the puck," Francis says.

Remember, this is two decades before Ron Hextall came to the NHL. "His ambition was always to score a goal and he damn near did," Francis says. "One night in Toronto, they pulled their goaltender in a 2–1 game, and he shot it down and hit the goal post."

Giacomin forced teams to consider his roaming in their game plan—much like today's teams factor Martin Brodeur's puckhandling into their defensive approach to the New Jersey Devils. "Teams would try to keep the puck away from Eddie," Francis says. "They would never shoot it to his left because it was on his forehand. They always shot it to the opposite corner so he would have to handle it with his backhand."

Giacomin was also a vocal goaltender. His voice could be heard in the second level of Madison Square Garden as he gave instructions to his defensemen, or warned them of potential danger.

Giacomin didn't wear a mask in games until 1970–71. "He was fearless," Francis says. "He would get hit, stitched up, and go back in. He was afraid of nothing."

Though goaltenders are often defined by a performance in a Stanley Cup championship game or at least a major playoff game, Giacomin's career might

Giacomin Was Underappreciated Because . . . The lack of a Stanley Cup championship masked how well he performed for the Rangers during his heyday. He is clearly one of the most popular players in Rangers history.

have been defined by a relatively meaningless regular-season game. It was in New York a few days after he had been shipped to the Detroit Red Wings for a $30,000 waiver price in October 1975. At the root of the deal was the Rangers' desire to rebuild without falling out of the playoffs and the team's desire to rid itself of Giacomin's $200,000 contract.

Fans began chanting "Eddie, Eddie, Eddie" during the national anthem and it quickly became a home game for the Red Wings. The picture of Giacomin wiping away tears during the ovation became a classic. He made 42 saves, and the Red Wings won 6–4. After the game New York defenseman Brad Park said Giacomin had beat the Rangers more with his "presence" than his goaltending.

Giacomin shared the Vezina Trophy with Gilles Villemure in 1970–71.

"They say that New York is a cold, heartless place," Giacomin told the media after the game. "But it's not true. Believe me, I know."

It was clear that night that Giacomin was one of the most popular players in team history, even though he hadn't helped the team win a Stanley Cup. Francis was vilified for letting him go.

An interesting twist on the Giacomin story is that he had almost ended up with Detroit in 1965. Even though Francis had been pondering the goalie for months, he didn't hustle to Providence until he heard the Red Wings and Montreal Canadiens were sniffing around for a possible swap.

Francis wanted to meet Pieri the night he arrived, but the Providence owner said the meeting had to be at 8:00 A.M. the following day. Francis was a little nervous when he ran into a Red Wings scout in the hotel elevator.

"He had been scouting with the Red Wings for 100 years," he says "I knew him because he was Glen Sonmor's father-in-law, and I had played with Glen in Cleveland. He got off the elevator with me, and said, 'Son, I know you will give me a straight answer on this: What do you think of Eddie Giacomin as a goalkeeper?'"

"That's a tough question," I said. "I wouldn't want to answer that on the spur of the moment. Call me tomorrow."

Francis started his meeting with Pieri at 8:00 A.M. sharp and had the deal for Giacomin done at 9:15.

261

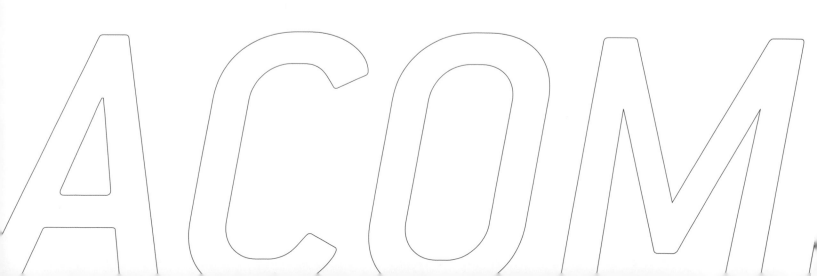

45 | CURTIS JOSEPH

BORN: Keswick, Ontario, April 29, 1965

SHOOTS: Left	HEIGHT: 5′10″	WEIGHT: 185 lbs.
King Clancy Trophies: 1		NHL All-Star Games: 2

NOTABLE ACHIEVEMENTS: Led Stanley Cup playoffs in shutouts, 1992–93; earned silver medal and second All-Star team with Canada at 1996 World Championships; won silver medal at 1996 World Cup; won gold medal at 2002 Olympics; made Western Collegiate Hockey Association All-Star and All-Freshman teams at Wisconsin; won 1990–91 Centennial Cup with Notre Dame Hounds; holds a 2.53 playoff goals-against average.

Johnny Bower's Commentary on Joseph

"Curtis Joseph is a big-money goaltender who is worth every penny that he is paid. When he was a teenager, he enrolled into my goalie school and was one of the best students I've ever had because he was willing to listen. Even back then he had his patented butterfly style, and I told him that he was very good at stopping the low shots. But I was concerned about his ability to stop the shots under the bar since he was down so soon. He had and still has the reflexes to get back up to make the stop, but I was a stand-up goalie and have always preached that style. Every so often, Curtis will remind me of what I tried to teach him back [then]. He doesn't believe me when I tell him that I was only teasing him."

Second Opinion: Toronto's Alyn McCauley on Joseph

"He gives you a lot of confidence. We know that he's going to make the saves and that allows us to play a more open style. Maybe it's a little risky, but we have that freedom when he's in net. Although I'm sure he doesn't like to face all of those rushes, he seems to make a lot of those saves. That's . . . what makes him so good. With the offensive power we have up front, we should be a little more risky, more free-flowing. CuJo allows us to be that team."

Down to their last breaths, the Dallas Stars and the Edmonton Oilers were doing battle in overtime of Game 7 of their first-round playoff series in 1997.

The Stars were the number two seed in the NHL's Western Conference, accumulating 23 more points than the seventh-seeded Oilers during regular-season competition. But Dallas couldn't overpower the one factor that so often makes the difference in playoff hockey. "You can outplay a team," ESPN analyst Bill Clement says. "But the one thing you can't control is goaltending."

Early in the overtime session Joseph went paddle down to make a save against his left post, but the puck hopped away from him, skipping in front of the gaping net, where Dallas center Joe Nieuwendyk, poised on the edge of the crease, smacked it goalward. Contorting to fling his glove hand across his prone body, the sprawling Joseph snared the disk right at his goal line.

"There was nothing but air," ESPN play-by-play man Gary Thorne says. "And then there was CuJo. That was as great a save as you'll ever see."

From the ensuing faceoff, Todd Marchant sprung down the left wing and whipped a wrist shot past Stars goalie Andy Moog for the series winner.

"People ask me about that save all the time," Joseph says. "It happened so fast, I wasn't sure if I had it, because I didn't feel the puck hit me. Judging from the crowd reaction, I figured I'd stopped it, though." A defining moment in Stanley Cup lore, that save wrote another chapter in the life of a man for whom defying the odds has become a way of life.

Born Curtis Monroe, he was adopted by Harold and Jeanne Joseph of Keswick, Ontario, as an infant. Unclaimed in the Ontario Hockey League draft, Joseph played Tier II junior in Richmond Hill, Ontario, sending his résumé to U.S. colleges in pursuit of a scholarship. When there were no takers, Joseph enrolled at Notre Dame, a Wilcox, Saskatchewan, prep school with a rich hockey tradition, leading the Hounds to a Centennial Cup Canadian junior A title and earning a scholarship to Wisconsin. Joseph was named Western Collegiate Hockey Association Player of the Year as a freshman with the Badgers and signed a free-agent deal with the St. Louis Blues.

With the Blues, Joseph secured his reputation as a goalie who thrived on work and vaulted mediocre squads to overachiever status. In the 1993 playoffs he posted two shutouts to help the Blues sweep the Western Conference–leading Blackhawks in the first round.

"I think he actually likes it when his team gets outshot," adds Derek King, Joseph's former teammate in Toronto. King just might have a point. "When you have a lot of work, when you're busy and handling a lot of shots, you're more into the game mentally and physically," Joseph says. "The bottom line is winning. And I know we play better when we don't tighten up."

Joseph Is Underappreciated Because . . . Even though he has knocked off a number one– or number two–seeded team four times in the playoffs, he has never been named to a first or second All-Star team based on regular-season play.

Overlooked in the NHL draft, Joseph was signed by St. Louis as a free agent.

48 | CHRIS OSGOOD

BORN: Peace River, Alberta, November 26, 1972

SHOOTS: Left	HEIGHT: 5'10"	WEIGHT: 160 lbs.
Stanley Cups: 2		Jennings Trophies: 1
NHL Second All-Star Team: 1		NHL All-Star Games: 3

NOTABLE ACHIEVEMENTS: Led NHL in wins, 1995–96; posted a shutout in first Stanley Cup game, 1994 vs. San Jose; set Detroit club marks with 13-game winning streak and 21-game unbeaten run in 1995–96; scored a goal during the 1995–96 season against Hartford; also scored a goal in junior hockey with Medicine Hat, Alberta.

Johnny Bower's Commentary on Osgood

"Chris Osgood has quick hands and plays the butterfly with ease. Osgood tends to stay square to the shooter even when he's rushed to make the second or third save. He's very good on shots in tight because he tends to cover his five-hole properly, that is with the blade of his stick. There have been a few times where I've seen him give up a goal from outside the blue line, but I really like how he has battled back from giving up a couple of weak goals in the 1998 Stanley Cup playoffs. The next game, Ozzie came up big for the Wings and was a big reason why they won the Cup."

Second Opinion: Islanders Teammate Michael Peca on Osgood

"I think when you play against him, he doesn't have that big-time superstar goaltender tag, but he's quietly had a great career and won some Stanley Cups. He's never quite gotten that level of respect that I think he deserves. He's a terrific goalie, a great teammate, and a hard worker who just loves playing hard for the guys in front of him. He's just a calming presence back there for us. He always seems to be in the right spot."

Chris Osgood remembers how the fear gripped his insides, stifling the flow from his salivary glands, as he fumbled yet another one.

A puck in the Stanley Cup playoffs? No, his lines in the sixth-grade school play. "That was the toughest thing I ever had to do," Osgood recalls of the time he starred as the lead in that show.

By comparison, the thought of following Stanley Cup MVP Mike Vernon in net for the reigning champion Detroit Red Wings during the 1997–98 season never cost Osgood a moment's sleep. "I love going out there and playing the big game," he says. "That's when I'm in my element."

The juxtaposition of Osgood's profession and his personality make for intriguing fodder. He's the first to admit he shies away from the limelight. "I don't want any attention," he says. And yet by positioning himself between the pipes in the NHL's red-light district, he guaranteed the spotlight would shine on him.

Especially during Detroit's 1998 road back to Stanley Cup glory. Vernon was the Conn Smythe Trophy winner in 1996–97 as Detroit ended its 42-year championship drought. But by the time training camp opened in the fall, Vernon had been dealt to the San Jose Sharks and the number one goaltending assignment was Osgood's.

"He was under the gun all season," recalls Detroit defenseman Larry Murphy. "No matter what he did, it was always, 'Can he do it in the playoffs?'"

Inside Osgood's heart, there was only belief, even after he committed some of the most infamous blunders in Stanley Cup history. He allowed goals from the neutral zone by St. Louis defenseman Al MacInnis and Dallas forward Jamie Langenbrunner, the latter tally in overtime.

Osgood followed up his colossal blunders with some colossal stops. He closed the door that night in St. Louis and the Wings won in OT. The game after Langenbrunner's long goal, he

Osgood Is Underappreciated Because . . .

Even though he has two Stanley Cup rings and has never posted a losing record in nine NHL seasons—with a career winning percentage of .627—he was let go by the Detroit Red Wings when Dominik Hasek became available.

blanked the Stars 2–0, putting the Red Wings back in the Stanley Cup final, where they swept Washington.

"Each time, I bounced back and played better," Osgood says. "I kind of thrived on the adversity."

His Detroit mates weren't surprised to see their goalie overcome his failings. "He's got everybody fooled," right wing Darren McCarty says. "He's not an outgoing person, but he's quietly confident. He doesn't get too excited and he doesn't get too upset. I guess that's what it takes to be a goaltender."

Detroit general manager Ken Holland first discovered this side of his future netminder while running a team in a summer ball hockey league in Medicine Hat, Alberta, a squad that listed a teenaged Osgood at forward. "He had great drive and competitiveness," Holland recalls. "I got to know him as a person, better than you usually get to know these kids heading into the draft."

Osgood had the last laugh on the skeptics when he helped keep the Cup in Detroit four years ago. "I didn't look for vindication or revenge," he says. "What I was looking for, I got. Ever since I was a little kid, I wanted to be the goalie on the team that won a Stanley Cup. It was very gratifying."

Osgood ranks second all time in wins and shutouts with the Red Wings.

49 | BILL RANFORD

BORN: Brandon, Manitoba, December 14, 1966

SHOT: Left	**HEIGHT:** 5'11"	**WEIGHT:** 185 lbs.
Stanley Cups: 2		Conn Smythe Trophies: 1
NHL All-Star Games: 1		

NOTABLE ACHIEVEMENTS: Won the Stanley Cup (1987–88, 1989–90), Canada Cup (1991), and World Championships (1994), Canada's first world title since 1961; named all-tournament goalie at the 1994 Worlds, posting a 6–0–0 record and a 1.17 goals-against average; named Canada Cup All-Star in 1991; his 77 games played in 1995–96 tied for second-most in an NHL season (with Martin Brodeur and Arturs Irbe); jumped right from New Westminster juniors to the Boston Bruins.

Johnny Bower's Commentary on Ranford

"Bill Ranford is one of the greatest athletes of all time to play this game. He had to be in order to play that classic triple-overtime game against Boston in the 1990 Stanley Cup finals. It was one of the most impressive single-game performances that I've ever witnessed. The difficulty of playing a game like that is not the physical but rather the mental exhaustion that a goaltender can suffer. You're so focused on the game that nothing else matters, but once the contest is over, you feel like you're going to collapse. Most of us goaltenders tend to replay the game in our sleep, so if you consider that he played more than two games that night, he might have gotten a couple of hours of true rest before having to get back up and start focusing on the next game. You could almost always count on Ranford to come up big during the playoffs.

Second Opinion: ESPN Analyst Darren Pang on Ranford

"Billy Ranford didn't get the credit he deserved throughout his career, probably because he played much of it with teams that were fighting to make the playoffs. But even before he won the Stanley Cup in Edmonton, he was highly rated. He was a guy who battled, who didn't let bad games stay with him, and who was capable of rising to the occasion and stealing games for his team. He was one of the last of the old-style goalies, who would slide across and stack the pads and make those big kick saves that sent the rebounds sailing."

Within the Northlands Coliseum crowd, there was an impending sense of doom. The Winnipeg Jets had whipped the Edmonton Oilers 7–5 in the 1990 playoff opener, and all eyes were fixed on Edmonton goalie Bill Ranford. The Oilers were missing four-time Stanley Cup winner Grant Fuhr because of a shoulder injury, and Ranford, the heir apparent, looked like an apparent error.

"In the first game of the playoffs he didn't play very well," recalls former Oilers forward Craig Simpson.

But what stayed with Simpson was the way the goalie responded to that setback. "I think what gave everybody the confidence in him was that he didn't back down," he says. "He focused on playing better from there."

Ranford did exactly that, rallying the Oilers from a 3–1 series deficit. "The team realized that Billy was a competitor and that when things went badly, instead of sulking, he got mad and tried to play better," Simpson says.

The Oilers swept the Los Angeles Kings in the next round, then took out the Chicago Blackhawks in the Western Conference final and readied to face the Boston Bruins for the Stanley Cup. The first game would be the longest in Cup final history, a three-overtime-period affair decided when Edmonton's Petr Klima finally dented the twine. "Winning that triple-overtime game, where he made some big, big saves and remained cool under pressure, it settled everybody on the team," Simpson says. "Billy was able to get it in his mind that he could shut the door, and the team followed along with him." The Oilers brought down the Bruins in five games and, along with the Stanley Cup, Ranford lifted the Conn Smythe Trophy as playoff MVP.

The Cup triumph launched Ranford on an impressive personal odyssey that saw him carry Canada to the Canada Cup one year later, posting the first unbeaten record (6–0–2) in tournament history.

The changing financial picture in the NHL put the small-market Oilers under duress, and they were forced to deal many of their stars in order to survive, falling from contender status to NHL bottom feeder by the midnineties.

The ways of goaltending were also changing, but Ranford wasn't. "Billy Ranford was a great goalie, but he was a feet-first goalie and he didn't adapt when the game changed and the butterfly became the new style," says television analyst John Davidson, a former NHL goalie. "You can't play feet-first anymore, too many goals come from scrambles, and once you slide and stack the pads, you can't get in position for the next shot."

Ranford's career sputtered toward the end, and he played for five teams in his last four seasons before retiring in 2000. But for a three-year span in the early nineties, many viewed him as hockey's top stopper.

Ranford Was Underappreciated Because . . .

He was never given the recognition due to the only netminder in hockey history with a Stanley Cup, Canada Cup, and World Championship on his résumé.

Ranford backstopped Edmonton to victory in the longest Stanley Cup final game ever played.

50 | JOHN VANBIESBROUCK

BORN: Detroit, Michigan, September 14, 1963

SHOT: Left	HEIGHT: 5'7"	WEIGHT: 175 lbs.
Vezina Trophies: 1	NHL First All-Star Team: 1	
NHL Second All-Star Team: 1	NHL All-Star Games: 3	

NOTABLE ACHIEVEMENTS: Second U.S.-born NHL goalie to post 300 wins; played in the 1996 Stanley Cup final with the Florida Panthers; led NHL goalies in wins, 1985–86; undrafted as a junior in 1980, made his NHL debut with the New York Rangers one year later; shared Central Hockey League's MVP award in 1983–84; helped Panthers establish first-year records for wins (33) and points (83) in 1993–94; runner-up in Vezina Trophy voting that season; played for the USA in World Junior Championships, World Champion-ships, Canada Cup, World Cup, and the Olympics.

Johnny Bower's Commentary on Vanbiesbrouck

"You can't play goal in the National Hockey League without confidence, and Vanbiesbrouck has always had his fair share. He has always been known for being strong on his angles, and he certainly challenged shooters. I like that in a goaltender. You didn't see John make the first move very often. He seems quite patient. Once a goaltender commits to a move, that's like opening the door for a shooter."

Second Opinion: Former NHL Goaltender John Davidson on Vanbiesbrouck

"John was always very energy efficient with his movements. He would always just make a series of small movements that were designed to let the puck hit him. He always had a lot of composure."

The secret to John Vanbiesbrouck's success might have been that the player he believed in most was the one he viewed in the mirror while shaving every morning.

"When he first came to the New York Rangers, he was pretty arrogant," recalls former teammate Tom Laidlaw. "At first guys were taken aback by that. But to his credit, he really backed it up."

Vanbiesbrouck's faith in himself was probably more valuable to him than his superb technique or his competitiveness. His inner strength often seemed contagious to teammates. NHL players often take a team's temperature based on how harried a goaltender looks, and Vanbiesbrouck always looked as if he were master of the house.

"When it comes to goaltending, it's not about just stopping the puck," Laidlaw says. "It's the way you stop it. Players don't want to see their goaltender flopping around, out of control. If a goalie gives the impression that he's just hanging on, or barely making a save, players start to think they are playing terrible. When John would make a key save, he made it seem routine, like he was in complete control. There were no wild rebounds, and his angles were covered. You would look at Beezer and say, 'OK, we are fine here.'"

Although Vanbiesbrouck played in the NHL at 18 and won a Vezina at age 23, his best season probably came at age 32 when he was able to lead the fledgling Florida Panthers to the Stanley Cup final in 1995–96. The Panthers had only been around for three seasons when Vanbiesbrouck helped them down the Boston Bruins, the Philadelphia Flyers, and the Pittsburgh Penguins before they lost to the Colorado Avalanche in the final.

"His mental preparation that year was as good as any goaltender I've ever seen," says Doug MacLean, the Panthers coach at the time. "He was so confident that even when he had the odd rough night, it was a nonissue about whether he was going to come back and play well."

Vanbiesbrouck won the Vezina Trophy in 1985–86.

What MacLean remembers most about those 1996 playoffs was how often the diminutive Vanbiesbrouck robbed Pittsburgh's Jaromir Jagr and Mario Lemieux during the seven-game Eastern Conference final.

"I can still remember him stoning Mario and Jagr, two of the greatest scorers in the history of the game, and I'm thinking, 'Man, how hot is this guy going to get?'" MacLean says.

Vanbiesbrouck Was Underappreciated Because . . .

Though he was capable of winning a Stanley Cup, he

never played on a team that had the talent to win one.

He got hot enough that it wasn't unthinkable that the Panthers could have won the Stanley Cup final. The Avalanche ended up sweeping, but the final game went to triple overtime before Uwe Krupp drilled a shot past Vanbiesbrouck to give Colorado a 1–0 win.

"Togetherness was the main factor on that team," Vanbiesbrouck recalls. "We were a tight group, more than any team that I've played on. We were able to predict what all of our teammates were going to do. We had a good relationship with the rats and the fans."

That was the season in which fans showered the ice with plastic rats after Florida goals because Scott Mellanby had killed a rat in the dressing room early in the season. As close as this team might have been, Vanbiesbrouck was the stabilizer. He was the Panthers' true rat slayer.

"John Vanbiesbrouck had the swagger about him that he allowed the tough saves to look easy," says ESPN analyst Bill Clement. "It's almost like Clint Eastwood walking in and not having to say anything to transmit to the world that he's cool."

Remember, Vanbiesbrouck was playing for an expansion team void of real stars. But his confidence never wavered. The Panthers wanted him because the team's first coach, Roger Neilson, said he had the right temperament for the expansion job.

"I coached John for three and a half years in New York," Neilson told *The Hockey News*, "and the one thing about him is that he comes back strong from a bad goal, a bad game, or a bad season."

Confident or not, Vanbiesbrouck did pay his dues to become an NHL standout. In 1983–84 he played for the financially challenged Tulsa Oilers in the Central Hockey League. The team had to practice in a mall and was forbidden from shooting pucks for fear of hurting shoppers. They could only skate. For the first half of the season, the Oilers played at an arena at the State Fairgrounds, where dirt would often remain on the ice from the previous day's rodeo. After games, players would have to wash off with hoses in the bathroom.

In the second half of the season, they played every game on the road, and yet the team won the CHL playoff championship. Vanbiesbrouck was named Minor League Player of the Year by *The Hockey News*.

He did indeed appreciate being in the NHL. In describing his style, he once said, "I know I don't have the talent of a [Grant] Fuhr or a [Patrick] Roy, but I've learned to scratch and claw back."

MacLean always felt as if Vanbiesbrouck's composure stemmed from his knowledge of how to play goal. His style was like a training video.

"Fundamentally, he was so sound that it was easy to look composed," MacLean says. "For a small guy to be as good as he was, he had to have outstanding fundamentals."

Laidlaw still believes that bravado carried Vanbiesbrouck even farther than his talent.

"In the end, he was a competitor," Laidlaw says. "He wasn't a wallflower. Right from the beginning he came in believing he was going to be a quality goaltender. And when I think back, I learned a good lesson from him. Whether you are a goaltender or a defenseman you have to believe in yourself."